# THE HERITAGE OF CHINESE CIVILIZATION

# The Heritage
# of Chinese Civilization

Albert M. Craig

*Harvard University*

Prentice
Hall

*Upper Saddle River, New Jersey 07458*

Library of Congress Cataloging-in-Publication Data

CRAIG, ALBERT M.

    The heritage of Chinese civilization / Albert M. Craig.
      p. cm.
    Includes bibliographical references and index.
    ISBN  0-13-576620-6
    1. China—History.  I. Title.
DS735.A2 C73 2001
951—dc21

                                  00-057460

Editorial Director *Charlyce Jones Owen*
Acquisitions Editor: *Charles Cavaliere*
AVP, Director of Production and Manufacturing: *Barbara Kittle*
Editorial Production/Supervision and Interior Design: *Judith Winthrop*
Cover Art: *American Heritage Publishing Co., Inc./Bibliotheque Nationale de France*
Prepress and Manufacturing Buyer: *Lynn Pearlman*
Supervisor of Production Services: *Guy Ruggiero*
Electronic Page Layout: *Rosemary Ross*
Cartographers: *Carto-Graphics, Mirella Signoretto*
Copy Editor: *Rene Lynch*

This book was set in 10/12.5 Caslon 540 by the HSS in-house formatting and
production services group and was printed and bound by RR Donnelley.
The cover was printed by Phoenix Color Corporation.

**Prentice Hall**

© 2001 by Prentice-Hall
A Unit of Pearson Education
Upper Saddle River, New Jersey 07458

Printed in the United States of America
10 9 8 7 6 5 4 3 2 1

ISBN 0-13-576620-6

Pearson Education (UK) Limited, *London*
Prentice-Hall of Australia Pty. Limited, *Sydney*
Prentice-Hall Canada Inc., *Toronto*
Prentice-Hall Hispanoamericana, S.A., *Mexico*
Prentice-Hall of India Private Limited, *New Delhi*
Prentice-Hall of Japan, Inc., *Tokyo*
Pearson Education Pte. Ltd., *Singapore*
Editora Prentice-Hall do Brasil, Ltda., *Rio de Janeiro*

For Sarah Craig *(1960–1992)*

# Contents

# 4
# *Late Imperial China: The Ming (1368–1644)*
# *and Ch'ing (1644–1912) Dynasties*     *95*

# *Maps*

# Documents

# *Preface*

China is one of the birthplaces of civilization. Of the original civilizations, it is the only one which has continued down to the present. The civilizations of ancient Mesopotamia, Egypt, and India were all submerged or supplanted by subsequent waves of very different cultures. Chinese civilization, to be sure, was not static. It continued to evolve, but while it absorbed from outside influences, it was never wholly swamped by them. During the seventh and eighth centuries C.E., China's writing system, philosophies, and technology spread to Japan, Korea, and Vietnam, defining the area known today as East Asia. Its poetry, literature, and arts were no less influential. Today China is a nuclear power with a fifth of the world's population. Its economy is burgeoning. To understand the world today, one must understand China, and to understand China, one must understand its past.

This volume consists in the main of the China chapters of *The Heritage of World Civilizations*, though they have been extensively revised. It provides a chronological framework and a short narrative of China's long history. It does not neglect the ruling dynasties, but it also treats social, economic, and cultural developments that cut across dynastic lines. There exist, of course, several excellent thick histories of China. Their only drawback is that length often precludes the assignment of other readings. For the instructor who wishes to approach Chinese history topically or assign monographs, collections of documents, novels, or movies, the brevity of this text may prove an advantage.

Since brevity was a goal, the author asserts with seeming confidence many things that may be true only in the balance. Proper qualifications would take up many pages.

The author has picked many key historical variables for his reconstruction of the past. In doing so, however, he has inevitably left out other variables that merit attention. Reading assignments in other works, perhaps from the bibliographies given at the end of each chapter, may provide a counterpoint to the account in the text.

Written history is an abstraction. In any society, change or stability is a consequence of the feelings and actions of hundreds of thousands or millions of people. Each person lives in a family, has social ties extending to the larger society, works for a living, and is constrained and protected by a structure of rule. The totality of such relationships shapes the actual history of a nation. The historian, at best, grasps bits and pieces of this past. In China, despite the fact that its written record in the premodern ear surpassed that of any other nation, most of the people lived in obscurity and left no traces. Writing its history from surviving sources is like doing a jigsaw puzzle with most of the pieces missing.

It is also difficult to see the past in the terms in which it saw itself. Even studying the West—our own civilization—we catch only glimpses of what it meant to be, say, a merchant in medieval Hamburg. What family, society, and the universe looked like to a merchant of Hangchow during the Southern Sung dynasty is even more difficult to ascertain. But some inkling may be gleaned from original sources. To this end, translations of poems, philosophy, essays, scenes from novels, and the like, are included both in the narrative and in the form of boxed quotations. The immediacy of these writings provides windows into the actual thought and feelings of the actors in China's history. They not only illuminate the history, but they remind us that Chinese living a thousand years ago had many of the same hopes, fears, joys, and sorrows that we do today. We recognize these shared feelings despite the powerful shaping of human experience by cultural modalities and social organization.

The text contains many maps. Peking in China's north is as different from Canton in the near tropical southeast as is Boston from El Paso. Most place names in the narrative may be found on the chapter maps. Also, the final section of each chapter attempts to review some of the chapter materials in a larger comparative perspective. Comparisons are useful in pointing out that similar processes occur in widely divergent societies. But the reader must remember that such similarities are usually embedded in dense structures that are quite dissimilar. Each chapter is followed by several review questions, which may be of use. The questions are followed by a short bibliography of further readings.

The author has drawn on many fine studies, his intellectual debts are legion and, as usual in a text, largely unacknowledged. But I would like to mention those to whom I owe a particular and personal debt, my first teachers in Chinese history—Benjamin Schwartz, Edwin Reischauer, Lien-sheng Yang, and John Fairbank—and also the colleagues from whom I have learned so much over the years—Peter Bol, Paul Cohen, Nicola DiCosmo, Merle Goldman, Philip Kuhn, Dwight Perkins, Michael Puitt, and Robin Yates. I would also like to mention my wife, Teruko Craig, who, in addition to moral support, read the manuscript many times and made valuable suggestions. Needless to say, errors in the text are my own.

Lastly, I would like to add a note on language. Until recently, most Western scholarship on Chinese history used the Wade-Giles system for the romanization of Chinese names and terms. I have used this system throughout so that students may move easily from this text to the scholarship on Chinese history listed in the bibliographies. China today, however, uses another system, known as *pinyin*. Virtually all Western newspapers have adopted this system, as have many scholars. For this reason, in treating Chinese history since 1949 I have included *pinyin* spellings in parentheses after the Wade-Giles. For example, Teng Hsiao-p'ing (Deng Hsiaoping). When the balance tips and the preponderance of scholarship is in *pinyin*, I will use it throughout.

# THE HERITAGE OF CHINESE CIVILIZATION

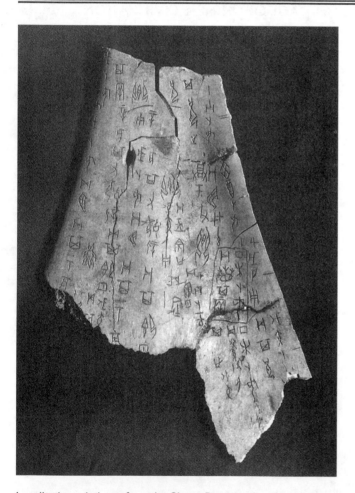

Inscribed oracle bone from the Shang Dynasty city of An Yang.
[From the Collection of the C. V. Starr East Asian Library, Columbia University]

*chapter one*

*Early China*

## ORIGINS: THE OLD AND NEW STONE AGES

Human life in China goes back several hundred thousand years to "Peking man" (*homo erectus*), whose remains were first found on the North China plain but have since been found in other areas as well. Peking man was about five feet tall and had a smaller cranial capacity than modern humans. "Peking man" was similar to "Java man" and to varieties of *homo erectus* found in Africa, the Middle East, and Europe. These early humans lived by hunting deer and other animals and by fishing and gathering. Men were slightly larger than women and there was probably a division of labor by gender, with women doing the gathering. Nothing is known of their language capability, social relations, or beliefs, but we do know that they made chipped stone tools and cooked with fire. Bashed-in skulls suggest that they ate brains in some circumstances.

Large-brained modern human beings (*homo sapiens*), who may have developed one hundred thousand years ago in Africa, entered China about fifty thousand years ago, supplanting Peking man. They made tools with finer stone blades: The history of progress during the Old Stone Age is dimly perceived through successive layers of tools found in archaeological sites, and distinctive regional variations in the tools have been noted. They buried their dead. Population remained sparse, however, for humans were still subject to ecological constraints of the kind that today maintain a balance, for example, between deer and wolves in Alaska.

Of the thousands of Old Stone Age cultures in the world, only a few developed the combination of agriculture, pottery, domesticated animals, and better polished stone tools that we characterize as the "New Stone Age." Better tools were useful both for hunting and agriculture. Perhaps it was women, gathering while men hunted, who discovered how to plant and care for seeds and gave crops the constant attention they required from planting to harvest. They stored dry food in baskets and liquids in pottery jars. The greater production of food led to denser populations, and they built permanent settlements in clusters near their best fields. These changes transformed the prehistoric world as science is transforming our own.

Agriculture began in China between 5600 and 4000 B.C.E. in the basin of the southern bend of the Yellow River. This is the northernmost of East Asia's four great river systems. The others are the Yangtze in central China, the West River in southern China, and the Red River in what is today northern Vietnam. All drain eastward into the Pacific

Ocean. In recent millennia, the Yellow River has flowed through a deforested plain, cold in winter and subject to periodic droughts. But in the sixth millennium B.C.E., the area was warm and moist, with forested highlands in the west and swampy marshes to the east. The bamboo rat that today can be found only in semitropical Southeast Asia lived along the Yellow River.

The chief crop of China's agricultural revolution was millet. A second independent discovery of agriculture may have occurred almost as early on China's southeast coast. It was based on yams and taro and may have been related to agricultural developments in what is today Vietnam. A third development, the cultivation of rice, may have occurred somewhat later on the Huai River between the Yellow River and the Yangtze near the coast in eastern China. In time, wheat also entered China from the west.

New Stone Age Chinese cleared land and burned its cover to plant millet, cabbage, and later rice and soybeans. When soil became exhausted, fields or whole villages were abandoned. Tools were of stone: axes, hoes, spades, and sickle-shaped knives. The early Chinese domesticated pigs, sheep, cattle, dogs, and chickens. Game was plentiful and hunting continued to be important to the village economy. In excavated garbage heaps of ancient villages are found the bones of deer, wild cattle, antelopes, rhinoceros, hares, and marmots. Grain was stored in pottery painted in bold, geometric designs

**Map 1–1    The four great river valley civilizations to ca. 1000 B.C.E.**    By ca. 2000 B.C.E. urban life was established along the Tigris and Euphrates rivers in Mesopotamia, the Nile River in Egypt, the Indus and Ganges rivers in India, and the Yellow River in China.

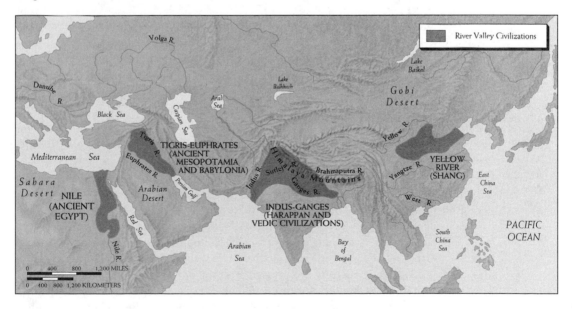

of red and black. This pottery gave way to a harder, thin black pottery, made on a potter's wheel, whose use spread west along the Yellow River and south to the Yangtze. The tripodal shapes of Neolithic pots prefigure later Chinese bronzes.

Early cultivators wove fabrics of hemp and learned to produce silk from the cocoons of silkworms fed on mulberry leaves. They lived in wattle-and-daub pit-dwellings with wooden support-posts and sunken, plastered floors. Their villages were located in isolated clearings along slopes of river valleys. Archaeological finds of weapons and remains of pounded earthen walls suggest tribal warfare between villages. Of their religion little is known, though some evidence suggests the worship of ancestral spirits. They practiced divination by applying heat to a hole drilled in the shoulder bone of a steer or the undershell of a tortoise and then interpreting the resulting cracks in the bone. They buried their dead in cemeteries with jars of food. Tribal leaders wore rings and beads of jade.

## EARLY BRONZE AGE: THE SHANG

The traditional history of China tells of three ancient dynasties:

| | | |
|---|---|---|
| 2205–1766 B.C.E. | Hsia |
| 1766–1050 B.C.E. | Shang |
| 1050–256 B.C.E. | Chou |

Until early in the twentieth century, modern historians saw the first two as legendary. Then, in the 1920s, archaeological excavations at "the wastes of Yin" near present-day An Yang uncovered the ruins of a walled city that had been a late Shang capital (see Map 1–2). Other Shang cities have been discovered more recently. The ruins contained the archives of the department of divination of the Shang court, with thousands on thousands of "oracle bones" incised with archaic Chinese writing. The names of kings on the bones fit almost perfectly those of the traditional historical record. The recognition that the Shang actually existed has led historians to suggest that the Hsia may also have been an actual dynasty. Perhaps the Hsia began as a late Neolithic red pottery kingdom; some scholars even identify a site just south of the Yellow River at Erlitou as the Hsia capital. Perhaps the Hsia developed black pottery, bronze, and the earliest, still-missing stage of Chinese writing.

The characteristic political institution of Bronze Age China was the city-centered state. The largest was the Shang capital, which, frequently moved, lacked the monumental architecture of Egypt or Mesopotamia. The walled city contained public buildings, altars, and the residences of the aristocracy; it was surrounded by a sea of Neolithic tribal villages. By late Shang times, several such cities were spotted across the north China plain. The characteristic form of social organization was the royal or noble clan.

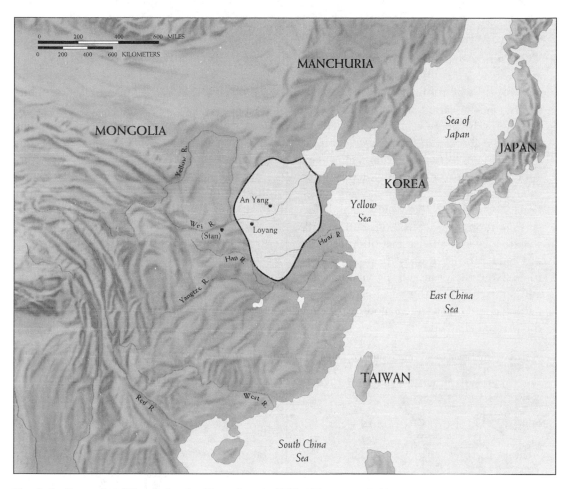

**Map 1-2   Bronze Age China during the Shang dynasty, 1766–1050 B.C.E.**   An Yang was a late Shang dynasty capital. Sian and Loyang were the capitals of the Western and the Eastern Chou.

The Shang kings possessed political, economic, social, and religious authority, and the rulers of other states acknowledged their authority. When they died, they were sometimes succeeded by younger brothers and sometimes by sons.

The military aristocracy went to war in chariots, supported by levies of foot soldiers. Their weapons were spears and powerful compound bows. Accounts tell of armies of three or four thousand troops and of a battle involving thirteen thousand. The Shang fought against barbarian tribes and, occasionally, against other city-states in rebellion against Shang rule. Captured prisoners were enslaved.

The three most notable features of Shang civilization were writing, bronzes, and the appearance of social classes. Scribes at the Shang court kept records on strips

## Chinese Writing

The Chinese system of writing dates back at least to the Shang dynasty (1766–1050 B.C.E.), when animal bones and tortoise shells (the so-called oracle bones) were incised for the purpose of divination. About half of the three thousand characters used in Shang times have been deciphered. They evolved over the centuries into the fifty thousand characters found in the largest dictionaries. But even today only about three or four thousand are in common use. A scholar may know twice that number.

Characters developed from little pictures. Note the progressive stylization. By 200 B.C.E., the writing had become standardized and close to the modern form of the printed character.

|  | Shang (1400 B.C.E.) | Chou (600 B.C.E.) | Seal Script (200 B.C.E.) | Modern |
|---|---|---|---|---|
| Sun | | | | |
| Moon | | | | |
| Tree | | | | |
| Bird | | | | |
| Mouth | | | | |
| Horse | | | | |

Other characters combined two pictures to express an idea. The following examples use modern characters:

| Sun | 日 | + moon | 月 | = bright | 明 |
|---|---|---|---|---|---|
| Mouth | 口 | + bird | 鳥 | = to chirp | 鳴 |
| Woman | 女 | + child | 子 | = good | 好 |
| Tree | 木 | + sun | 日 | = east | 東 |

It was a matter of convention that the sun behind a tree meant the rising sun in the east and not the setting sun in the west.

Characters were formed several other ways. In one, a sound element was combined with a meaning element. Chinese has many homophones, or words with the same sound. The character 台, for example, is read *tai* and means "elevation" or "to raise up." But in spoken Chinese, there are other words with the same sound that mean "moss," "trample," a "nag," and "idle." Thus

| Tai | 台 | + grass | 艹 | = moss | 苔 |
|---|---|---|---|---|---|
| Tai | 台 | + foot | 足 | = trample | 跆 |
| Tai | 台 | + horse | 馬 | = a nag | 駘 |
| Tai | 台 | + heart | 心 | = idle | 怠 |

In each case the sound comes from the 台, and the meaning from the other element. Note that the 台 may be at the bottom, the top, or the right. This positioning, too, is a matter of convention.

Table by author; calligraphy by Teruko Craig.

of bamboo, but these have not survived. What survived are inscriptions on bronzes and the oracle bones. Some bones contain the question put to the oracle, the answer, and the outcome of the matter. Representative questions were: Which ancestor is causing the king's earache? If the king goes hunting at Ch'i, will there be a disaster? Will the king's child be a son? If the king sends his army to attack an enemy, will the deity help him? Was a sacrifice acceptable to ancestral deities?

What we know of Shang religion is based on the bones. The Shang Chinese believed in a supreme "Deity Above," who had authority over the human world. Lesser natural deities—the sun, moon, earth, rain, wind, and the six clouds—served at the court of the Deity Above. The Shang king sacrificed not to the Deity Above but to his own ancestors, who interceded with the Deity Above on his behalf. Kings, while alive at least, were not considered divine but were the high priests of the state.

In Shang times, as later, religion in China was often associated with cosmology. The Shang people observed the movements of the planets and stars and reported eclipses. Celestial happenings were seen as omens from the gods above. The chief cosmologists also recorded events at the court. The Shang calendar had a month of 30 days and a year of 360 days, and adjustments were made periodically by adding an extra month. The calendar was used by the king to tell his people when to sow and when to reap.

Bronze appeared in China about 2000 B.C.E., a thousand years later than in Mesopotamia and five hundred years later than in India. The Shang likely developed bronze technology independently, however, because Shang methods of casting were more advanced than those of Mesopotamia and because the designs emerge directly from the preceding black-pottery culture. Bronze was used for weapons, armor, and chariot fittings, and for a variety of ceremonial vessels of amazing fineness and beauty.

Among the Shang, as with all early river valley civilizations, the increasing control of nature through agriculture and metallurgy was accompanied by the emergence of a highly stratified society in which the many were compelled to serve the few. A monopoly of bronze weapons enabled aristocrats to exploit other groups. A hierarchy of class defined life in the Chinese city-state. The king and the officials of his court lived within the walled city. Their houses were spacious, built above the ground with roofs supported by rows of wooden pillars, resting on foundation stones. Their lifestyle was, for ancient times, opulent: They wore fine clothes, feasted at banquets, and drank wine from bronze vessels. In contrast, a far larger population of agricultural workers lived outside the city in cramped pit-dwellings. Their life was meager and hard; archaeological excavations of their underground hovels have uncovered only earthenware pots.

Nowhere was the gulf between the royal lineage and the baseborn more apparent than in the Shang institution of human sacrifice. One Shang tomb 39 feet long, 26 feet wide, and 26 feet deep contained the decapitated bodies of humans, horses, and dogs, as well as ornaments of bone, stone, and jade. When a king died, hundreds of slaves or prisoners of war, together with some who had served the king during his lifetime, might be buried with him. Sacrifices also were made when a palace or an altar was built.

**Human Sacrifice in Early China**

By the seventh century B.C.E., human sacri-fice was less frequent in China, but they still happened. This poem was composed when Duke Mu of the state of Ch'in died in 631. (For want of better terms, Chinese titles are usually translated into roughly equivalent titles among the English nobility.) Were human feelings different, as Professor K. C. Chang has asked, a thousand years earlier during the Shang? The poem suggests that despite religious belief and the honor accorded the victims, they may not have gone gladly to the grave. Note the identification of Heaven with "that blue one," the sky.

*We believe today that it is honorable to die in war for one's nation. How is that different from dying to serve one's lord in the afterlife?*

*"Kio" sings the oriole*
*As it lights on the thorn-bush.*
*Who went with Duke Mu to the grave?*
*Yen-hsi of the clan Tsu-chu.*

*Now this Yen-hsi*
*Was the pick of all our men;*
*But as he drew near the tomb-hole*
*His limbs shook with dread.*
*That blue one, Heaven,*
*Takes all our good men.*
*Could we but ransom him*
*There are a hundred would give their lives.*
*"Kio" sings the oriole*
*As it lights on the mulberry-tree.*
*Who went with Duke Mu to the grave?*
*Chung-hang of the clan Tsu-chu.*
*Now this Chung-hang*
*Was the sturdiest of all our men;*
*But as he drew near the tomb-hole*
*His limbs shook with dread.*
*That blue one, Heaven,*
*Takes all our good men.*
*Could we but ransom him*
*There are a hundred would give their lives.*

From *The Book of Songs*, trans. by Arthur Waley (New York: Grove Press, 1960), p. 311.

## LATER BRONZE AGE: THE WESTERN CHOU

To the west of the area of Shang rule, in the valley of the Wei River, a tribu-tary of the Yellow River, and near the present-day city of Sian, lived the Chou people. Culturally closer to the Neolithic black-pottery culture, they were less civilized and more warlike than the Shang. References to the Chou in the Shang oracle bones indicate that the Shang had relations with them—sometimes friendly, sometimes hostile. According to the traditional historical record, the last Shang kings were weak, cruel, and tyrannical. By 1050 B.C.E., they had been debilitated by cam-paigns against nomads in the north and rebellious tribes in the east. Taking advan-tage of this opportunity, the Chou made alliances with disaffected city-states and swept in, conquering the Shang.

| **Early China** | |
| --- | --- |
| 4000 B.C.E. | Neolithic agricultural villages |
| 1766 B.C.E. | Bronze Age city-states, aristocratic chari14oteers, pictographic writing |
| 771 B.C.E. | Iron Age territorial states |
| 500 B.C.E. | Age of philosophers |
| 221 B.C.E. | China is unified |

In most respects, the Chou continued the Shang pattern of life and rule. The agrarian-based city-centered state continued to be the basic unit of society, and it is estimated that there were about two hundred of them in the eighth century B.C.E. The Chou social hierarchy was not unlike that of the Shang, with kings and lords at the top, officials and warriors below them, and peasants and slaves at the bottom. Slaves served primarily as domestic servants. Themselves backward, the Chou assimilated Shang culture, continuing the development of ideographic writing. The Chou also maintained the practice of casting bronze ceremonial vessels, but their vessels lacked the fineness that set the Shang above the rest of the Bronze Age world.

The Chou kept their capital in the west but set up a secondary capital at Loyang, along the southern bend of the Yellow River (see Map 1–2). They appointed their kinsmen or other aristocratic allies to rule in other city-states. Blood or lineage ties were essential to the Chou pattern of rule. The Chou king was the head of the senior branch of the family and he performed the sacrifices to the Deity Above for the entire family. The rankings of the lords of other princely states, which, for want of better terms, are usually translated into the titles of English feudal nobility—duke, marquis, earl, viscount, and baron, reflected their degree of closeness to the senior line of Chou kings.

One difference between the Shang and the Chou was in the nature of political legitimacy. The Shang kings, descended from shamanistic (priestly) rulers, enjoyed a hereditary religious authority and needed no theory to justify their rule. But the Chou, having conquered the Shang, needed a rationale for why they, and not the Shang, were now the rightful rulers. Their argument was that Heaven (the new name for the supreme being that gradually replaced the "Deity Above" during the early Chou), appalled by the wickedness of the last Shang king, had withdrawn its mandate to rule from the Shang, awarding it instead to the Chou. This concept of the Mandate of Heaven was subsequently invoked by every dynasty in China down to the twentieth century. The ideograph for Heaven is related to that for man, and the concept originally had human, or anthropomorphic, overtones. In the later Chou, how-ever, although it continued to have a moral will, Heaven became less anthropomor-phic and more of an abstract metaphysical force.

## IRON AGE: THE EASTERN CHOU

In 771 B.C.E., the Wei valley capital of the Western Chou was overrun by bar-barians. The explanation of the event in Chinese tradition calls to mind the story of "the boy who cried wolf." The last Western Chou king was so infatuated with a favorite concubine that he repeatedly lit bonfires signaling a barbarian attack. His concubine would clap her hands in delight at the sight of the army assembled in martial splen-dor. But the army tired of the charade, and when invaders actually came, the king's beacons were ignored. The king was killed and the Chou capital sacked. The heir to the throne, with some members of the court, escaped to the secondary capital at Loyang, two hundred miles to the east and just south of the bend in the Yellow River, begin-ning the Eastern Chou period.

The first phase of the Eastern Chou is sometimes called the Spring and Autumn period after the classic history by that name and lasted until 481 B.C.E. After their flight to Loyang, the Chou kings were never able to reestablish their old authority. Loyang remained a center of culture and ritual observances, but by the early seventh century B.C.E., its political power was nominal. Kinship and religious ties to the Chou house had worn thin, and it no longer had the military strength to reimpose its rule. During the seventh and sixth centuries B.C.E., the political configuration in China was an equi-librium of many little principalities on the north-central plain surrounded by larger, wholly autonomous territorial states along the borders of northern China (see Map 1–3). The larger states consolidated the areas within their borders, absorbed tribal peoples, and expanded, conquering states on their periphery.

To defend themselves against the more aggressive territorial states, and in the absence of effective Chou authority, smaller states entered defensive alliances. The ear-liest alliance, of 681 B.C.E., was directed against the half-barbarian state of Ch'u, which straddled the Yangtze in the south. Princes and lords of smaller states elected as their hegemon (or military overlord) the lord of a northern territorial state and pledged him their support. At the formal ceremony that established the alliance, a bull was sacrificed. The hegemon and other lords smeared its blood on their mouths and before the gods swore oaths to uphold the alliance. That the oaths were not always upheld can be sur-mised from the Chinese expression "to break an oath while the blood is still wet on one's lips." During the next two centuries, alliances shifted and hegemons changed. At best, alliances only slowed down the pace of military aggrandizement.

The second phase of the Eastern Chou is known as the Warring States period after a chronicle of the same name treating the years from 401 to 256 B.C.E. By the

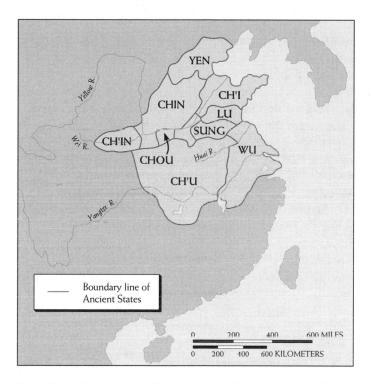

**Map 1-3   Early Iron Age territorial states in China during the sixth century B.C.E.**   After the fall of the Western Chou in 771 B.C.E., large territorial states formed in China that became increasingly independent of the later Chou kings.

fifth century B.C.E., all defensive alliances had collapsed. Strong states swallowed their weaker neighbors. The border states grew in size and power. Interstate stability disappeared. By the fourth century B.C.E., only eight or nine great territorial states remained as contenders. The only question was which one would defeat the others and go on to unify China.

Three basic changes in Chinese society contributed to the rise of large territorial states. One was the expansion of population and agricultural lands. The walled cities of the Shang and Western Chou had been like oases in the wilds, bounded by plains, marshes, and forests. Game was plentiful, so hunting, along with the pasturage of sheep and cattle, supplemented agriculture. But in the Eastern Chou, as population grew, wilds began to disappear, the economy became almost entirely agricultural, and hunting became an aristocratic pastime. Friction arose over boundaries as states began to abut. These changes accelerated in the late sixth century B.C.E. after the start of the Iron Age. Iron tools cleared new lands and plowed deeper, raising yields and increasing agricultural surpluses. Irrigation and drainage canals became important for the first time. Serfs gave way to independent farmers, who bought and sold land. By the third century B.C.E., China had about twenty million people, making it the most populous country in the world, a distinction it has never lost.

A second development was the rise of commerce, which further disrupted the formerly stable agricultural economy. Roads built for war were used by merchants. Goods were transported by horses, oxcarts, riverboats, and the camel, which entered China in the third century B.C.E. The products of one region were traded for those of another. Copper coins joined bolts of silk and precious metals as media of exchange. Rich merchants rivaled in lifestyle the landowning lower nobility. New outer walls were added to cities to provide for expanded merchant quarters. Bronze bells and mirrors, clay figurines, lacquer boxes, and musical instruments found in late Chou tombs give ample evidence that the material and artistic culture of China leaped ahead during this period, despite its endemic wars.

A third change that benefited larger states was the rise of a new kind of army. The war chariots of the old aristocracy, practical only on level terrain, were replaced by cavalry armed with crossbows. Most of the fighting was done by conscript foot soldiers. The upstart armies of the territorial states numbered in the hundreds of thousands. Against these, little states were helpless. The old nobility gave way to professional commanders. The old aristocratic etiquette, which affected behavior even in battle, gave way to military tactics that were bloody and ruthless. Prisoners were often massacred.

Change also affected government. Lords of the new territorial states began to style themselves as kings, taking the title that previously only Chou royalty had enjoyed. At some courts, the hereditary nobility began to decline, supplanted by ministers appointed for their knowledge of statecraft. To survive, new states had to transform their agricultural and commercial wealth into military strength. To collect taxes, conscript soldiers, and administer the affairs of state required records and literate officials. Academies were established to fill the need. Beneath the ministers, a literate bureaucracy developed. Its members were referred to as *shih*, a term that had once meant "warrior" but gradually came to mean "scholar-bureaucrat." The *shih* were of mixed social origins, including petty nobility, literate members of the old warrior class, landlords, merchants, and rising commoners. From this class came the philosophers who created the "one hundred schools" and transformed the culture of China.

## IRON AGE: THE BIRTH OF CHINESE PHILOSOPHY

Shang bronzes are breathtakingly beautiful, but they also have an archaic strangeness. Like Mayan stone sculpture, they are products of a culture so far removed from our own as to be almost incomprehensible. By contrast, the humanism of the Confucian writings and poetry of the Eastern Chou (771–256 B.C.E.) speaks to us directly.

However much the philosophies of these centuries grew out of the earlier matrix of archaic culture, they mark a break with it and the beginning of what we think of today as the Chinese tradition.

The break with the past that occurred during the Eastern Chou culture had parallels, it is important to note, in other parts of the globe. In the Middle East there appeared Greek philosophy and the monotheistic Judaism from which would later develop the world religions of Christianity and Islam. In South Asia there rose Hinduism and Buddhism. The simultaneity of their appearance was striking. Confucius, Lao-tzu, the Hebrew prophets, Buddha, and Socrates, if not exact contemporaries, were grouped within a few hundred years of each other in the first millennium B.C.E. The founders of these great philosophies and religions based their teachings on intensely personal experiences that cannot be analyzed in historical terms. Yet we can examine their historical contexts and note certain similarities.

1. It was not accidental that each philosophical or religious revolution occurred in an area of one of the original river valley civilizations: the Yellow River, the Nile, the Tigris-Euphrates, and along the Indus and Ganges. These areas contained the most advanced cultures of the ancient world. They had sophisticated agriculture, cities with many literate inhabitants, and specialized trades and professions. In short, they had the material preconditions for breakthroughs in religion and thought.

2. Each of the revolutions in thought and ethos was born of a crisis in the ancient world. The appearance of iron meant better tools and weapons and, by extension, greater riches and more powerful armies. Old societies began to change and then to disintegrate. Old aristocratic and priestly codes of behavior broke down, producing a demand for more universalized rules of behavior, that is to say, for ethics. The very relation of humans to nature or to the universe seemed to be changing. This predicament led to new visions of social and political order. There is, thus, more than an accidental similarity between the Chinese sage-king, the Jewish Messiah, and Plato's philosopher-king. Each was a response to a crisis in a society of the ancient world. Each would reconnect ethics to history and restore order in a troubled society.

3. What distinguished the visions embodied in the new religions and philosophies was their universalism. Each held that its doctrines were true for all peoples and times. Because of this, Buddhism, Christianity, and Islam became missionary religions; because of this, Greek and Chinese philosophies could spread far beyond their countries of origin. Confucianism eventually spread to Vietnam, Korea, and Japan, countries with customs quite different from those of China. It could provide a basis for social ethics and law in those countries just because some aspects of its moral teachings transcended particular Chinese institutions.

Of the four great revolutions in thought of the first millennium B.C.E., the Chinese was more akin to the Greek than to the Indian or Judaic. Just as Greece had a gamut of philosophies, so in late Chou China there were the "one hundred schools." (When Mao Tse-tung in 1956 said, "Let the one hundred flowers bloom"—encouraging a momentary easing of intellectual oppression—he was referring back to the creative era of Chou philosophy.) Whereas Greek thought was speculative and more concerned with the world of nature, Chinese thought was sociopolitical and more practical. Even Taoist sages, who were inherently apolitical, found it necessary to offer a political philosophy.

Chinese thought also had far greater staying power than the Greek. Only a few centuries after the glory of Athens, Greek thought was submerged by Christianity. It became the handmaiden of theology and did not reemerge as an independent force until the Renaissance. In contrast, Chinese philosophy, although challenged for centuries by Buddhism, reemerged and remained dominant down to the early twentieth century. How were these early philosophies, and particularly Confucianism, able to maintain such a grip on China when the cultures of every other part of the world fell under the sway of religions?

Part of the answer is that most Chinese philosophy had a religious dimension. But it was another kind of religion, with assumptions quite different from those derived from Judaic roots. In the Christian or Islamic worldview, there is a God, who, however concerned with humankind, is not of this world. This conception leads to dualism, the distinction between an otherworld, which is supernatural, and this world, which is natural.

In the Chinese worldview, the two spheres are not separate: The cosmos is single, continuous, and nondualistic. It includes heaven, earth, and man. Heaven is above. Earth is below. Man, ideally guided by a wise and virtuous ruler, stands in between and regulates or harmonizes the cosmological forces of heaven and earth by the power of his virtue and by performing the sacrifices. The form that this cosmology took under the last Manchu dynasty can be seen today in the city of Peking (Beijing): The Temple of Heaven is in the south; the Temple of Earth is in the northeast; and the Imperial Palace is, symbolically at least, in between. To say that the emperor's sacrifices at the Temple of Heaven were secular (and, therefore, not religious) or religious (and not secular) misses the point. It projects our own dualistic assumptions onto China. Similarly, when we speak of the Taoist sage becoming one with nature, it is not the nature of a twentieth-century natural scientist; rather, it is a nature that contains metaphysical and cosmological forces of a kind that our worldview might label as religious.

Most of the one hundred schools—if, in fact, there were that many—are unknown today. Many writings disappeared in the book burning of the Ch'in dynasty (256–221 B.C.E.). But even apart from the three major schools of Confucianism, Taoism, and Legalism, enough have survived to convey a sense of the range and vitality of Chou thought:

1. *Rhetoricians.* This school taught the arts of persuasion to be used in diplomatic negotiations. Its principal work instructed the rulers of territorial states by using historical anecdote. A practical work, it was popular for its humor and lively style.

2. *Logicians.* This school taught logic and relativity. For example, one proposition was: "The south has no limit and has a limit." Another was: "A white horse is not a horse": That is to say, the concept of *horse* is not the same as the concept of *white horse.*

3. *Strategists: The Art of War* by Sun-tzu became the classic of military science in China and is studied today by guerrillas and in military academies around the world. It praises the general who wins victories without battles, and also talks of organizing states for war, of supply, of spies, and of propaganda.

4. *Cosmologists.* This school described the functions of the cosmos in terms of *yin* and *yang,* the complementary negative and positive forces of nature, and in terms of the five elements (metal, wood, earth, fire, and water). Its ideas were later absorbed by other schools.

5. *Mohists.* Mo-tzu (470–391 B.C.E.) was an early critic of Confucius. His goals were peace, wealth, and the increase of population. He taught an ethic of universal love—to overcome a selfish human nature. He preached discipline and austerity and was critical of whatever lacked utility, including music, other arts, elaborate funerals, wasteful rites, and, above all, war. To achieve his goals, Mo-tzu argued for a strong state: Subjects must obey their rulers, who, in turn, must obey Heaven. Heaven will punish evil and reward good. To promote peace, Mo-tzu organized his followers into military units to aid states that were attacked.

## Confucianism

Confucius was born in 551 B.C.E. in a minor state in northeastern China. As he received an education in writing, music, and rituals, he probably belonged to the lower nobility or the knightly class. His father died when Confucius was young, so he may have known privation. He made his living by teaching. He traveled with his disciples from state to state, seeking a ruler who would put his ideas into practice. His techniques,

| China | |
|---|---|
| 551–479 B.C.E. | Confucius |
| 370–290 B.C.E. | Mencius |
| Fourth century B.C.E. | Lao-tzu |
| 221 B.C.E. | Ch'in unifies China |

however, were rejected as impractical, although he may once have held a minor position. He died in 479 B.C.E., having failed to find a ruler to advise but honored as a teacher and scholar. The name *Confucius* is the Latinized form of K'ung Fu-tzu, or Master K'ung, as he is known in China.

We know of Confucius only through *The Analects*, his sayings collected by his disciples, or perhaps by their disciples. They are mostly in the form of "The Master said," followed by his words. The picture that emerges is of a man of moderation, propriety, optimism, good sense, and wisdom. In an age of cruelty and superstition, he was humane, rational, and upright, demanding much of others and more of himself. Asked about death, he replied, "You do not understand even life. How can you understand death?"[1] Asked about how to serve the spirits and the gods, in which he did not disbelieve, he answered, "You are not able even to serve man. How can you serve the spirits?"

Confucius described himself as a transmitter and a conservator of tradition, not an innovator. He idealized the early Shang and Chou kings as paragons of virtue and particularly saw early Chou society as a golden age. He sought the secrets of this golden age in its writings. Some of these writings, along with later texts, became the Confucian classics, which through most of subsequent Chinese history had an authority not unlike Scripture in the West. Five of the thirteen classics were the following:

1. *The Book of Changes* (also known as the *Classic of Divination*). A handbook for diviners, this book was later seen as containing metaphysical truths about the universe.
2. *The Book of History*. This book contains documents and speeches from the early Chou, some authentic. Chinese tradition holds that it was edited by Confucius. It was interpreted as the record of sage-kings.
3. *The Book of Poetry*. This book contains some three hundred poems from the early Chou. Representing a sophisticated literary tradition, it includes love songs as well as poems of friendship, ritual, and politics. Many were given political and moral interpretations in later times.
4. *The Book of Rites*. This book includes both rituals and rules of etiquette. Rites were important to Confucians, both as a support for proper behavior and because they were seen as corresponding to forces within nature.
5. *The Spring and Autumn Annals*. A brief record of the major occurrences from 722 to 481 B.C.E. in the state where Confucius was born, this book, according to Chinese tradition, was edited by Confucius and reflected his moral judgments on past historical figures.

---

[1]This quotation and all quotations from Confucius in this passage are from Confucius, *The Analects*, trans. by D. C Lau (Penguin Books, 1979).

## Confucius Defines the Gentleman

For over two thousand years in China, the cultural ideal was the gentleman, who combined knowledge of the ancient sages with an inner morality and outer propriety.

---

*How does the injunction "to repay an injury with straightness" compare to the Christian injunction to turn the other cheek? Which do you think is more appropriate?*

---

*The Master said, "I never enlighten anyone who has not been driven to distraction by trying to understand a difficulty or who has not got into a frenzy trying to put his ideas into words.*

*"When I have pointed out one corner of a square to anyone and he does not come back with the other three, I will not point it out to him a second time."*

*The Master said, "Yu, shall I tell you what it is to know. To say you know when you know, and to say you do not when you do not, that is knowledge."*

*The Master said, "Is it not a pleasure, having learned something, to try it out at due intervals? Is it not a joy to have friends come from afar? Is it not gentlemanly not to take offence when others fail to appreciate your abilities?"*

*Someone said, "Repay an injury with a good turn. What do you think of this saying?" The Master said, "What, then, do you repay a good turn with? You repay an injury with straightness, but you repay a good turn with a good turn."*

*Lin Fang asked about the basis of the rites. The Master said, "A noble question indeed! With the rites, it is better to err on the side of frugality than on the side of extravagance; in mourning, it is better to err on the side of grief than on the side of formality."*

*The Master said, "I suppose I should give up hope. I have yet to meet the man who is as fond of virtue as he is of beauty in women."*

*The Master said, "The gentleman agrees with others without being an echo. The small man echoes without being in agreement."*

*The Master said, "The gentleman is at ease without being arrogant; the small man is arrogant without being at ease."*

*The Master said, "There is no point in seeking the views of a gentleman who, though he sets his heart on the Way, is ashamed of poor food and poor clothes."*

Confucius, *The Analects*, trans. by D. C. Lau (New York: Penguin Classics, 1979), © D. C. Lau, 1979.

Basing his teachings on these writings, Confucius proposed to solve the turmoil of his own age by a return to the good old ways of the early Chou. When asked about government, he said, "Let the ruler be a ruler, the subject a subject, the father a father, the son a son." (The five Confucian relationships were ruler-subject, father-son, husband-wife, older brother-younger brother, and friend-friend.) If everyone fulfilled the duties of his or her status, then harmony would prevail. Confucius understood the fundamental truth that the well-being of a society depends on the morality of its members. His vision was of an unbroken social harmony extending from the individual family member to the monarch.

But a return to the early Chou was impossible. China was undergoing a dynamic transition from hundreds of small city-states to a few large territorial states. New, specialized classes were appearing. Old rituals no longer worked. It was thus not enough to stress basic human relationships. The genius of Confucius was to transform the old aristocratic code into a new ethic that could be practiced by any educated Chinese. His reinterpretation of the early Chou tradition can be seen in the concept of the *chun-tzu*. This term literally meant "the son of the ruler" (or the aristocrat). Confucius redefined it to mean one of noble behavior, a person with the inner virtues of humanity, integrity, righteousness, altruism, and loyalty, and an outward demeanor and propriety to match.

This redefinition was not unlike the change in the meaning of *gentleman* in England from "one who is gentle-born" to "one who is gentle-behaved." But whereas *gentleman* remained a fairly superficial category in the West, in China *chun-tzu* went deeper. Confucius saw ethics as grounded in nature. The true *chun-tzu* was in touch with his own basic nature, which, in turn, was a part of the cosmic order. Confucius expressed this saying: "Heaven is the author of the virtue that is in me." Confucius's description of his own passage through life goes far beyond the question of good manners: "At fifteen I set my heart on learning; at thirty I took my stand; at forty I came to be free from doubts; at fifty I understood the Decree of Heaven; at sixty my ear was attuned; at seventy I followed my heart's desire without overstepping the line."

Confucius often contrasted the gentleman with the small or common person. The gentleman, educated in the classics and cultivating the Way, understands moral action. The common people, in contrast, "can be made to follow a path but not to understand it." Good government for Confucius depended on the appointment to office of good men, who would serve as examples for the multitude: "Just desire the good yourself and the common people will be good. The virtue of the gentleman is like wind; the virtue of the small man is like grass. Let the wind blow over the grass and it is sure to bend." Beyond the gentleman was the sage-king, who possessed an almost mystical virtue and power. For Confucius, the early Chou kings were clearly sages. But Confucius wrote, "I have no hopes of meeting a sage. I would be content if I met someone who is a gentleman."

Confucianism was not adopted as the official philosophy of China until the second century B.C.E., during the Han dynasty. But two other important Confucian philosophers had appeared in the meantime. Mencius (370–290 B.C.E.) represents an idealistic extension of Confucius's thought. His interpretation was accepted during most of subsequent history. He is famous for his argument that humans tend toward the good just as water runs downward. The role of education, therefore, is to uncover and cultivate that innate goodness. Moreover, just as humans tend toward the good, so does Heaven possess a moral will. The will of Heaven is that a government should see to the education and well-being of its people. The rebellion of people against a government is the primary evidence that Heaven has withdrawn its mandate. At times in Chinese history, only lip service was paid to a concern for the people. In fact, rebellions occurred more often against weak governments than against harsh ones. But the idea that government ought to care for the people became a permanent part of the Confucian tradition.

The other influential Confucian philosopher was Hsun-tzu (300–237 B.C.E.), who represents a tough-minded extension of Confucius's thought. Hsun-tzu felt Heaven was amoral, indifferent to whether China was ruled by a tyrant or a sage. He believed human nature was bad or, at least, that desires and emotions, if unchecked and unrefined, led to social conflict. So he emphasized etiquette and education as restraints on an unruly human nature, and good institutions, including punishments and rewards, as a means for shaping behavior. These ideas exerted a powerful influence on thinkers of the Legalist school.

## Taoism

It is sometimes said that the Chinese have been Confucian while in office and Taoist (pronounced "Dah-oh-ist") in their private lives. Taoism offered a refuge from the burden of social responsibilities. The classics of the school are the *Lao-tzu*, dating from the fourth century B.C.E., and the *Chuang-tzu*, dating from about a century later.

The central concept is the *Tao*, or Way. It is mysterious, ineffable, and cannot be named. It is the creator of the universe, the sustainer of the universe, and the process or flux of the universe. The *Tao* functions on a cosmic, not a human, scale. As the *Lao-tzu* put it, "Heaven and Earth are ruthless, and treat the myriad creatures as straw dogs; the sage (in accord with the *Tao*) is ruthless, and treats the people as straw dogs."[2]

What does it mean to be a sage? How does a human join the rhythms of nature? The answer given by the *Lao-tzu* is by regaining or returning to an original simplicity. Various similes describe this state: "to return to the infinite," "to return to being a babe," or "to return to being the uncarved block." To attain this state, one must "learn to be without learning." Knowledge is bad because it creates distinctions, because it leads to the succession of ideas and images that interfere with participation in the *Tao*. One must also learn to be without desires beyond the immediate and simple needs of nature: "The nameless uncarved block is but freedom from desire."

If the sage treats the people as straw dogs, it would appear that he is beyond good and evil. But elsewhere in the *Lao-tzu*, the sage is described as one who "excels in saving people." If not a contradiction, this is at least a paradox. The resolution is that the sage is clearly beyond morality but is not immoral or even amoral. Quite to the contrary, by being in harmony with the *Tao* the sage is impeccably moral— as one who clings to the forms of morality or makes morality a goal could never be.

---

[2]All quotations from the *Lao-tzu* are from *Lao-Tzu Tao Te Ching*, trans. by D. C. Lau (Penguin Books, 1963).

## Taoism

Can inner, transformative, religious experience take people beyond everyday worldly concerns and imbue them with moral charisma or moral authority? What other religions might call "supernatural," Taoism sees as truly natural.

---

*How does the "Way" in Taoism compare with Confucius's use of the same term?*

---

### Lao-tzu Tells of the Way of the Sage

*The way that can be spoken of*
*Is not the constant way;*
*The name that can be named*
*Is not the constant name.*
*The nameless was the beginning of heaven and*
*    earth;*
*The named was the mother of the myriad*
*    creatures.*

*The spirit of the valley never dies*
*This is called the mysterious female.*
*The gateway of the mysterious female*
*Is called the root of heaven and earth.*
*Dimly visible, it seems as if it were there,*
*Yet use will never drain it.*

*There is a thing confusedly formed,*
*Born before heaven and earth.*
*Silent and void*
*It stands alone and does not change,*
*Goes round and does not weary.*
*It is capable of being the mother of the world.*
*I know not its name*
*So I style it "the way."*
*When the way prevails in the empire, fleetfooted*
*    horses are relegated to ploughing the fields;*
*    when the way does not prevail in the empire,*
*    war-horses breed on the border.*

So in the *Lao-tzu*, it is written, "Exterminate benevolence, discard rectitude, and the people will again be filial; exterminate ingenuity, discard profit, and there will be no more thieves and bandits." In this formulation, we also see the basis for the political philosophy of Taoism, which can be summed up as "not doing" (*wu wei*). What this means is something between "doing nothing" and "being, but not acting." This concept has some overlap with Confucianism. The Confucian sage-king, we recall, exerts a moral force by dint of his internal accord with nature. A perfect Confucian sage could rule without doing. Confucius said, "If there was a ruler who achieved order without taking any action, it was, perhaps, Shun [an early Chou sage emperor]. There was nothing for him to do but to hold himself in a respectful posture and to face due south." In Taoism, all true sages had this Shun-like power to rule without action: "The way never acts yet nothing is left undone. Should lords and princes be able to hold fast to it, the myriad creatures will be transformed of their own accord." Or, says the *Lao-tzu*, "I am free from desire and the people of themselves become simple like the uncarved block." The sage acts without acting, and "when his task is accomplished and his work is done, the people will say, 'It happened to us naturally.'"

*One who knows does not speak; one who speaks does not know.*

*Therefore the sage puts his person last and it comes first,*

*Treats it as extraneous to himself and it is preserved.*

*Is it not because he is without thought of self that he is able to accomplish his private ends?*

**Chuang-tzu Compares**
**Governmental Office to a Dead Rat**

When Hui Tzu was prime minister of Liang, Chuang Tzu set off to visit him. Someone said to Hui Tzu, "Chuang Tzu is coming because he wants to replace you as prime minister!" With this Hui Tzu was filled with alarm and searched all over the state for three days and three nights trying to find Chuang Tzu. Chuang Tzu then came to see him and said, "In the south there is a bird called the Yuan-ch'u—I wonder if you've ever heard of it? The Yuan-ch'u rises up from the South Sea and flies to the North Sea, and it will rest on nothing but the Wu-t'ung tree, eat nothing but the fruit of the Lien, and drink only from springs of sweet water. Once there was an owl who had gotten hold of a half-rotten old rat, and as the Yuan-ch'u passed by, it raised its head, looked up at the Yuan-ch'u, and said, "Shoo!' Now that you have this Liang state of yours, are you trying to shoo me?"

Lao-tzu selection from *Lao-tzu, Tao Te Ching*, trans. by D. C. Lau (New York: Penguin Classics, 1963). © D. C. Lau. Chuang-tzu selection from *The Complete Works of Chuang-tzu*, trans. by Burton Watson © 1968 by Columbia University Press. Reprinted by permission of the publisher.

Along with the basic Taoist prescription of becoming one with the Tao are two other assumptions or principles. One is that any action pushed to an extreme will initiate a countervailing reaction in the direction of the opposite extreme. The other is that too much government, even good government, can become oppressive by its very weight. As the *Lao-tzu* put it, "The people are hungry; it is because those in authority eat up too much in taxes that the people are hungry. The people are difficult to govern; it is because those in authority are too fond of action that the people are difficult to govern." Elsewhere, the same idea was expressed in even homelier terms: "Govern a large state as you would cook small fish," that is, without too much stirring.

## Legalism

A third great current in classical Chinese thought, and by far the most influential in its own age, was Legalism. Like the philosophers of other schools, the Legalists were concerned to end the wars that plagued China. True peace, they felt, required a united country, and thus a strong state. They favored conscription and considered war a means of extending state power.

## Legalism

According to Legalism, the state can only regulate behavior, it cannot affect the inner dimensions of human life. Rewards and punishments, furthermore, are far more efficient in controlling behavior than moral appeals.

---

*Do the tenets of Legalism have any modern parallels? What do you think of Legalism as a philosophy of government? As an approach to the problem of crime? How does Legalism compare with other approaches to law, leadership, and governments?*

---

### Han Fei-Tzu Argues for the Efficacy of Punishments

Now take a young fellow who is a bad character. His parents may get angry at him, but he never makes any change. The villagers may reprove him, but he is not moved. His teachers and elders may admonish him but he never reforms. The love of his parents, the efforts of the villagers, and the wisdom of his teachers and elders—all the three excellent disciplines are applied to him, and yet not even a hair on his shins is altered. It is only after the district magistrate sends out his soldiers and in the name of the law searches for wicked individuals that the young man becomes afraid and changes his ways and alters his deeds. So while the love of parents is not sufficient to discipline the children, the severe penalties of the district magistrate are. This is because men became naturally spoiled by love, but are submissive to authority. . . .

That being so, rewards should be rich and certain so that the people will be attracted by them; punishments should be severe and definite so that the people will fear them; and laws should be uniform and steadfast so that the people will be familiar with them. Consequently, the sovereign should show no wavering in bestowing rewards and grant no pardon in administering punishments, and he should add honor to rewards and disgrace to punishments—when this is done, then both the worthy and the unworthy will want to exert themselves. . . .

### Han Fei-Tzu Attacks Confucianism

There was once a man of Sung who tilled his field. In the midst of his field stood the

The Legalists did not seek a model in the distant past. In ancient times, said one, there were fewer people and more food, so it was easier to rule; different conditions require new principles of government. Nor did the Legalists model their state on a heavenly order of values. Human nature is selfish, argued both of the leading Legalists, Han Fei-tzu (d. 233 B.C.E.) and Li Ssu (d. 208 B.C.E.). It is human to like rewards or pleasure and to dislike punishments or pain. If laws are severe and impartial, if what strengthens the state is rewarded and what weakens the state is punished, then a strong state and a good society will ensue.

stump of a tree, and one day a hare, running at full speed, bumped into the stump, broke its neck, and died. Thereupon the man left his plow and kept watch at the stump, hoping that he would get another hare. But he never caught another hare, and was only ridiculed by the people of Sung. Now those who try to rule the people of the present age with the conduct of government of the early kings are all doing exactly the same thing as that fellow who kept watch by the stump. . . .

Those who are ignorant about government insistently say: "Win the hearts of the people." If order could be procured by winning the hearts of the people, then even the wise ministers Yi Yin and Kuan Chung would be of no use. For all that the ruler would need to do would be just to listen to the people. Actually, the intelligence of the people is not to be relied upon any more than the mind of a baby. If the baby does not have his head shaved, his sores will recur; if he does not have his boil cut open, his illness will go from bad to worse. However, in order to shave his head or open the boil someone has to hold the baby while the affectionate mother is performing the work,

and yet he keeps crying and yelling incessantly. The baby does not understand that suffering a small pain is the way to obtain a great benefit.

Now, the sovereign urges the tillage of land and the cultivation of pastures for the purpose of increasing production for the people, but they think the sovereign is cruel. The sovereign regulates penalties and increases punishments for the purpose of repressing the wicked, but the people think the sovereign is severe. Again he levies taxes in cash and in grain to fill up the granaries and treasuries in order to relieve famine and provide for the army, but they think the sovereign is greedy. Finally, he insists upon universal military training without personal favoritism, and urges his forces to fight hard in order to take the enemy captive, but the people think the sovereign is violent. These four measures are methods for attaining order and maintaining peace, but the people are too ignorant to appreciate them.

From *Sources of Chinese Tradition*, translated by William Theodore de Bary. © 1960 by Columbia University Press. Reprinted by permission of the publisher.

Laws, therefore, should contain incentives for loyalty and bravery in battle, and for obedience, diligence, and frugality in everyday life. The Legalists despised merchants as parasites and approved of productive farmers. They particularly despised purveyors of doctrines different from their own and criticized rulers who honored philosophers while ignoring their philosophies.

Legalism was the philosophy of the state of Ch'in, which destroyed the Chou in 256 B.C.E. and unified China in 221 B.C.E. Because Ch'in laws were cruel and severe, and because Legalism put human laws above an ethic modeled on Heaven, later generations of Chinese have execrated its doctrines. They saw it, not without justification, as a philosophy that consumed its founders: Han Fei-tzu became an official of the Ch'in state but was eventually poisoned in a prison cell by Li Ssu, who was jealous of his growing influence. Li Ssu, although he became prime minister of Ch'in, was killed in 208 B.C.E. in a political struggle with a court eunuch. Yet, for all of the abuse heaped on Legalist doctrines, their legacy of administrative and criminal laws became a vital part of subsequent dynastic China. Even Confucian statesmen could not do without them.

## REVIEW QUESTIONS

1. "The 'New Stone Age' is a shorthand designation for many complex changes in China's society and economy." Discuss.
2. What are the most important differences between the Eastern and Western Chou periods?
3. What conditions gave rise to the one hundred schools of philosophy?
4. What solution to China's predicament did Confucianism offer? Taoism? Legalism?

## SUGGESTED READINGS

CHANG, K. C. *Shang Civilization* (1980).

CHANG, K. C. *Art, Myth, and Ritual: The Path to Political Authority in Ancient China* (1984). A study of the relation between shamans, gods, agricultural production, and political authority during the Shang and Chou dynasties.

CHANG, K. C. *The Archeology of Ancient China*, 4th ed. (1986). The standard work on the subject.

CREEL, H. G. *The Origins of Statecraft in China* (1970). On the political structure of the Western Chou kingdom.

CREEL, H. G. *What Is Taoism? And Other Studies in Chinese Cultural History* (1970).

DE BARY, W. T. ET AL. *Sources of Chinese Tradition* (1960). A reader in China's philosophical and historical literature. It should be consulted for the later periods as well as for the Chou.

FINGARETE, H. *Confucius—the Secular as Sacred* (1998). An influential study of Confucius.

FUNG, Y. L. *A Short History of Chinese Philosophy*, ed. D. Bodde (1948). A survey of Chinese philosophy from its origins down to recent times.

GRAHAM, A. C. *Disputers of the Tao* (1989). On early Chou intellectual history.

HAWKES, D. *Ch'u Tz'u: The Songs of the South* (1985). Chou poems from the southern state of Ch'u, superbly translated.

HSU, C. Y. *Ancient China in Transition: An Analysis of Social Mobility 722–222 B.C.* (1965). A study of the Eastern Chou dynasty.

HSU, C. Y. *Western Chou Civilization* (1988).

KEIGHTLEY, D. N., ED. *The Origins of Chinese Civilization* (1983).

LAU, D. C., TRANS. *Lao-Tzu, Tao Te Ching* (1963).

LAU, D. C., TRANS. *Confucius, The Analects* (1979).

LEWIS, M. E. *Sanctioned Violence in Early China* (1990).

LI, X. Q. *Eastern Zhou and Qin Civilizations* (1986). This work includes fresh interpretations based on new archaeological finds.

MOTE, F. W. *Intellectual Foundations of China* (1971).

SCHWARTZ, B. I. *The World of Thought in Ancient China* (1985).

WALEY, A. *Three Ways of Thought in Ancient China* (1956). An easy yet sound introduction to Confucianism, Taoism, and Legalism.

WALEY, A. *The Book of Songs* (1960).

WATSON, B., TRANS. *Basic Writings of Mo Tzu, Hsun Tzu, and Han Fei Tzu* (1963).

WATSON, B., TRANS. *The Complete Works of Chuang-tzu* (1968).

WELCH, H. *Taoism, the Parting of the Way* (1967).

Cast bronze horses and warriors excavated in 1969 from the vaulted brick and earth mounded tomb (circa 186–219 C.E.) of a general of the Later Han dynasty. The general may have served on China's western frontier since the tomb was at Lei T'ai in Kansu province. The tomb also contained coins, silver seals, model chariots, and inscribed figures of male and female slaves. The beauty and energy of these bronzes suggest a continuity between Han art and that of the T'ang dynasty several centuries later. [National Museum, Beijing, China]

## chapter two

# China's First Empire (221 B.C.E.–220 C.E.) and Its Aftermath

## CHAPTER OUTLINE

One hallmark of Chinese history is its striking continuity of culture, language, and geography. The Shang and Chou dynasties were centered in north China along the Yellow River or its tributary, the Wei. The capitals of China's first empire were in exactly the same areas, and north China would remain China's political center down through history to the present. If Western civilization had experienced similar continuity, it would have progressed from Thebes in the valley of the Nile to Athens on the Nile, Rome on the Nile, and then, in time, to Paris, London, and Berlin on the Nile, and each of these centers of civilization would have spoken Egyptian and used a single writing system based on Egyptian hieroglyphics.

The many continuities in its history did not mean, however, that China was unchanging. One key turning point came in the third century B.C.E. when the old, quasifeudal, multistate Chou system gave way to a centralized bureaucratic government. The new centralized state built an empire stretching from the steppe in the north to Vietnam in the south.

The history of the first empire is composed of three segments: The Ch'in dynasty, the Former Han dynasty, and the Later Han dynasty. The English word *China* is derived from the name of the first dynasty. The Ch'in overthrew the previous Chou dynasty in 256 B.C.E. It went on to unify China in 221 B.C.E. In reshaping China, the Ch'in developed such momentum that it became overextended and collapsed a single generation after the unification. The succeeding Han dynasties each lasted about two hundred years, the Former Han from 206 B.C.E. to 8 C.E., the Later Han (founded by a descendant of the Former Han rulers, from 25 to 220 C.E. Historians usually treat each of the Han dynasties as a separate period of rule, although they were almost back to back and shared many institutions and cultural traits. So deep was the impression left by these two dynasties on the Chinese that even today they call themselves—in contrast to Mongols, Manchus, Tibetans, and other minorities—the "Han people," and their ideographs, "Han writing."

## CH'IN UNIFICATION OF CHINA

Of the territorial states of the late Chou era, none was more innovative and ruthless than Ch'in. Its location on the Wei River in northwest China—the same area from which the Chou had launched their expansion a millennium earlier—gave it strategic advantages: It controlled the passes leading out onto the Yellow River plain and so was easy to defend and was a secure base from which to launch attacks on other states. From the late fourth century B.C.E., the Ch'in conquered a part of Szechwan and thus controlled two of the most fertile regions of ancient China. It welcomed Legalist administrators, who developed policies for enriching the country and strengthening its military. Despite its harsh laws, farmers moved to Ch'in from other areas, attracted by the order and stability of its society. Its armies had been forged by centuries of warfare against the nomadic raiders by whose lands it was half encircled. To counter these raiders, Ch'in armies adopted nomadic skills, developing cavalry in the fourth century. Other states regarded the Ch'in as tough, crude, and brutal but recognized its formidable strengths.

In 246 B.C.E., the man who would unify China succeeded to the Ch'in throne at the age of thirteen. He grew to be vigorous, ambitious, intelligent, and decisive. He is famous as a Legalist autocrat; but he was also well liked by his ministers, whose advice he usually followed. In 232 B.C.E., at the age of twenty-seven, he began the campaigns that destroyed the six remaining territorial states. On completing his conquests in 221 B.C.E., he adopted the glorious title we translate as "emperor"—a combination of ideographs hitherto used only for gods or mythic heroes—to raise himself above the kings of the former territorial states. Then, aided by officials of great talent, this First Ch'in Emperor set about applying to all of China the reforms that had been tried and found effective in his own realm. His accomplishments in the eleven years before his death in 210 B.C.E. were stupendous.

Having conquered the civilized world of north China and the Yangtze River basin, the First Emperor sent his armies to conquer new lands. They reached the northern edge of the Red River basin in what is now Vietnam. They occupied China's southeastern coast and the area about the present-day city of Canton (see Map 2–1). In the north and the northwest, the emperor's armies fought against the Hsiung Nu, Altaic-speaking Hunnish nomads organized in a tribal confederation. During the late Chou, northern border states had built long walls to protect settled lands from incursions by horse-riding raiders. The Ch'in emperor had them joined into a single Great Wall that extended 1400 miles from the Pacific Ocean into central Asia. (By way of comparison, Hadrian's Wall in England was 73 miles long.) Construction of the Great Wall cost the lives of vast numbers of conscripted laborers—by some accounts, one hundred thousand; by others, as many as one million.

The most significant Ch'in reform, carried out by the Legalist minister, Li Ssu, extended the Ch'in system of bureaucratic government to the entire empire. Li Ssu divided China into forty prefectures, which were further subdivided into counties. The county heads were responsible to prefects, who, in turn, were responsible to the central government. Officials were chosen by ability. Bureaucratic administration was impersonal, based on laws to which all were subject. No one, for example, escaped Ch'in taxation. This kind of bureaucratic centralism broke sharply with the old Chou pattern of establishing dependent principalities for members of a ruler's family. Furthermore, to ensure the smooth functioning of local government offices, former aristocrats of the territorial states were removed from their lands and resettled in the Ch'in capital,

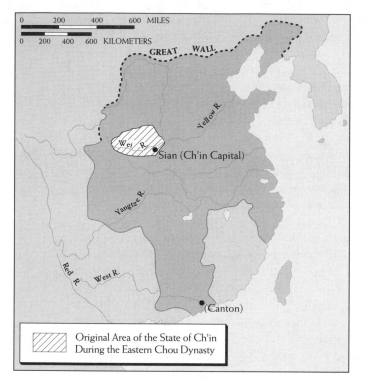

**Map 2-1   The unification of China by the Ch'in State.**   Between 221 and 206 B.C.E. the Ch'in state expanded and unified China.

near present-day Sian. They were housed in mansions on one side of the river, from which they could gaze across at the enormous palace of the First Emperor.

Other reforms further unified the First Emperor's vast domain. Roads were built radiating out from the capital city. The emperor decreed a system of uniform weights and measures. He unified the Chinese writing system, establishing standard ideographs to replace the great variety that had hitherto prevailed. He established uniform axle lengths for carts. Even ideas did not escape the drive toward uniformity. Following the precepts of Legalism, the emperor and his advisers launched a campaign for which they subsequently have been execrated throughout Chinese history. They collected and burned the books of Confucianism and other schools, and were said to have buried alive several hundred scholars opposed to the Legalist philosophy. Only useful books on agriculture, medicine, and Legalist teachings were spared.

But the Ch'in had changed too much too quickly. To pay for the roads, canals, and the Great Wall, burdensome taxes were levied on the people. Commoners hated conscription and labor service, and nobles resented their loss of status. Merchants were despised and exploited; scholars, except for Legalists, were oppressed. A Chinese historian wrote afterward: "The condemned were an innumerable multitude; those who had been tortured and mutilated formed a long procession on the roads. From the princes and ministers down to the humblest people everyone was terrified and in fear of their lives."[1] After the First Emperor died in 210 B.C.E., intrigues broke out at court and rebellions arose in the land. At the end, the Ch'in was destroyed by the domino effect of its own legal codes. When the generals sent to quell a rebellion were defeated, they joined the rebellion rather than return to the capital and incur the severe punishment decreed for failure. The dynasty collapsed in 206 B.C.E.

In 1974, a farmer digging a well near Sian discovered the army of eight thousand life-sized terra-cotta horses and soldiers that guarded the tomb of the First Emperor. The historical record tells us that in the tomb itself, under a mountain of earth, are a replica of his capital; a relief model of the Chinese world with quicksilver rivers; other warriors with chariots of bronze; and the remains of horses, noblemen, and criminals sacrificed to accompany in death the emperor whose dynasty was to have lasted for ten thousand generations.

## FORMER HAN DYNASTY (206 B.C.E.–8 C.E.)

### The Dynastic Cycle

Confucian historians of China have seen a pattern in every dynasty of long duration. They call it the *dynastic cycle*. The stages of the cycle are interpreted in terms of the "Mandate of Heaven." The cycle begins with internal wars that eventually lead to the military unification of China. Unification is proof that Heaven has given the unifier the mandate to rule. Strong and vigorous, the first ruler, in the process of consolidating his political power, restores peace and order to China. His rule is harmonious. Economic growth follows, almost automatically. The peak of the cycle is marked by public works, further energetic reforms, and aggressive military expansion. During this phase, China appears invincible. But then the cycle curves downward. The costs of expansion, coupled with an increasing opulence at the court, place a heavy burden on tax revenues just as they are beginning to decline. The vigor of monarchs wanes. Intrigues develop at the court. The central controls loosen, and provincial governors and military commanders gain autonomy. Finally, canals and other public works fall into disrepair, floods and pestilence occur, rebellions break out, and the dynasty collapses. In the view of Confucian historians, the last emperors in a cycle are not only politically weak but morally culpable as well.

### Early Years of the Former Han Dynasty

The first sixty years of the Han may be thought of as the early phase of its dynastic cycle. After the collapse of the Ch'in, one rebel general gained control of the Wei basin and went on to unify China. He became the first emperor of the Han dynasty

---

[1]C. P. Fitzgerald, *China, a Short Cultural History* (New York, Praeger, 1935), p. 147.

and is known by his posthumous title of Kao Tsu. He rose from plebeian origins to become emperor, which would happen only once again in Chinese history. Kao Tsu built his capital at Ch'ang-an, not far from the former capitals of the Western Chou and the Ch'in. It took Kao Tsu and his immediate successors many years to consolidate their power because they consciously avoided actions that would remind the populace of the hated Ch'in despotism. They made punishments less severe and reduced taxes. Good government prevailed, the economy rebounded, granaries were filled, and vast cash reserves accumulated. Later historians often singled out the early Han rulers as model sage emperors.

## Han Wu Ti

The second phase of the dynastic cycle began with the rule of Wu Ti (the "martial emperor"), who came to the throne in 141 B.C.E. at the age of sixteen and remained there for fifty-four years. Wu Ti was daring, vigorous, and intelligent but also superstitious, suspicious, and vengeful. He wielded tremendous personal authority.

Building on the prosperity achieved by his predecessors, Wu Ti initiated new economic policies. A canal was built from the Yellow River to the capital in northwest China, linking the two major economic regions of north China. "Ever-level granaries" were established throughout the country so that the surplus from bumper crops could be bought and then resold in time of scarcity. To increase revenues, taxes were levied on merchants, the currency was debased, and some offices were sold. Wu Ti also moved against merchants who had built fortunes in untaxed commodities by reestablishing government monopolies—a practice of the Ch'in—on copper coins, salt, iron, and liquor. For fear of Wu Ti, no one spoke out against the monopolies, but a few years after his death, a famous debate was held at the court.

Known after the title of the chronicle as the "Salt and Iron Debate," it was frequently cited thereafter in China, and in Japan and Korea as well. On one side, quasi-Legalist officials argued that the state should enjoy the profits from the sale of salt and iron. On the other side, Confucians argued that these resources should be left in private hands, for the moral purity of officials would be sullied by dealings with merchants. The Confucian scholars who compiled the chronicle made themselves the winner in the debate; but state monopolies became a regular part of Chinese government finance.

Wu Ti also aggressively expanded Chinese borders—a policy that would characterize every strong dynasty. His armies swept south into what is today northern Vietnam and northeast across Manchuria to establish a military outpost in northern Korea that would last until 313 C.E.

The principal threat to the Han was from the Hsiung Nu empire to the north; mounted archers could raid China and flee before an army could be sent against them. To combat them, Wu Ti employed the entire repertoire of policies that would become standard thereafter. When possible he "used the barbarian to control the barbarian," making allies of border nomads against those more distant. Allies were permitted to trade with Chinese merchants; they were awarded titles and honors; and their kings were sent Chinese princesses as brides. When this tactic did not work, he used force. Between 129 and 119 B.C.E., Wu Ti sent several armies of over one hundred thousand troops into the steppe, destroying Hsiung Nu power south of the Gobi Desert in southern Mongolia. To establish a strategic line of defense aimed at the heart of the Hsiung Nu empire further to the west, Wu Ti then sent seven hundred thousand Chinese colonists to the arid Kansu panhandle and extended the Great Wall to the Jade Gate outpost at the eastern end of the Tarim Basin. From this outpost, Chinese influence was extended over the rim oases of Central Asia, thereby establishing the Silk Road that linked Ch'ang-an with Rome (see Map 2–2).

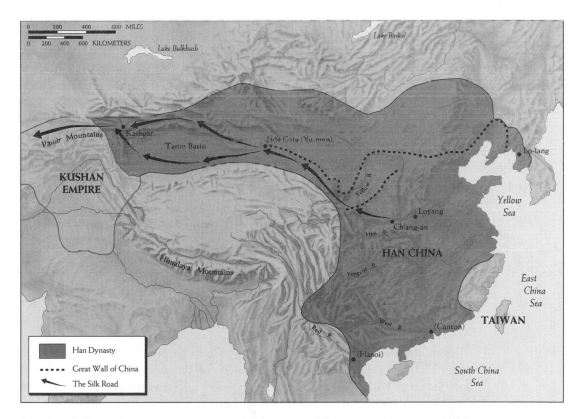

**Map 2–2   The Han Empire 206 B.C.E.–220 C.E.**   At the peak of the Han expansion, the Han armies advanced far out into the steppe north of the Great Wall and west into Central Asia. The Silk Road to Rome passed through the Tarim Basin and the Kushan Empire.

## Chinese Women Among the Nomads

The first of these selections is the lament of Hsi-chun, a Chinese lady sent by Wu Ti in about 105 B.C.E. to be the wife of a nomad king of the Wu-sun people of central Asia. When she got there, she found her husband to be old and decrepit. He saw her only once or twice a year, when they drank a cup of wine together. They could not converse, as they had no language in common. The second selection, written centuries later, is by the T'ang poet Tu Fu, who visited the village of another woman sent to be the wife of a nomad king.

*What does the fate of the women in these poems suggest about the foreign policy of the rulers of ancient China?*

### 1

*My people have married me*
*In a far corner of Earth;*
*Sent me away to a strange land,*
*To the king of the Wu-sun.*
*A tent is my house,*
*Of felt are my walls;*
*Raw flesh my food*
*With mare's milk to drink.*

*Always thinking of my own country,*
*My heart sad within.*
*Would I were a yellow stork*
*And could fly to my old home!*

### 2

*Ten thousand ranges and valleys approach the*
*    Ching Gate*
*And the village in which the Lady of Light was*
*    born and bred.*
*She went out from the purple palace into the*
*    desert-land;*
*She has now become a green grave in the yel-*
*    low dusk.*
*Her face!—Can you picture a wind of the*
*    spring?*
*Her spirit by moonlight returns with a tinkling*
*Telling her eternal sorrow.*

1. From *Chinese Poems* by Arthur Waley. Copyright © 1946 by George Allen and Unwin Ltd., London, p. 43. Reprinted by permission of the Arthur Waley Estate.

2. From *The Jade Mountain: A Chinese Anthology* by Witter Bynner, trans. Copyright © 1929 and renewed 1956 by Alfred A. Knopf Inc. Reprinted by permission of Alfred A. Knopf, a Division of Random House Inc.

## Government During the Former Han

To demonstrate their difference from the Ch'in emperor, and to reward their allies, the early Han emperors set up a few Chou-like principalities: small, semi-autonomous states with independent lords. This arrangement was, however, a token gesture. The principalities were closely superintended and then curtailed after several generations. Basically, despite the formal repudiation of the Ch'in and all its works, the Han continued the Ch'in form of centralized bureaucratic administration. Officials were organized by grades and were paid salaries in grain, plus cash or silk. They were recruited by sponsorship or recommendation: Provincial officials had the duty of recommending promising candidates. A school established at Ch'ang-an was said to have had thirty thousand students by the Later Han. The bureaucracy grew until, by the first century B.C.E., there were more than one hundred thirty thousand officials—perhaps not too many for a population that, by that time, had reached sixty million.

During the Han dynasty, this Legalist structure of government became partially Confucianized. It did not happen overnight. The first Han emperor, Kao Tsu, despised Confucians as bookish pedants—he once urinated in the hat of a scholar. But Confucian ideas proved useful. The Mandate of Heaven provided a moral basis for dynastic rule. A respect for old records and the written word fit in well with the vast bookkeeping the empire entailed. The Confucian classics were gradually accepted as the standard for education. Confucianism was seen as shaping moral men who would be upright officials, even in the absence of external constraints. For Confucius had taught the transformation of self by ethical cultivation and had presented a vision of benevolent government by men who were virtuous as well as talented. To be sure, no one attempted to replace laws with a code of etiquette, but increasingly laws were interpreted and applied by men with a Confucian education.

The court during the Han dynasty exhibited features that would appear in later dynasties as well. All authority centered on the emperor, who was the all-powerful "son of heaven." The will of a strong adult emperor was paramount. When the emperor was weak, however, or ascended to the throne when still a child, others competed to rule in his name. Four contenders for this surrogate role appeared and reappeared through Chinese history: court officials, the empress dowager, court eunuchs, and military commanders.

Court officials were selected for their ability to govern. They staffed the apparatus of government and advised the emperor directly. Apart from the emperor himself, they were usually the most powerful men in China. Yet their position was often precarious. Few officials escaped being removed from office or banished once or twice during their careers, and of the seven prime ministers who served Wu Ti, five were executed by his order.

Of the emperor's many wives, the empress dowager was the one whose child had been named as the heir to the throne. Her influence sometimes continued even after her child became an adult emperor. But she was most powerful as a regent for a child emperor. On Kao Tsu's death in 195 B.C.E., for example, the Empress Lu became the regent for her child, the new emperor. Aided by her relatives, she seized control of the court and murdered a rival, and when her son was about to come of age, she had him killed and a younger son made the heir in order to continue her rule as regent. When she died in 180 B.C.E., loyal adherents of the imperial family who had opposed her rule massacred her relatives.

Court eunuchs came mostly from families of low social status. They were brought to the court as boys, castrated, and assigned to work as servants in the emperor's harem. In contact with the future emperor from the day he was born, they became his childhood

## Pan Chao's Admonitions for Women

Pan Chao (45–116) was the sister of the famous historian Pan Ku. Her guide to morality, *Admonitions for Women*, was widely used during the Han Dynasty. Humility is one of the seven womanly virtues about which she wrote; the others are resignation, subservience, self-abasement, obedience, cleanliness, and industry.

*Given the range of female personalities in Chinese society, what are some of the likely responses to this sort of moral education? Are self-control and self-discipline more likely to be associated with weakness or with strength of character?*

### Humility

In ancient times, on the third day after a girl was born, people placed her at the base of the bed, gave her a pot shard to play with, and made a sacrifice to announce her birth. She was put below the bed to show that she was lowly and weak and should concentrate on humbling herself before others. Playing with a shard showed that she should get accustomed to hard work and concentrate on being diligent. Announcing her birth to the ancestors showed that she should focus on continuing the sacrifices. These three customs convey the unchanging path for women and the ritual traditions.

Humility means yielding and acting respectful, putting others first and oneself last, never mentioning one's own good deeds or denying one's own faults, enduring insults and bearing with mistreatment, all with due trepidation. Industriousness means going to bed late, getting up early, never shirking work morning or night, never refusing to take on domestic work, and completing everything that needs to be done neatly and carefully. Continuing the sacrifices means serving one's husband-master with appropriate demeanor, keeping oneself clean and pure, never joking or laughing, and preparing pure wine and food to offer to the ancestors.

There has never been a woman who had these three traits and yet ruined her reputation or fell into disgrace. If a woman loses these three traits, she will have no name to preserve and will not be able to avoid shame.

Reprinted with the permission of The Free Press, a Division of Simon & Schuster, Inc. From *Chinese Civilizations: A Sourcebook* by Patricia Buckley Ebrey. © 1993 by Patricia Buckley Ebrey.

confidants, and often continued to advise him after he had gained the throne. Emperors found eunuchs useful as counterweights to officials. But to the scholars who wrote China's history, the eunuchs were greedy half men, given to evil intrigues.

Military leaders, whether generals or rebels, were the usual founders of dynasties. In the later phase of most dynasties, regional military commanders often became semi-independent rulers. A few even usurped the throne. Yet they were less powerful at the Chinese court than they were, for example, in imperial Rome, partly because the military constituted a separate social stratum, lower in prestige than the better educated civil officials. It was also partly because the court took great pains to prevent its generals from establishing a base of personal power. An appointment to command a

Han army was given only for a specific campaign, and commanders were appointed in pairs so that each would check the other.

Another characteristic of government during the Han and subsequent dynasties was that its functions were limited. It collected taxes, maintained military forces, administered laws, supported the imperial household, and carried out public works that were beyond the powers of local jurisdictions. But government in a district that remained orderly and paid its taxes was left largely in the hands of local notables and large landowners. This pattern was not, to be sure, unique to China. Most premodern governments, even those that were bureaucratic, floated on top of local society and were not able to to reach down and interfere in the everyday lives of their subjects.

## Decline and Usurpation

During the last decade of Wu Ti's rule in the early first century B.C.E., military expenses ran ahead of revenues. His successor cut back on military costs, eased economic controls, and reduced taxes. But over the next several generations, large landowners began to use their growing influence in provincial politics to avoid paying taxes. State revenues declined. The tax burden on smaller landowners and free peasants grew heavier. In 22 B.C.E., rebellions broke out in several parts of the empire. At the court, too, a decline set in. There was a succession of weak emperors. Intrigues, nepotism, and factional struggles grew apace. Even officials began to sense that the dynasty no longer had Heaven's approval. The dynastic cycle approached its end.

Many at the court urged Wang Mang, the regent for the infant emperor and a nephew of an empress, to take the throne and begin a new dynasty. Wang Mang refused several times—to demonstrate a modest lack of eagerness—and then accepted in C.E. 8. He drew up a program of sweeping reforms based on ancient texts. He was Confucian, yet he relied on new institutional arrangements, rather than moral reform, to improve society. He revived ancient titles, expanded state monopolies, abolished private slavery (about 1 percent of the population), made loans to poor peasants, and then moved to confiscate large private estates.

These reforms, however, alienated many. Merchants disliked the monopolies. Large landowners resisted the expropriation of their lands. Nature also conspired to bring down Wang Mang: The Yellow River overflowed its banks and changed its course, destroying the northern Chinese irrigation system. Several years of poor harvests produced famines. The Hsiung Nu overran China's northern borders. In 18 C.E., the Red Eyebrows, a peasant secret society, rose in rebellion. In 23 C.E., rebels attacked Ch'ang-an, and Wang Mang was killed and eaten by rebel troops. Wang Mang had tried to found a new dynasty from within a decrepit court without an independent military base. The attempt was futile. Internal wars continued in China for two more years until a large landowner, who had become the leader of a rebel army, emerged triumphant in 25 C.E. Because he was from a branch line of the imperial family, his new dynasty was viewed as a restoration of the Han.

## LATER HAN (25–220 C.E.) AND ITS AFTERMATH

### First Century

The founder of the Later Han moved his capital east to Loyang. Under the first emperor and his two successors, there was a return to strong central government and a laissez-faire economy. Agriculture and population recovered from the devastation of war. By the end of the first century C.E., China was as prosperous as it had been during the good years of the Former Han. The shift from pacification and recuperation to military expansion came earlier than it had in the previous dynasty. Even during the reign of the first emperor, south China and Vietnam were retaken. Dissension among the Hsiung Nu enabled the Chinese to secure an alliance with some of the southern tribes in 50 C.E., and in 89 C.E. Chinese armies crossed the Gobi Desert and defeated the northern Hsiung Nu. This defeat sparked the migrations, some historians say, that brought the Hsiung Nu to the southern Russian steppes and then, in the fifth century C.E., to Europe, where they were known as the Huns of Attila. In 97 C.E., a Chinese general led an army as far west as the shores of the Caspian Sea. The Chinese expansion in inner Asia, coupled with more lenient government policies toward merchants, facilitated the camel caravans that carried Chinese silk across the Tarim Basin to Iran, Palestine, and Rome.

### Decline During the Second Century

Until 88 C.E., the emperors of the Later Han were vigorous; afterward they were ineffective and short-lived. Empresses plotted to advance the fortunes of their families. Emperors turned for help to palace eunuchs, whose power at times surpassed that of officials. In 159 C.E., a conspiracy of eunuchs in the service of an emperor slaughtered the family of a scheming empress dowager and ruled at the court. When officials and students protested against the eunuch dictatorship, over a hundred were killed and over a thousand were tortured or imprisoned. In another incident in 190 C.E., a general deposed one emperor, installed another, killed the empress dowager, and massacred most of the eunuchs at the court.

In the countryside, large landowners who had been powerful from the start of the dynasty grew more so. They harbored private armies. Farmers on the estates of the mighty were reduced to serfs. The landowners used their influence to avoid taxes. Great numbers of free farmers fled south to avoid taxes. As a result, the remaining freeholders paid ever heavier taxes and labor services. Many peasants turned to neo-Taoist religious movements—the Yellow Turbans in the east and the Five Pecks of Rice Band in Szechwan—that provided the ideology and organization to channel their discontent into action. In 184 C.E., rebellions organized by members of the religious movements broke out against the government. Han generals suppressed the rebellions but stayed on to rule in the provinces they had pacified. In 220 C.E., they deposed the last Han emperor.

## Aftermath of Empire

For more than three-and-a-half centuries after the fall of the Han, China was disunited. For several generations, it was divided into three kingdoms, whose heroic warriors and scheming statesmen were made famous by wandering storytellers. These figures later peopled the *Romance of the Three Kingdoms*, a great epic of Chinese literature.

Chinese history during the post-Han centuries had two characteristics. The first was the dominant role played by the great aristocratic landowning families. With vast estates, huge numbers of serfs, fortified manor houses, and private armies, they were beyond the control of most governments. Because they took over many of the functions of local government, some historians describe post-Han China as having reverted to the quasi-feudalism of the Chou. The second characteristic of these centuries was that northern and southern China developed in quite different ways.

In the south, there followed a succession of ever weaker dynasties with capitals at Nanking. Although these six southern states were called dynasties—and the entire period of Chinese history from 220 C.E. to 589 is called the Six Dynasties era after them—they were in fact short-lived kingdoms, plagued by intrigues, usurpations, and coups d'état. They frequently warred with northern states and were in constant fear of their own generals. The main developments in the south were (1) continuing economic growth and the emergence of Nanking as a thriving center of commerce; (2) the ongoing absorption of tribal peoples into Chinese society and culture; (3) large-scale immigrations of Chinese fleeing the north; and (4) the spread of Buddhism and its penetration to the heart of Chinese culture.

In the north, state formation depended on the interaction of nomads and Chinese. During the Han dynasty, Chinese invasions of the steppe had led to the incorporation of semi-Sinicized Hsiung Nu as the northernmost tier of the Chinese defense system—just as Germanic tribes had acted as the teeth and claws of the late Roman Empire. But as the Chinese state weakened, the highly mobile nomads broke loose, joined with other tribes, and began to invade China. The short-lived states that they formed are usually referred to as the "Sixteen Kingdoms." One kingdom was founded by invaders of Tibetan stock. Most spoke Altaic languages: the Hsien Pi (proto-Mongols), the Toba (proto-Turks), and the Juan Juan (who would later appear in eastern Europe as the Avars). But differences of language and stock were less important than these tribes' similarities:

1. All began as steppe nomads with a way of life different from that of agricultural China.

2. After forming states, all became at least partially Sinicized. Chinese from great families, which had preserved Han traditions, served as their tutors and administrators.

3. All were involved in wars—among themselves, against southern dynasties, or against conservative steppe tribes that resisted Sinicization.

## The Peach Blossom Spring

The poet Ta'o Ch'ien wrote in 380 C.E. of a lost village without taxes and untouched by the barbarian invasions and wars of the post-Han era. The simplicity and naturalness of his utopian vision were in accord, perhaps, with certain strains of Neo-Taoist thought. It struck a chord in the hearts of Chinese, and then Koreans and Japanese, inspiring a spate of paintings, poetry, and essays.

---

*Utopias are often based on religion, but this one is not. What does this suggest regarding the Chinese view of human nature?*

---

During the T'ai-yuan period of the Ch'in dynasty a fisherman of Wuling once rowed upstream, unmindful of the distance he had gone, when he suddenly came to a grove of peach trees in bloom. For several hundred paces on both banks of the stream there was no other kind of tree. The wild flowers growing under them were fresh and lovely, and fallen petals covered the ground—it made a great impression on the fisherman. He went on for a way with the idea of finding out how far the grove extended. It came to an end at the foot of a mountain whence issued the spring that supplied the stream. There was a small opening in the mountain and it seemed as though light was coming through it. The fisherman left his boat and entered the cave, which at first was extremely narrow, barely admitting his body; after a few dozen steps it suddenly opened out onto a broad and level plain where well-built houses were surrounded by rich fields and pretty ponds. Mulberry, bamboo and other trees and plants grew there, and criss-cross paths skirted the fields. The sounds of cocks crowing and dogs barking could be heard from one courtyard to the next. Men and women were coming and going about their work in the fields. The clothes they wore were like those of ordinary people. Old men and boys were carefree and happy.

When they caught sight of the fisherman, they asked in surprise how he had got there. The fisherman told the whole story, and was invited to go to their house, where he was served wine while they killed a chicken for a feast. When the other villagers heard about the fisherman's arrival they all came to pay him a visit. They told him that their ancestors had fled the disorders of Ch'in times and, having taken refuge here with wives and children and neighbors, had never ventured out again; consequently they had lost all contact with the outside world. They asked what the present ruling dynasty was, for they had never heard of the Han, let alone the Wei and the Chin. They sighed unhappily as the fisherman enumerated the dynasties one by one and recounted the vicissitudes of each. The visitors all asked him to come to their houses in turn, and at every house he had wine and food. He stayed several days. As he was about to go away, the people said, "There's no need to mention our existence to outsiders."

After the fisherman had gone out and recovered his boat, he carefully marked the route. On reaching the city, he reported what he had found to the magistrate, who at once sent a man to follow him back to the place. They proceeded according to the marks he had made, but went astray and were unable to find the cave again.

From *The Poetry of Ta'o Ch'ien* by J. R. Hightower. Copyright © 1970 Clarendon Press. pp. 254–255. Reprinted by permission of Oxford University Press.

---

**Languages of East Asia**

The two main language families in present-day East Asia are the Sinitic and the Ural-Altaic. They are as different from each other as they are from European tongues. The Sinitic languages are Chinese, Vietnamese, Thai, Burmese, and Tibetan. Within Chinese are several mutually unintelligible dialects. Standard Chinese, based on the Peking dialect, is further from Cantonese than Spanish is from French. Ural-Altaic languages are spoken to the east, north, and west of China. They include Japanese, Korean, Manchurian, Mongolian, the Turkic languages, and, in Europe, Finnish and Hungarian.

---

4. Buddhism was powerful in the north as in the south. As a universal religion, it acted as a bridge between "barbarians" and Chinese—just as Christianity was a unifying force in post-Roman Europe. The barbarian rulers of the north were especially attracted to its magical side. Usually Buddhism was made the state religion. Of the northern states, the most durable was the Northern Wei (386–534 C.E.), famed for its Buddhist sculpture.

## HAN THOUGHT AND RELIGION

Poems describe the splendor of Ch'ang-an and Loyang: broad boulevards, tiled gateways, open courtyards, watchtowers, and imposing walls. Most splendid of all were the palaces of the emperors, with their audience halls, vast chambers, harem quarters, and parks containing artificial lakes and rare animals and birds. But today little remains of the grandeur of the Han. Whereas Roman ruins abound in Italy and circle the Mediterranean, in China nothing remains above ground. Only from the pottery, bronzes, musical instruments, gold and silver jewelry, lacquerware, and clay figurines that were buried in tombs do we gain an inkling of the rich material culture of the Han period. And only from paintings on the walls of tombs do we know of its art. But a wealth of written records convey the sophistication and depth of Han culture. Perhaps the two most important areas were philosophy and history.

### Han Confucianism

A major accomplishment of the early Han was the recovery of texts that had been lost during the Ch'in persecution of scholars. Some were retrieved from the walls of houses where they had been hidden; others were reproduced from memory by scholars. Debate arose regarding the relative authenticity of the old and new texts—a controversy that has continued until modern times. In 51 B.C.E. and again in 79 C.E., councils were held to determine the true meaning of the Confucian classics. In 175 C.E., an approved, official version of the texts was inscribed on stone tablets.

In about 100 C.E., the first Chinese dictionary was compiled. Containing about nine thousand characters, it helped promote a uniform system of writing. In Han times, as today, Chinese from the north could not converse with Chinese from the southeastern coast. But a common written language bridged differences of pronunciation, contributing to Chinese unity.

It was also in Han times that scholars began writing commentaries on the classics, a major activity for scholars throughout Chinese history. Scholars learned the classics by heart and used classical allusions in their writing.

Han philosophers extended Chou Confucianism by adding to it the teachings of cosmological naturalism. Chou Confucianists had assumed that the moral force of a virtuous emperor would not only order society but also harmonize nature. Han Confucianists explained why. Tung Chung-shu (ca. 179–104 B.C.E.), for example, held that all nature was a single, interrelated system. Just as summer always followed spring, so did one color, one virtue, one planet, one element, one number, and one officer of the court always take precedence over another. All reflected the systematic workings of *yang* and *yin* and the five elements. And just as one dressed appropriately to the season, so was it important for the emperor to choose policies appropriate to the sequences inherent in nature. If he was moral, if he acted in accord with Heaven's natural system, then all would go well. But if he acted inappropriately, then Heaven would send a portent as a warning—a blue dog, a rat holding its tail in its mouth, an eclipse, or a comet. If the portent went unheeded, wonders and then misfortunes would follow. It was the Confucian scholars, of course, who claimed to understand nature's messages and advised the emperor.

It is easy to criticize Han philosophy as a pseudoscientific or mechanistic view of nature. But it represented a new effort by the Chinese to encompass and comprehend the interrelationships of the natural world. This effort led to inventions like the seismograph and to advances in astronomy, music, and medicine. It was also during the Han that the Chinese invented paper, the wheelbarrow, the stern-post rudder, and the compass (known as the "south-pointing chariot").

## History

The Chinese were the greatest historians of the premodern world. They wrote more history than anyone else, and what they wrote was usually more accurate. Apart from a few early works such as the *Spring and Autumn Annals* and the scholarship of Confucius himself, history writing in China began during the Han dynasty. Why the Chinese were so history-minded has been variously explained: because the Chinese tradition is this-worldly; because Confucians were scholarly and their veneration for the classics carried over to the written word; because history was seen as a lesson book (the Chinese called it a mirror) for statesmen, and thus a necessity for the literate men who operated the centralized Chinese state.

The practice of using actual documents and first-hand accounts of events began with Ssu-ma Ch'ien (d. 85 B.C.E.), who set out to write a history of the known world from the most ancient times down to the age of the Emperor Wu Ti. His *Historical Records* consisted of 130 substantial chapters (with a total of over seven hundred thousand characters) divided into "Basic Annals"; "Chronological Tables"; "Treatises" on rites, music, astronomy, the calendar, and so on; "Hereditary Houses"; and seventy chapters of "Biographies," including descriptions of foreign peoples. A second great work, *The Book of the Han*, was written by Pan Ku (d. 92 C.E.). It applied the analytical schema of Ssu-ma Ch'ien to a single dynasty, the Former Han, and established the pattern by which each dynasty wrote the history of its predecessor.

## Neo-Taoism

As the Han dynasty waned, the effort to realize the Confucian ethic in the sociopolitical order became more and more difficult. Some scholars abandoned Confucianism altogether in favor of Neo-Taoism, or "mysterious learning," as it was called at the time.

**A second century Chinese seismograph.** When an earthquake occurs, a weight suspended in the vase swings in the direction of the quake. This moves a lever, dropping a ball from the dragon head on that side of the vase into the mouth of a waiting frog.

### Ssu-ma Ch'ien on the Wealthy

More than half of the chapters in Ssu-ma Ch'ien's *Historical Records* (early first century B.C.E.) were biographies of extraordinary men and women. He wrote of scholars, wandering knights, diviners, harsh officials and reasonable officials, wits and humorists, doctors, and money makers. The following is his description of the vibrant economic life of Han cities and his judgments regarding the wealthy.

---

*What economic "principles" can you derive from this passage? Can you detect an echo of Ssu-ma Ch'ien's claims in current debates on economic policy?*

---

Anyone who in the market towns or great cities manages in the course of a year to sell the following items: a thousand brewings of liquor; a thousand jars of pickles and sauces; a thousand jars of sirups; a thousand slaughtered cattle, sheep, and swine; a thousand chung of grain; a thousand cartloads or a thousand boat-lengths of firewood and stubble for fuel; a thousand logs of timber; ten thousand bamboo poles; a hundred horse carriages; a thousand two-wheeled ox carts; a thousand lacquered wooden vessels; brass utensils weighing thirty thousand catties; a thousand piculs of plain wooden vessels, iron vessels, or gardenia and madder dyes; two hundred horses; five hundred cattle; two thousand sheep or swine; a hundred male or female slaves; a thousand catties of tendons, horns, or cinnabar; thirty thousand catties of silken fabric, raw silk, or other fine fabrics; a thousand rolls of embroidered or patterned silk; a thousand piculs of fabrics made of vegetable fiber or raw or tanned hides; a thousand pecks of lacquer; a thousand jars of leaven or salted bean relish; a thousand catties of globefish or mullet; a thousand piculs of dried fish; thirty thousand catties of salted fish; three thousand piculs of jujubes or chestnuts; a thousand skins of fox or sable; a thousand piculs of lamb or sheep skins; a thousand felt mats; or a thousand chung of fruits or vegetables—such a man may live as well as the master of an estate of a thousand chariots. The same applies for anyone who has a thousand strings of cash [i.e., a million in cash] to lend out on interest. Such loans are made through a moneylender, but a greedy merchant who is too anxious for a quick return will only manage to revolve his working

A few wrote commentaries on the classical Taoist texts that had been handed down from the Chou. The *Chuang-tzu* was especially popular. Other scholars, defining the natural as the pleasurable, withdrew from society to engage in witty "pure conversations." They discussed poetry and philosophy, played the lute, and drank wine. The most famous were the Seven Sages of the Bamboo Grove of the third century C.E. One sage was always accompanied by a servant carrying a jug of wine and a spade— the one for his pleasure, the other to dig his grave should he die. Another wore no clothes at home. When criticized, he replied that the cosmos was his home, and his

capital three times while a less avaricious merchant has revolved his five times. These are the principal ways of making money. There are various other occupations which bring in less than twenty percent profit, but they are not what I would call sources of wealth.

Thrift and hard work are without doubt the proper way to gain a livelihood. And yet it will be found that rich men have invariably employed some unusual scheme or method to get to the top. Plowing the fields is a rather crude way to make a living, and yet Ch'in Yang did so well at it that he became the richest man in his province. Robbing graves is a criminal offense, but T'ien Shu got his start by doing it. Gambling is a wicked pastime, but Huan Fa used it to acquire a fortune. Most fine young men would despise the thought of traveling around peddling goods, yet Yung Loch'eng got rich that way. Many people would consider trading in fats a disgraceful line of business, but Yung Po made a thousand catties of gold at it. Vending sirups is a petty occupation, but the Chang family acquired ten million cash that way. It takes little skill to sharpen knives, but because the Chih family didn't mind doing it, they could eat the best of everything. Dealing in dried sheep stomachs seems like an insignificant enough trade, but thanks to it the Cho family went around with a mounted retinue. The calling of a horse doctor is a rather ignominious profession, but it enabled Chang Li to own a house so large that he had to strike a bell to summon the servants. All of these men got where they did because of their devotion and singleness of purpose.

From this we may see that there is no fixed road to wealth, and money has no permanent master. It finds its way to the man of ability like the spokes of a wheel converging upon the hub, and from the hands of the worthless it falls like shattered tiles. A family with a thousand catties of gold may stand side by side with the lord of a city; the man with a hundred million cash may enjoy the pleasures of a king. Rich men such as these deserve to be called the "untitled nobility," do they not?

From *Records of the Grand Historian of China,* trans. by Burton Watson. Copyright © 1961 by Columbia University Press. Reprinted by permission of the publisher.

house his clothes. "Why are you in my pants?" he asked a discomfited visitor. Still another took a boat to visit a friend on a snowy night, but on arriving at his friend's door, turned around and went home. When pressed for an explanation, he said that it had been his pleasure to go, and that when the impulse died, it was his pleasure to return. These anecdotes reveal a scorn for convention coupled with an admiration for inner spontaneity, however eccentric.

Another concern of what is called Neo-Taoism was immortality. Some sought it in dietary restrictions and yoga-like meditation, some in sexual abstinence or orgies.

## The Castration of Ssu-ma Ch'ien

*Why did the historian Ssu-ma Ch'ien let himself be castrated? When he incurred the wrath of the Emperor Wu Ti for defending a general defeated by the Hsiung Nu and was condemned to suffer this shame in 98 B.C.E., why did he not choose an honorable suicide? Read his explanation.*

A man has only one death. That death may be as weighty as Mount T'ai, or it may be as light as a goose feather. It all depends upon the way he uses it. It is the nature of every man to love life and hate death, to think of his relatives and look after his wife and children. Only when a man is moved by higher principles is this not so. Then there are things which he must do. The brave man does not always die for honor, while even the coward may fulfill his duty. Each takes a different way to exert himself. Though I might be weak and cowardly and seek shamefully to prolong my life, yet I know full well the difference between what ought to be followed and what rejected. How could I bring myself to sink into the shame of ropes and bonds? If even the lowest slave and scullery maid can bear to commit suicide, why should not one like myself be able to do what has to be done? But the reason I have not refused to bear these ills and have continued to live, dwelling among this filth, is that I grieve that I have things in my heart that I have not been able to express fully, and I am shamed to think that after I am gone my writings will not be known to posterity.

I too have ventured not to be modest but have entrusted myself to my useless writings. I have gathered up and brought together the old traditions of the world which were scattered and lost. I have examined the deeds and events of the past and investigated the principles behind their success and failure, their rise and decay, in one hundred and thirty chapters. I wished to examine into all that concerns heaven and man, to penetrate the changes of the past and present, completing all as the work of one family. But before I had finished my rough manuscript, I met with this calamity. It is because I regretted that it had not been completed that I submitted to the extreme penalty without rancor. When I have truly completed this work, I shall deposit it in some safe place. If it may be handed down to men who will appreciate it and penetrate to the villages and great cities, then though I should suffer a thousand mutilations, what regret would I have?

W. T. de Bary, W. T. Chan, and B. Watson, eds., *Sources of Chinese Tradition* (New York: Columbia University Press, 1960), pp. 272–273.

Others, seeking elixirs to prolong life, dabbled in alchemy, and although no magical elixir was ever found, the schools of alchemy to which the search gave rise are credited with the discovery of medicines, dyes, glazes, and gunpowder.

Meanwhile, among the common people, there arose popular religious cults that, because they included the Taoist classics among their sacred texts, are also called Neo-Taoist. Like most folk religions, they contained an amalgam of beliefs, practices, and superstitions. They featured a pantheon of gods and immortals and taught that the good or evil done in this life would be requited in the innumerable heavens or hells of an afterlife. These cults had priests, shamans who practiced faith healing, seers, and sorceresses. For a time, they also had hierarchical church organizations, but these were broken when the Yellow Turbans and Five Pecks of Rice rebellions were suppressed at the end of the second century C.E. Local Taoist temples and monasteries, however, continued until modern times. With many Buddhist accretions, they furnished the religious beliefs of the bulk of the Chinese population. Even today, these sects continue in Taiwan and in Chinese communities in Southeast Asia.

## Buddhism

Central Asian missionaries, following the trade routes east, brought Buddhism to China in the first century C.E. It was at first viewed as a new Taoist sect, which is not surprising since early translators used Taoist terms to render Buddhist concepts. *Nirvana*, for example, was translated as "not doing" (*wu-wei*). In the second century C.E., confusion about the two religions led to the very Chinese view that Lao-tzu had gone to India, where the Buddha had become his disciple, and that Buddhism was the Indian form of Taoism.

Then, as the Han sociopolitical order collapsed in the third century C.E., Buddhism spread rapidly. We are reminded of the spread of Christianity at the end of the Roman Empire. Although an alien religion in China, Buddhism had some advantages over Taoism:

1. It was a doctrine of personal salvation, offering several routes to that goal.
2. It contained high standards of personal ethics.
3. It had systematic philosophies, and during its early centuries in China, it continued to receive inspiration from India.
4. It drew on the Indian tradition of meditative practices and psychologies, which were the most sophisticated in the world.

By the fifth century C.E., Buddhism had spread over all of China (see Map 2–3). Occasionally it was persecuted by Taoist emperors—in the north between 446 and 452 C.E. and again between 574 and 578 C.E. But most courts supported Buddhism. The "Bodhisattva Emperor" Wu of the southern Liang dynasty three times gave himself to a monastery and had to be ransomed back by his disgusted courtiers. Temples and monasteries abounded in both the north and the south. There were communities of nuns as well as of monks. Chinese artists produced Buddhist painting and sculpture of surpassing beauty, and thousands of monk-scholars labored to translate sutras and philosophical treatises. Chinese monks went on pilgrimages to India. The record left by Fa Hsien, who traveled to India overland and back by sea between 399 and 413 C.E., became a prime source of Indian history. The T'ang monk Hsuan Tsang went to India from 629 until 645. Several centuries later, his pilgrimage was novelized as *Journey to the West* (later dubbed *Monkey* by Arthur Waley in his abridged English translation). The novel joins faith, magic, and adventure.

A comparison of Indian and Chinese Buddhism highlights some distinctive features of its spread. Buddhism in India had begun as a reform movement. Forget speculative philosophies and elaborate metaphysics, taught the Buddha, and concentrate on simple truths: Life is suffering, the cause of suffering is desire, death does not stop the endless cycle of birth and rebirth; only the attainment of *nirvana* releases one from the "wheel of *karma*." Thus, in this most otherworldly of the world's religions, all of the cosmic drama of salvation was compressed into the single figure of the Buddha meditating under the Bodhi tree. Over the centuries, however, Indian Buddhism developed contending philosophies and conflicting sects and, having become virtually indistinguishable from Hinduism, was reabsorbed after 1000 C.E.

In China, there were a number of sects with different doctrinal positions. But the Chinese genius was more syncretic. It took in the sutras and meditative practices of early Buddhism. It took in the Mahayana philosophies that depicted a succession of Buddhas, cosmic and historical, past and future, all embodying a single ultimate reality. It also took in the sutras and practices of Buddhist devotional sects. Finally, in the T'ien-t'ai sect, the Chinese joined together these various elements as different levels of a single truth. Thus the monastic routine of a T'ien-tai monk would include reading sutras, sitting in meditation, and also practicing devotional exercises.

Socially, too, Buddhism adapted to China. Ancestor worship demanded that there be heirs to perform the sacrifices. Without progeny, ancestors might become "hungry ghosts." Hence, the first son would be expected to marry and have children, whereas the second son, if he were so inclined, might become a monk. The practice also arose of holding Buddhist masses for dead ancestors. Still another difference between China and India was the more extensive regulation of Buddhism by the state in China. Just as Buddhism was not to injure the family, so Buddhism was not to reduce the taxes paid on land. As a result, limits were placed on the number of monasteries, nunneries, and monastic lands, and the requirement was made that the state must give its permission before men or women abandoned the world to enter a religious establishment. The regulations, to be sure, were not always enforced.

## CHINA'S FIRST EMPIRE IN HISTORICAL PERSPECTIVE

Were there world-historical forces that produced at roughly the same time great empires in China, India, and the Mediterranean? Certainly there were similar features in these empires. All three came after revolutions in thought. The Han built on

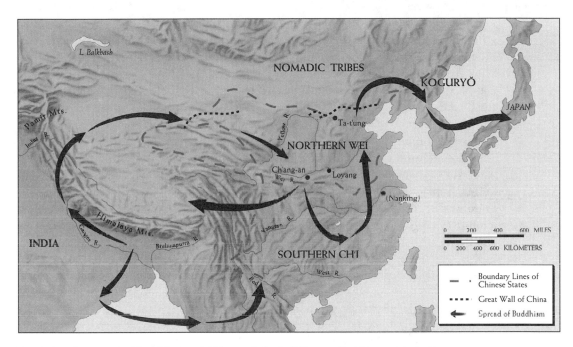

**Map 2–3   The spread of Buddhism and Chinese states in 500 C.E.**   Buddhism originated in a Himalayan state in northwest India. It spread in one wave south in India and on to Southeast Asia as far as Java. It also spread into northwest India, Afghanistan, Central Asia, and then to China, Korea, and Japan.

Chou thought (it would be hard to imagine the Han bureaucratic state without Legalism and Confucianism), just as Rome used Greek thought and the Mauryan empire used Buddhist thought. In each case, the conception of universal political authority that sustained the empire derived from earlier philosophies. All three were Iron Age empires, joining their respective technologies with new organizational techniques to create superb military forces.

The differences between the empires are also instructive. Contrast China and Rome. In China the pervasive culture—the only higher culture in the area—was Chinese even before the first empire arose. This culture had been slowly spreading for centuries and in places outran the polity. Even the Ch'u peoples south of the Yangtse, while viewed as "semibarbarian" by northern Chinese, had only a variation of the common culture. Thus cultural unity paved the way for political unity. In contrast, the polyglot empire of Rome encompassed quite different peoples, including older civilizations. The genius of Rome, in fact, was to fashion a government and a set of laws that could contain its cultural diversity.

Geographically, however, Rome had an easier time of it, for the Mediterranean offered direct access to most parts of the empire and was a thoroughfare for commerce. China, in contrast, was largely landlocked. It was composed of several regional economic units, each of which, located in a segment of a river basin separated from the others by natural barriers, looked inward. It was the genius of Chinese administration, overcoming physical and spatial barriers, to integrate the country politically.

A second difference was that government in Han China was more orderly, more complex, and more competent than that of Rome. For example, civil officials controlled the Chinese military almost until the end, whereas in later Roman times, emperor after emperor was set on the throne by the army or the Praetorian Guard. The Roman empire was not a Chinese-type, single-family dynasty.

A third difference was in the military dynamics of the two empires. Roman power was built over centuries. Its history is the story of one state growing in power by increments, imposing its will on others, and little by little piecing together an empire. Not until the early centuries C.E. was the whole empire in place. China, in contrast, remained a multistate system right up to 232 B.C.E. and then, in a sudden surge, was unified by one state in the space of eleven years. The greater dynamism of China can be explained, perhaps, by the military challenge it faced along its northern border: an immense Hunnish nomadic empire, far more united than the tribes that threatened Rome. Because the threat was more serious than that posed to Rome by any European barbarian enemy, the Chinese response was correspondingly massive.

## REVIEW QUESTIONS

1. How did Legalism help the Ch'in to unify China? What other factors played a part? Why did the Ch'in collapse?

2. What was the "dynastic cycle"? In what sense was it a Confucian moral rationalization? Was a cycle of administrative and military decline especially true of Chinese government, or can we see the same pattern elsewhere?

3. Who were the players who sought power at the court? Did the means they used reflect differences in their positions?

4. Did Buddhism "triumph" in China in the same sense in which Christianity triumphed in the Roman world? Compare China to the Roman Empire. What problems did both face and how did they try to resolve them?

## SUGGESTED READINGS

BODDE, D. *China's First Unifier* (1938). A study of the Ch'in unification of China, viewed through the Legalist philosopher and statesman Li Ssu.

CH'U, T. T. *Law and Society in Traditional China* (1961). Treats the sweep of Chinese history from 202 B.C.E. to 1911.

CH'U, T. T. *Han Social Structure* (1972).

COTTERELL, A. *The First Emperor of China* (1981).

COULBORN, R. *Feudalism in History* (1965). One chapter interestingly compares the quasifeudalism of the Chou with that of the Six Dynasties period.

FAIRBANK, J. K., REISCHAUER, E. O., AND CRAIG, A. M. *East Asia: Tradition and Transformation* (1989). A widely read single-volume history covering China, Japan, and other countries in East Asia from antiquity to recent times.

GERNET, J. *A History of Chinese Civilization* (1982). An excellent survey of Chinese history.

HSU, C. Y. *Ancient China in Transition* (1965). On social mobility during the Eastern Chou era.

HSU, C. Y. *Han Agriculture* (1980). A study of the agrarian economy of China during the Han dynasty.

LEVI, J. *The Chinese Emperor* (1987). A novel about the First Ch'in Emperor based on scholarly sources.

LOEWE, M. *Everyday Life in Early Imperial China* (1968). A social history of the Han dynasty.

NEEDHAM, J. *The Shorter Science and Civilization in China* (1978). An abridgement of the multivolume work on the same subject with the same title—minus *Shorter*—by the same author.

ROBINET, I. *Taoism: Growth of a Religion* (1987). A survey of Taoist religion.

SCHIROKAUER, C. *A Brief History of Chinese and Japanese Civilizations* (1978). A standard text, especially good on literature and art.

SULLIVAN, M. *The Arts of China* (1967). An excellent survey history of Chinese art.

TWITCHETT, D. AND LOEWE, M. EDS. *The Ch'in and Han Empires, 221* B.C.E.–A.D. 220 (1986). (Vol. 1 of *The Cambridge History of China*.)

WANG, Z. S. *Han Civilization* (1982).

WATSON, B. *Ssu-ma Ch'ien, Grand Historian of China* (1958). A study of China's premier historian.

WATSON, B. *Records of the Grand Historian of China*, Vols. 1 and 2 (1961). Selections from the *Shih-chi* by Ssu-ma Ch'ien.

WATSON, B. *The Columbia Book of Chinese Poetry* (1986).

WRIGHT, A. *Buddhism in Chinese History* (1959).

YU, Y. S. *Trade and Expansion in Han China* (1967). A study of economic relations between the Chinese and their neighbors.

During the T'ang dynasty (618–907), well-to-do families placed glazed pottery figurines in the tombs of their dead. Perhaps they were intended to accompany and amuse the dead in the afterlife. Note the fancy chignon hairstyle of this female flutist, one figure in a musical ensemble. Today these figurines are sought by collectors around the world. [Art Resource, N.Y.]

*chapter three*

# Imperial China (589–1368)

If Chinese dynasties from the late sixth to the mid-fourteenth centuries were given numbers like those of ancient Egypt, the Sui and T'ang dynasties would be called the Second Empire; the Sung, the Third; and the Yuan, the Fourth. Numbers, however, would not convey the distinct personalities of these dynasties. The T'ang (618–907) is everyone's favorite dynasty: open, cosmopolitan, expansionist, exuberant, and creative. It was the example of T'ang China that decisively influenced the formation of states and high cultures in Japan, Korea, and Vietnam. Poetry during the T'ang attained a peak that has not been equaled since. The Sung (960–1279) rivaled the T'ang in the arts; it was China's great age of painting and was the most significant period for philosophy since the Chou, when Chinese philosophy began. Although not militarily strong, the Sung dynasty also witnessed an important commercial revolution. The Yuan (1279–1368) was a short-lived dynasty of rule by Mongols during which China became the most important unit in the largest empire the world has yet seen.

## REESTABLISHMENT OF EMPIRE: SUI (589–618) AND T'ANG (618–907) DYNASTIES

In the period corresponding to the European early Middle Ages, the most notable feature of Chinese history was the reunification of China, the recreation of a centralized bureaucratic empire consciously modeled on the earlier Han dynasty (206 B.C.E.–220 C.E.). Reunification, as usual, began in the north. The first steps were taken by the Northern Wei (386–534), the most enduring of the northern Sino-Turkic states. It moved its court south to Loyang, made Chinese the language of the court, and adopted Chinese dress and surnames. It also used the leverage of its nomadic cavalry to impose a new land tax, mobilizing resources for state use. The Northern Wei was followed by several short-lived kingdoms. Because the emperors, officials, and military commanders of these kingdoms all came from the same stratum of aristocratic families, the social distance between them was small, and the throne was often usurped.

## THE SUI DYNASTY

The general of mixed Chinese-Turkic ancestry, Sui Wen-ti, who came to power in 581 and began the Sui dynasty (589–618), was no exception to the above rule. But he displayed great talent, unified the north, restored the tax base, reestablished a centralized bureaucratic government, and went on to conquer southern China and unify the country. During his reign, all went well. Huge palaces were built in his Wei valley capital. The Great Wall was rebuilt. The Grand Canal was constructed, linking the Yellow and Yangtze rivers. This canal enabled the northern conquerors to tap the wealth of central and southern China. Peace was maintained with the Turkic tribes along China's northern borders. Eastern Turkic khans (chiefs) were sent Chinese princesses as brides.

The early years of the Second Sui emperor were also constructive, but then, Chinese attempts to meddle in steppe politics led to hostilities and wars. The hardships and casualties in campaigns against Korea and along China's northern border produced rising discontent. Natural disasters occurred. The court became bankrupt and demoralized. Rebellions broke out, and once again, there was a free-for-all among the armies of aristocratic military commanders. The winner, and the founder of the T'ang dynasty, was a relative of the Sui empress and a Sino-Turkic aristocrat of the same social background as those who had ruled before him.

Chinese historians often compare the short Sui dynasty with that of the Ch'in (256–206 B.C.E.). Each brought all of China under a single government after centuries of disunity. Each did too much, fell, and was replaced by a long dynasty. The T'ang built on the foundations that had been laid by the Sui, just as the Han had built on those of the Ch'in.

## THE T'ANG DYNASTY

The first T'ang emperor took over the Sui capital, renamed it Ch'ang-an, and made it his own. Within a decade or so, the T'ang dynasty had extended its authority over all of China. Government was frugal and tax revenues were adequate to meet the needs of government and to support the military campaigns that would push Chinese borders out further than ever (see Map 3–1). Confucian scholars were employed at the court, Buddhist temples and monasteries flourished, and peace and order prevailed in the land. The years from 624 to 755 were the good years of the dynasty.

### Government

The first T'ang emperor had been a provincial governor before he became a rebel general. Many of those whom he appointed to posts in the new T'ang administration were former Sui officials who had served with him. In building the new administration, he and his successors had to reconcile two conflicting sets of interests. On the one

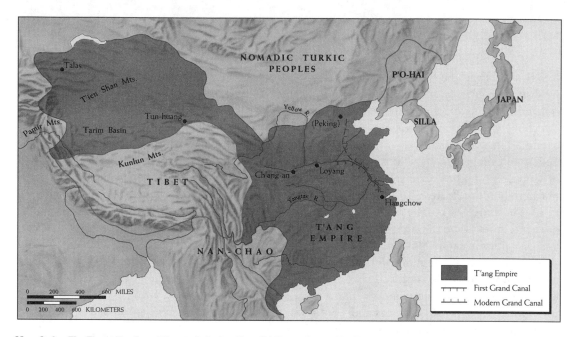

**Map 3–1 The T'ang Empire at its peak during the eighth century.** The T'ang expansion into Central Asia reopened trade routes to the Middle East and Europe. Students from P'o-Hai, Silla (Korea), and Japan studied in the T'ang capital of Ch'ang-an, and then returned, carrying with them T'ang books and technology.

hand, the emperor wanted a bureaucratic government in which authority was centralized in his own person. On the other hand, he had to make concessions to the aristocrats—the dominant elements in Chinese society since the late Han—who staffed his government and continued to dominate early T'ang society.

The degree to which political authority was centralized was apparent in the formal organization of the bureaucracy. At the highest level were three organs: Military Affairs, the Censorate, and the Council of State. Military Affairs supervised the T'ang armies, with the emperor, in effect, the commander-in-chief. The Censorate had watchdog functions: It reported instances of misgovernment directly to the emperor and could also remonstrate with the emperor when his behavior was improper. The Council of State was the most important body. It met daily with the emperor and was made up of the heads of the Secretariat, which drafted policies; the Chancellery, which reviewed them; and State Affairs, which carried them out. Beneath State Affairs were the Six Ministries, which continued as the core of the central government down to the twentieth century; beneath them were the several levels of provincial and local administration.

Concessions to the interests of the aristocratic families were embodied in the tax system. All land was declared to be the property of the emperor and was then redistributed to able-bodied cultivators, who paid taxes in labor and grain. Because all able-bodied adult males received an equal allotment of land (women got less), the land

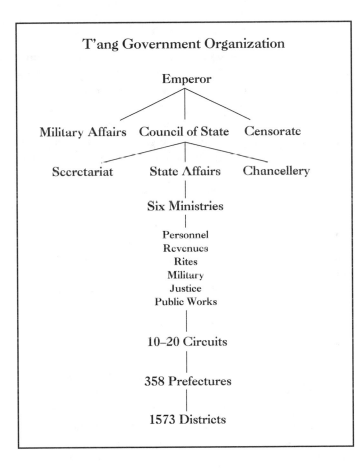

**T'ang Government Organization**

Emperor

Military Affairs  Council of State  Censorate

Secretariat  State Affairs  Chancellery

Six Ministries

Personnel
Revenues
Rites
Military
Justice
Public Works

10–20 Circuits

358 Prefectures

1573 Districts

tax system was called the "equal field system." But the system was not egalitarian. Aristocrats enjoyed special exemptions and grants of "rank" and "office" lands that, in effect, confirmed their estate holdings.

Aristocrats were also favored in the recruiting of officials. Most officials either were recommended for posts or received posts because their fathers had been high officials. They were drawn almost exclusively from the aristocracy, at first from the northwestern aristocratic families that had supported the establishment of the dynasty, and then, in time, from the aristocracies of other areas. Only a tiny percentage were recruited by examinations. Those who passed the examinations had the highest prestige and were more likely to have brilliant careers. But as only well-to-do families could afford the years of study needed to master the Confucian classics and pass the rigorous examinations, even the examination bureaucrats were usually the able among the noble. Entrance to government schools at Ch'ang-an and the secondary capital at Loyang was restricted to the sons of nobles and officials.

## The Empress Wu

Women of the inner court also continued to play a role in government. For example, Wu Chao (626–ca. 706), a young concubine of the strong second emperor, had so entranced his weak heir by her charms that when he succeeded to the throne, she was recalled from the nunnery to which all the former wives of deceased emperors were routinely consigned and was installed at the court. She poisoned or otherwise removed her rivals and became his empress. She also had murdered or exiled the statesmen who opposed her growing influence. When the emperor suffered a stroke in 660, she completely dominated the court. After his death in 683, she ruled for seven years as regent and then, deposing her son, became emperor herself, the only woman in Chinese history to hold the title. She moved the court to Loyang in her native area and proclaimed a new dynasty. A fervent Buddhist with an interest in magic, she saw herself as the incarnation of the Buddha Maitreya and built temples throughout the land. She patronized the White Horse Monastery, appointing one of her favorites as its abbot. Her sexual appetites were said to have been prodigious. She ruled China until 705, when at the age of eighty she lost her hold and was deposed.

After Empress Wu, no woman would ever become emperor again; yet, remarkably enough, her machinations do not appear to have seriously weakened the court. So highly centralized was power during these early years of the dynasty that the ill effects of her intrigues could be absorbed without provinces breaking away or military commanders becoming autonomous. In fact, her struggle for power may have strengthened the central government, for, to overcome the old northwestern Chinese aristocrats, she turned not to members of her family but to the products of the examination system and to a group known as the Scholars of the North Gate. This policy broadened the base of government by bringing in aristocrats from other regions of China. The dynamism of a young dynasty may also explain why her rule coincided with the maximal geographical expansion of T'ang military power.

## The Ch'ang-an of Emperor Hsuan-tsung

Only a few years after Empress Wu was deposed—years filled with tawdry intrigues—Hsuan-tsung came to the throne. In reaction to Empress Wu, he appointed special government commissions headed by distinguished aristocrats to superintend the reform of government finances. Examination bureaucrats lost ground during his reign. The Grand Canal was repaired and extended. A new census extended the tax rolls. Wealth and prosperity returned to the court. Hsuan-tsung's reign (713–756) was also the most brilliant culturally. Years later, while in exile, Li Po wrote a poem in which memories of youthful exhilaration merged with the glory of the capital of Hsuan-tsung:

Long ago, among the flowers and willows,
We sat drinking together at Ch'ang-an.

The Five Barons and Seven Grandees were of our company,
But when some wild stroke was afoot
It was we who led it, yet boisterous though we were
In the arts and graces of life we could hold our own
With any dandy in the town—
In the days when there was youth in your cheeks
And I was still not old.
We galloped to the brothels, cracking our gilded whips,
We sent in our writings to the palace of the Unicorn,
Girls sang to us and danced hour by hour on tortoise-shell mats.
We thought, you and I, that it would be always like this.
How should we know the grasses would stir and dust rise on the wind?
Suddenly foreign horsemen were at the Hsien-ku Pass
Just when the blossom at the palace of Ch'in was opening on the sunny
    boughs. . . .[1]

Ch'ang-an was an imperial city, an administrative city that lived on taxes. It was designed to exhibit the power of the emperor and the majesty of his court. At the far north of the city, the palace faced south. The placement was traditional: Confucius, speaking of Shun, said he had only "to hold himself in a respectful posture and to face due south." In front of the palace was a complex of government offices, from which an imposing five-hundred-foot-wide avenue led to the main southern gate. The city was laid out on a north–south, east–west grid, which one T'ang poet compared to a chessboard. Each block of the city was administered as a ward with interior streets and gates that were locked at night. Enclosed by great walls, the city covered 30 square miles. Its population was over a million—half within the walls, the other half in suburbs—the largest city in the world. (The population of China in the year 750 was about fifty million—about 4 percent of its present-day population.) Ch'ang-an was also a trade center from which caravans set out across Central Asia. Merchants from India, Iran, Syria, and Arabia hawked the wares of the Near East and all of Asia in its two government-controlled markets.

## The T'ang Empire

A Chinese dynasty is like an accordion, first expanding into the territories of its barbarian neighbors and then contracting back to its original, densely populated core area. The principal threats to the T'ang state were from Tibetans in the west, Turks in the northwest and north, and Khitan Mongols in Manchuria.

To protect their borders, the T'ang employed a four-tier policy. When nothing else would work, the T'ang sent armies. But armies were expensive, and using them

[1]Arthur Waley, *The Poetry and Career of Li Po* (New York, Macmillan, 1950) pp. 87–88.

against nomads was like sweeping back the waves with a broom. A victory might dissolve a confederation, but a decade or two later, it would reappear under a new tribal leader. For instance, in 630, T'ang armies defeated the eastern Turks; in 648, they took the Tarim Basin, opening trade routes to western Asia for almost a century; and in 657, they defeated the western Turks and extended Chinese influence across the Pamir Mountains to petty states near Samarkand. By 698, however, the Turks were back, invading northeastern China, and between 711 and 736, they were in control of all of the steppe from the Oxus River to China's northern frontier.

Chinese efforts against Tibet were much the same. From 670, Tibet expanded and threatened China. In 679, it was defeated. In 714, it rose again; wars were fought from 727 to 729; and a settlement was reached in 730. But wars broke out anew. In 752, Tibet entered an alliance with the state of Nan Chao in Yunnan (a province in southwestern China that abuts on Tibet). In 763, Tibetan forces captured and looted Ch'ang-an. They were driven out, but the point is that even during the good years of the T'ang, no final victory was possible.

The human costs of sending armies far afield was detailed in a poem by Li Po:

Last year we were fighting at the source of the Sang-kan;
This year we are fighting on the Onion River road.
We have washed our swords in the surf of Parthian seas;
We have pastured our horses among the snows of the T'ien Shan,
The King's armies have grown grey and old
Fighting ten thousand leagues away from home.
The Huns have no trade but battle and carnage;
They have no fields or ploughlands,
But only wastes where white bones lie among yellow sands.
Where the House of Ch'in built the great wall that was to keep away the
    Tartars.
There, in its turn, the House of Han lit beacons of war.
The beacons are always alight, fighting and marching never stop.
Men die in the field, slashing sword to sword;
The horses of the conquered neigh piteously to Heaven.
Crows and hawks peck for human guts,
Carry them in their beaks and hang them on the branches of withered
    trees.
Captains and soldiers are smeared on the bushes and grass;
The General schemed in vain.
Know therefore that the sword is a cursed thing
Which the wise man uses only if he must.[2]

---

[2]Waley, pp. 34–35.

The second tier of Chinese defenses was to use nomads against other nomads. The critical development for the T'ang was the rise to power of the Uighur Turks. From 744 to 840, the Uighurs controlled Central Asia and were staunch allies of the T'ang. Without their support, the T'ang dynasty would have ended sooner.

A third tier was defenses along China's borders, including the Great Wall. At mid-dynasty, whole frontier provinces in the north and the northwest were put under military commanders who, in time, came to control the provinces' civil governments as well. The bulk of the T'ang military was in such frontier commands. At times, their autonomy and potential as rebels were as much a threat to the T'ang court as to the nomadic enemy.

Diplomacy is always cheaper than war. The fourth line of defense was to bring the potential enemy into the empire as a tributary. The T'ang defined the position of "tributary" with great elasticity. It included principalities truly dependent on China, Central Asian states conquered by China, enemy states such as Tibet or the Thai state of Nan Chao in Yunnan when they were not actually at war with China, the Korean state Silla, which had unified the peninsula with T'ang aid but had then fought T'ang armies to a standstill when they attempted to impose Chinese hegemony, and wholly independent states such as Japan. All sent embassies bearing gifts to the T'ang court, which housed and fed them and bestowed costly gifts in return.

For some countries, these embassies had a special significance. As the only "developed nation" in East Asia, China was a model for countries still in the throes of forming a state. An embassy gained access to the entire range of T'ang culture and technology: its philosophy and writing, governmental and land systems, Buddhism, arts, architecture, and medicine. In 640 there were eight thousand Koreans, mostly students, in Ch'ang-an. Never again would China exert such an influence, for never again would its neighbors be at that formative stage of development.

## Rebellion and Decline

From the mid-eighth century, signs of decline began to appear. China's frontiers started to contract. Tribes in Manchuria became unruly. Tibetans threatened China's western border. In 751, an overextended T'ang army led by a Korean general was defeated by Arabs near Samarkand in western Asia, shutting down China's caravan trade with the West for more than five centuries. Furthermore, in 755, a Sogdian general, An Lu-shan, who commanded three Chinese provinces on the northeastern frontier, led 160,000 troops in a rebellion that swept across northern China, capturing Loyang and then Ch'ang-an. The emperor fled to Szechwan.

The event contained an element of romance. Ten years earlier, the emperor Hsuan-tsung had taken a young woman, Yang Kuei Fei, from the harem of his son (he gave his son another in exchange). So infatuated was he that he neglected not only the other "three thousand beauties of his inner chambers" but the business of government as well. For a while his neglect did not matter because he had an able chief minister, but when the minister died, Hsuan-tsung appointed his concubine's second cousin to the post, initiating a train of events that resulted in the rebellion. En route to Szechwan, his soldiers, blaming Yang Kuei Fei for their plight, strangled her. Her death was later immortalized in a poem that described her "snow-white skin," "flowery face," and "moth eyebrows," as well as the "eternal sorrow" of the emperor, who, in fact, was seventy-two at the time.

After a decade of wars and devastation, a new emperor restored the dynasty with the help of the Uighur Turks, who looted Ch'ang-an as part of their reward. The recovery and the century of relative peace and prosperity that followed illustrate the resilience of T'ang institutions. China was smaller, but military governors maintained the diminished frontiers. Provincial governors were more autonomous, but taxes were still sent to the capital. Occasional rebellions were suppressed by imperial armies, sometimes led by eunuchs. Most emperors were weak, but there were three strong emperors who carried out reforms. Edwin O. Reischauer, after translating the diary of a Japanese monk who studied in China during the early ninth century, commented that the "picture of government in operation" that emerges "is amazing for the ninth century, even in China":

> The remarkable degree of centralized control still existing, the meticulous attention to written instructions from higher authorities, and the tremendous amount of paper work involved in even the smallest matters of administration are all the more striking just because this was a period of dynastic decline.[3]

Of the reforms of this era, none was more important than that of the land system. The official census, on which land allotments and taxes were based, showed a drop in population from 53 million before the An Lu-shan rebellion to 17 million afterward. Unable to put people back on the registers, the government abandoned the equal field system and replaced it with a tax collected twice a year. The new system, begun in 780, lasted until the sixteenth century. Under it, a fixed quota of taxes was levied on each province and then apportioned out to prefectures and districts. But the government revenues from salt and iron nevertheless surpassed those from land.

During the second half of the ninth century, government weakened further. Most provinces became autonomous, often under military commanders, and resisted central control. Wars were fought with the state of Nan Chao in the southwest. Bandits appeared. Droughts led to peasant uprisings. By the 880s, warlords had carved all of China into independent kingdoms, and in 907, the T'ang dynasty fell. But within half a century, a new dynasty arose. The fall of the T'ang did not lead to centuries of division of the kind that had followed the Han. Something had changed within China.

---

[3]E. O. Reischauer, *Ennin's Travels in T'ang China* (New York, Ronald Press, 1955) p. 7.

### A Poem by Li Po

The great T'ang poet Li Po reputedly wrote twenty thousand poems, of which eighteen hundred have survived.

*It has been said that concreteness of imagery is the genius of Chinese poetry. How does this example support that contention?*

### The River Merchant's Wife: A Letter

*While my hair was still cut straight across my forehead*
*I played about the front gate, pulling flowers.*
*You came by on bamboo stilts, playing horse,*
*You walked about my seat, playing with blue plums.*
*And we went on living in the village of Chokan:*
*Two small people, without dislike or suspicion.*

*At fourteen I married My Lord you.*
*I never laughed, being bashful.*
*Lowering my head, I looked at the wall.*
*Called to, a thousand times, I never looked back.*

*At fifteen I stopped scowling,*
*I desired my dust to be mingled with yours*
*Forever and forever and forever.*
*Why should I climb the look out?*

*At sixteen you departed,*
*You went into far Ku-to-yen, by the river of swirling eddies,*
*And you have been gone five months.*
*The monkeys make sorrowful noise overhead.*

*You dragged your feet when you went out.*
*By the gate now, the moss is grown, the different mosses,*
*Too deep to clear them away!*
*The leaves fall early this autumn, in wind.*
*The paired butterflies are already yellow with August*
*Over the grass in the West garden;*
*They hurt me. I grow older.*
*If you are coming down through the narrows of the river Kiang,*
*Please let me know beforehand,*
*And I will come out to meet you*
*As far as Cho-fu-Sa.*

"The River Merchant's Wife: A Letter" by Ezra Pound, from *Personae*. Copyright © 1926 by Ezra Pound. Reprinted by permission of New Directions Publishing Corp.

## T'ang Culture

The creativity of the T'ang period arose from the juxtaposition and interaction of cosmopolitan, medieval Buddhist and secular elements. The rise of each of these cultural spheres was rooted in the wealth and the social order of the recreated empire.

T'ang culture was cosmopolitan not just because of its broad contacts with other cultures and peoples but because of its openness to them. Buddhist pilgrims to India and a flow of Indian art and philosophies to China were a part of it. The voluptuousness of Indian painting and sculpture, for example, helped shape the T'ang representation of the *bodhisattva*. Commercial contacts were widespread. Foreign goods were vended in Ch'ang-an marketplaces. Communities of central and western Asians were established in the capital, and Arab and Iranian quarters grew up in the seaports of southeastern China. Merchants brought their religions with them. Nestorian Christianity, Zoroastrianism, Manichaeism, Judaism, and Islam entered China at this time. Most would be swept away in the persecutions of the ninth century, but Islam and a few small pockets of Judaism survived until the twentieth century.

Central Asian music and musical instruments entered along the trade routes and became so popular as almost to displace the native tradition. T'ang ladies adopted foreign hairstyles. Foreign dramas and acrobatic performances by western Asians could be seen in the streets of the capital. Even among the pottery figurines customarily placed in tombs, there were representations of West Asian traders and Central Asian grooms, along with those of horses, camels, and court ladies that today are avidly sought by collectors and museums around the world. In T'ang poetry, too, what was foreign was not shunned but judged on its own merits or even presented as exotically attractive. Of a gallant of Ch'ang-an, Li Po wrote:

A young man of Five Barrows suburb east of the Golden Market,
Silver saddle and white horse cross through wind of spring.
When fallen flowers are trampled all under, where is it he will roam?
With a laugh he enters the tavern of a lovely Turkish wench.[4]

Later in the dynasty, another poet, Li Ho wrote of service on the frontier:

A Tartar horn tugs at the north wind,
Thistle Gate shines whiter than the stream.
The sky swallows the road to Kokonor.
On the Great Wall, a thousand miles of moonlight.[5]

The T'ang dynasty, although slightly less an age of faith than the preceding Six Dynasties, was the golden age of Buddhism in China nonetheless. Patronized by emperors and aristocrats, the Buddhist establishment acquired vast landholdings and great wealth. Temples and monasteries were constructed throughout China. To gain even an inkling of the beauty and sophistication of the temple architecture, the wooden

---

[4]S. Owen, *The Great Age of Chinese Poetry: The High T'ang* (New Haven, CT; Yale University Press, 1980), p. 130.

[5]A. C. Graham, *Poems of the Late T'ang* (Baltimore, MD: Penguin, 1965), p. 9.

sculpture, or the paintings on the temple walls, one must see Horyuji or the ancient temples of Nara in Japan, for little of note has survived in China. The single exception is the Caves of the Thousand Buddhas at Tunhuang in China's far northwest, which were sealed during the eleventh century for protection from Tibetan raiders and were not rediscovered until the twentieth century. They were found to contain stone sculptures, Buddhist frescoes, and thousands of manuscripts in Chinese and Central Asian languages.

Only during the T'ang did China have a "church" establishment that was at all comparable to that of medieval Europe, and even then it was subservient to the far stronger T'ang state. Buddhist wealth and learning brought with them secular functions. T'ang temples served as schools, inns, or even bathhouses. They lent money. Priests performed funerals and dispensed medicines. Occasionally, the state moved to recapture the revenues monopolized by temples. The severest persecution, which marked a turn in the fortunes of Buddhism in China, occurred from 841 to 845, when an ardently Taoist emperor confiscated millions of acres of tax-exempt lands, put back on the tax registers 260,000 monks and nuns, and destroyed 4,600 monasteries and 40,000 shrines.

During the early T'ang, the principal Buddhist sect was the T'ien-t'ai, but after the mid-ninth-century suppression, other sects came to the fore:

1. One devotional sect focused on Maitreya, a Buddha of the future who will appear and create a paradise on earth. Maitreya (*Mi Lo* in Chinese and *Miroku* in Japanese) was a cosmic messiah, not a human figure. The messianic teachings of the sect often furnished the ideology for popular uprisings and rebellions like the White Lotus, which claimed that it was renewing the world in anticipation of Maitreya's coming.

2. Another devotional or faith sect worshiped the Amitabha (*A Mi T'o* in Chinese, *Amida* in Japanese) Buddha, the Lord of the Western Paradise or Pure Land. This sect taught that in the early centuries after the death of the historical Buddha, his teachings had been transmitted properly and people could obtain enlightenment by their own efforts, but that at present, the Buddha's teachings had become so distorted that only by reliance on Amitabha could humans obtain salvation. All who called on Amitabha with a pure heart and perfect faith would be saved. Developing a congregational form of worship, this sect became the largest in China and deeply influenced Chinese popular religion.

3. A third sect, and the most influential among the Chinese elites, was known in China, where it began, as *Ch'an* but is better known in the West by its Japanese name, *Zen*. Zen had no cosmic Buddhas. It taught that the historical Buddha was only a man and exhorted each person to attain enlightenment by his or her own efforts. Although its monks were often the most learned in China, Zen was

anti-intellectual in its emphasis on direct intuition into one's own Buddha-nature. Enlightenment was to be obtained by a regimen of physical labor and meditation. To jolt the monk into enlightenment—after he had been readied by long hours of meditation—some Zen sects used little problems not answerable by normal ratiocination: "What was your face before you were conceived?" "If all things return to the One, what does the One return to?" "From the top of a hundred-foot pole, how do you step forward?" The psychological state of the novice attempting to deal with these problems is compared to that of "a rat pursued into a blocked pipe" or "a mosquito biting an iron ball." The discipline of meditation, combined with a Zen view of nature, profoundly influenced the arts in China and subsequently in Korea and Japan as well.

A third characteristic of T'ang culture was the reappearance of secular scholarship and letters. The reestablishment of centralized bureaucratic government stimulated the tradition of learning that had been partially interrupted after the fall of the Han dynasty in the third century C.E. A scholarly-bureaucratic complex emerged. Most men of letters were also officials, and most high-ranking officials painted or wrote poems. This secular stream of T'ang culture was not ideologically anti-Buddhist; officials were often privately sympathetic to Buddhism. But as men involved themselves in the affairs of government, their values became increasingly this-worldly.

Court historians of the T'ang revived the Han practice of writing an official history of the previous dynasty. For the first time, scholars wrote comprehensive institutional histories and regional and local gazetteers. They compiled dictionaries and wrote commentaries on the Confucian classics. Other scholars wrote ghost stories or tales of adventure, using the literary language. (Buddhist sermons, in contrast, were often written in the vernacular.) More paintings were Buddhist than secular, but Chinese landscape painting had its origins during the T'ang. Nowhere, however, was the growth of a secular culture more evident than in poetry, the greatest achievement of T'ang letters. An anthology of T'ang poetry compiled during the Ming period (1368–1644) contained 48,900 poems by almost 2,300 authors.

Li Po (701–762) was not wholly secular. He was clearly not Buddhist, but he was influenced somewhat by Taoism. Born in Szechwan, he was exceptional among T'ang poets in never having sat for the civil service examinations, although he briefly held an official post at Ch'ang-an, given in recognition of his poetry. Large and muscular, he was a swordsman and a carouser. Of the twenty thousand poems he is said to have composed, eighteen hundred have survived, and a fair number have titles like "Bring on the Wine" or "Drinking Alone in the Moonlight." According to legend, he drowned while drunkenly attempting to embrace the reflection of the moon in a lake. His poetry is clear, powerful, passionate, and always sensitive to beauty. It also contains a sense of fantasy, as when he climbed a mountain and saw a star-goddess, "stepping in emptiness, pacing pure ether, her rainbow robes trailed broad sashes." Li Po, nearer to heaven than to earth, looked down below where

> Far and wide Tartar troops were speeding,
> And flowing blood mired the wild grasses
> Where wolves and jackals all wore officials' caps.[6]

According to Li Po, life is brief and the universe is large, but this view did not lead him to renounce the world. His perception of the Way was not quietistic. Rather, he exulted, identifying with the primal flux of *yin* and *yang*:

> I'll wrap this Mighty Mudball of a world all up in a bag
> And be wild and free like Chaos itself![7]

Tu Fu (712–770), an equally famous T'ang poet, was from a literary family. He failed the metropolitan examination at the age of twenty-three and spent years in wandering and poverty. At thirty-nine, he received an official appointment after presenting his poetry to the court. Four years later, he was appointed to a military post. He fell into rebel hands during the An Lu-shan rebellion, escaped, and was reappointed to a civil post. But he was then dismissed and suffered further hardships. His poetry is less lyrical and more allusive than Li Po's. It also reflects more compassion for human suffering: for the mother whose sons have been conscripted and sent to war; for brothers scattered by war; for his own family, to whom he returned after having been given up for dead. Like Li Po, he felt that humans are short-lived and that nature endures. Visiting the ruins of the palace of the second T'ang emperor, he saw "grey rats scuttling over ancient tiles" and "in its shadowed chambers ghost fires green." "Its lovely ladies are the brown soil" and only "tomb horses of stone remain." But his response to this sad scene was to

> Sing wildly, let the tears cover your open hands.
> Then go ever onward and on the road of your travels,
> Meet none who prolong their fated years.[8]

His response was unlike that of Li Po. It was close to Stoicism but equally non-Buddhist.

[6]Owen, p. 134.
[7]Owen, p. 125.
[8]Owen, pp. 223–224.

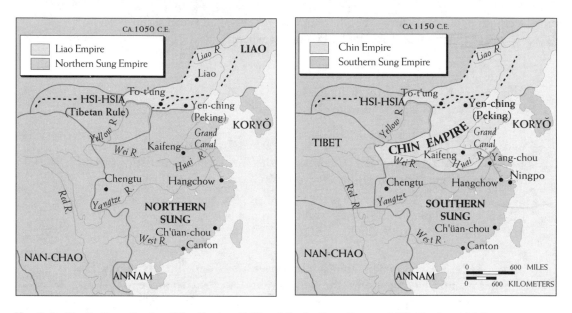

**Map 3–2 The Northern Sung and Liao Empires (left) and the Southern Sung and Chin Empires (right).**
During the Northern Sung, the Mongol Liao dynasty ruled only the extreme northern edge of China. During the Southern Sung, in contrast, the Manchurian Chin dynasty ruled half of China.

# TRANSITION TO LATE IMPERIAL CHINA: THE SUNG DYNASTY (960–1279)

Most traditional Chinese history was written in terms of the dynastic cycle, and for good reason: The pattern of rise and fall, of expansion and contraction, within each dynasty cannot be denied. Certainly, the Sung can be viewed from this perspective. It reunified China in 960, establishing its capital at Kaifeng on the Yellow River (see Map 3–2). Mobilizing its resources effectively, it ruled for 170 years. This period is called the Northern Sung. Then it weakened. In 1127, it lost the north but continued to rule the south for another 150 years from a new capital at Hangchow in east-central China. The Southern Sung fell before the Mongol onslaught in 1279.

But there is more to Chinese history than the inner logic of the dynastic cycle. Longer-term changes that cut across dynastic lines were ultimately more important. One such set of changes began during the late T'ang and continued on into the Sung, affecting its economy, society, state, and culture. Taken together, these changes help to explain why China after the T'ang did not relapse into centuries of disunity as it had after the Han, and why China would never again experience more than brief intervals of disunity. In this section, we will skip over emperors and empresses, eunuchs and generals, and focus instead on more fundamental transformations.

## AGRICULTURAL REVOLUTION OF THE SUNG: FROM SERFS TO FREE FARMERS

Landed aristocrats had dominated local society during the Sui and the T'ang periods. The tillers of their lands were little more than serfs. Labor service was the heaviest tax, and whether performed on the office or rank lands of aristocrats or on other government lands, it created conditions of social subordination.

The aristocracy weakened, however, over the course of the T'ang and after its fall. Estates became smaller as they were divided among male children at each change of generation. Drawn to the capital, the aristocracy became less a landed, and more a metropolitan, elite. After the fall of the T'ang, the aristocratic estates were often seized by warlords. As the aristocracy declined, the claims of those who worked the soil grew stronger, aided by changes in the land and tax systems. With the collapse of the equal field system (described earlier), farmers could buy and sell land. The ownership of land as private property gave the cultivators greater independence. They could now move about as they pleased. Taxes paid in grain gave way during the Sung to taxes in money. The commutation of the labor tax to a money tax gave farmers more control over their own time. Conscription, the cruelest and heaviest labor tax of all, disappeared as the conscript armies of the early and middle T'ang gave way to a professional soldiery.

Changes in technology also benefited the cultivator. New strains of an early-ripening rice permitted double cropping. In the Yangtze region, extensive water-control projects were carried out, and more fertilizers were used. New commercial crops were developed. Tea, which had been introduced during the Six Dynasties as a medicine and had been drunk by monks during the T'ang, became widely cultivated; cotton also became a common crop. Because taxes paid in money tended to become fixed, much of the increased productivity accrued to the cultivator. Of course, not all benefited equally; there were landlords and landless tenants as well as independent small farmers.

The disappearance of the aristocrats also increased the authority of the district magistrate, who no longer had to contend with their interference in local affairs. The Sung magistrate became the sole representative of imperial authority in local society. But there were too many villages in his district for him to be involved regularly in their internal governance. As long as taxes were paid and order was maintained, the affairs of the village were left in the hands of the village elites. So the Sung farmer enjoyed not only a rising income and more freedom, but also substantial self-government.

One other development that began during the Sung—and became vastly more important later on—was the appearance of a scholar-gentry class. The typical gentry family lived in a district seat or market town and had at least one member who had passed the provincial civil service examination. Socially and culturally, these gentry were closer to magistrates than to villagers, but they usually owned land in the villages and thus shared some interests with the local landholders. Although much less powerful than the former aristocrats, they took a hand in local affairs and at times functioned as a buffer between village and magistrate.

## COMMERCIAL REVOLUTION OF THE SUNG

Stimulated by changes in the countryside, and contributing to them in turn, were demographic shifts, innovative technologies, the growth of cities, the spread of money, and rising trade. These developments varied by region, but overall propelled the Sung economy to new levels of prosperity.

### Emergence of the Yangtze Basin

Until late in the T'ang, north China had been the most populous and productive region. But from the late ninth century, the center of gravity of China's population, agricultural production, and culture shifted to the lower and eastern Yangtze region. Between 800 and 1100, the population of the region tripled as China's total population increased to about one hundred million. Its rice paddies yielded more per acre than the wheat or millet fields of the north, making rice the tax base of the empire. Its wealth led to the establishment of so many schools that regional quotas for the examination system were set by the government to prevent the Yangtze region from dominating all of China. The Northern Sung capital itself was kept in the north for strategic reasons, but it was situated at Kaifeng, further east than Loyang, at the point where the Grand Canal, which carried tax rice from the south, joined the Yellow River.

### New Technology

During the Northern Sung, there developed in north China a coal and iron-smelting industry that provided China with better tools and weapons. Using coke and bellows to heat furnaces to the temperatures required for carbonized steel, it was the most advanced in the world.

Printing began with the use of carved seals. The earliest woodblock texts, mostly on Buddhist subjects, appeared in the seventh century. By the tenth century, a complete edition of the classics had been published, and by the mid-Sung, books printed with movable type were fairly common.

Other advances during the Sung were the abacus, the use of gunpowder in grenades and projectiles, and finer textiles and porcelains.

## Rise of a Money Economy

Exchange during the T'ang had been based on silk. Coins had been issued, but their circulation was limited. During the Northern Sung, large amounts of copper cash were coined, but the demand outstripped the supply. Coins were made with holes in the center, and one thousand on a string constituted the usual unit for large transactions. Beginning in the Southern Sung, silver was minted to complement copper cash, ten times as much silver in the late twelfth century as in the early eleventh century. Merchants used letters of credit, and various kinds of paper money also were issued. The penetration of money into the village economy was such that by 1065, tax receipts paid in money had risen to thirty-eight million strings of cash—in comparison with a mere two million in mid-T'ang.

## Trade

The growth of trade spurred the demand for money. One may distinguish between trade within economic regions, trade between regions, and foreign trade. During the T'ang, most cities had been administrative, supported by taxes from the countryside. Official salaries and government expenditures created a demand for services and commercial products, making the cities into islands of commerce in a noncommercial hinterland. In most of China's seven or eight economic regions, this pattern continued during the Sung, but in the capital, and especially in the economically advanced regions along the Yangtze, cities became the hubs of regional commercial networks, with district seats or market towns serving as secondary centers for the local markets beneath them.

As this transition occurred, cities with more than 100,000 households almost quadrupled in number. The Northern Sung capital at Kaifeng is recorded as having had 260,000 households—probably more than one million inhabitants—and the Southern Sung capital at Hangchow had 391,000 households. Compare these capitals to those of backward Europe: London during the Northern Sung had a population of about 18,000; Rome during the Southern Sung had 35,000; and Paris even a century later had fewer than 60,000.

Furthermore, these Sung capitals, unlike Ch'ang-an with its walled wards that closed at night, were open within and spread beyond their outer walls. As in present-day Chinese cities, their main avenues were lined with shops. Merchant guilds replaced government officials as the managers of marketplaces. Growing wealth also led to a taste for luxury and an increasingly secular lifestyle. Restaurants, theaters, wine shops, and brothels abounded. Entertainment quarters with fortune tellers, jugglers, chess masters, acrobats, and puppeteers sprang up. Such activity had not been absent from Ch'ang-an, but their numbers increased, and they now catered to traders and rich merchants as well as officials.

### "Chaste Woman" Shi

Hung Mai (1123–1202 C.E.) was a collector of stories—fantastic, folkloric, and factual. Unlike the usual Confucian homilies on the proper virtues of women, his stories, and those told by other Sung storytellers, contained broader perspectives. They reflected the actual diversity of Chinese society. In this story the Chinese belief in ghosts enables the wronged Ning to have a hand in the villain's downfall.

---

*Is the moral of this tale simply that justice ultimately prevails? Can a more complex interpretation be made? What does it say about the dynamics of Sung society?*

---

Ning Six of South Meadow village, in the southern suburbs of Jianchang, was a simple-minded man who concentrated on his farming. His younger brother's wife, Miss Shi, was a little sleeker than her peers. She was also ruthless and licentious, and had an adulterous affair with a youth who lived there. Whenever Ning looked askance at her she would scold him and there was not much he could do.

Once Miss Shi took a chicken, wanting to cook it. When Ning learned of it, he went into her room, demanded that she give it to him, then left with it. Miss Shi quickly cut her arm with a knife, then went to the neighbors screaming, "Because my husband is not home, brother-in-law offered me a chicken and tried to force me to have sex with him. I resisted, threatening to kill myself with the knife I was holding, and so just managed to escape."

Ning at that time had no wife, so the neighbors thought she might be telling the truth. They took them to the village headman, then the county jail. The clerks at the jail reviewed the evidence and demanded 10,000 cash to set things right. Ning was poor and stingy, and moreover, knew himself to be in the right, so stubbornly refused. The clerks sent up the dossier to the perfect Dai Qi. Dai was unable to examine it but noted that it involved an ordinary village wife who was able to protect her virtue and her body and not be violated. The administrative supervisor, Zhao Shiqing, concurred with Qi, and they sent up the case making Ning look guilty. Ning received the death penalty and Miss Shi was granted 100,000 cash, regular visits from the local officials, and a banner honoring her for her chastity. From this, she acquired a reputation as a chaste wife. The local people all realized Ning had been wronged and resented how overboard she had gone.

In the end Miss Shi had an affair with a monk at the nearby Lintian temple. Charges were brought and she received a beating and soon became ill. She saw Ning as a vengeful demon and then died. The date was the sixth month of 1177.

From *Chinese Civilization: A Sourcebook*, second edition by Patricia Buckley Ebrey. Copyright © 1993 by Patricia Buckley Ebrey. Reprinted with permission of The Free Press, a Division of Simon & Schuster, Inc.

Trade between regions during the Sung was limited mainly to luxury goods like silk, lacquerware, medicinal herbs, and porcelains. Only where transport was cheap—along rivers, canals, or the coast—was interregional trade in bulk commodities economical, and even then, it was usually carried on only to make up for periodic shortages.

Foreign trade also reached new heights during the Sung. In the north, Chinese traders bought horses from Tibetan, Turkic, and Mongol border states, and sold silks, tea, and rhubarb. Along the coast, Chinese merchants took over the port trade that during the T'ang had been in the hands of Korean, Arab, and Persian merchants. The new hegemony of Chinese merchants was based on improved ships using both sail and oars and equipped with watertight compartments and better rudders. Chinese captains, navigating with the aid of the compass, came to dominate the sea routes from Japan in the north to Sumatra in the south. The content of the overseas trade reflected China's advanced economy: It imported raw materials and exported finished goods. Porcelains were sent to Southeast Asia and then were carried by Arab ships to medieval trading centers on the Persian Gulf and down the coast of East Africa as far south as Zanzibar.

## GOVERNMENT: FROM ARISTOCRACY TO AUTOCRACY

The millennium of late imperial China after the T'ang is often spoken of as the age of autocracy or as China's age of absolute monarchy. Earlier emperors, as we have noted, were often personally powerful, but beginning with the Sung, changes occurred that made it easier for emperors to be autocrats.

One change was that Sung emperors had direct personal control over more offices than their T'ang predecessors. For example, the Board of Academicians, an advisory office, presented the emperor with policy options separate from those presented by the Secretariat-Chancellery. The emperor could thus use the one against the other and prevent bureaucrats in the Secretariat-Chancellery from dominating the government.

A second change was that the central government was better funded than it had been previously. Revenues in 1100 were three times the peak revenues of the T'ang, partly as a result of the growth of population and agricultural wealth, and partly as a result of the establishment of government monopolies on salt, wine, and tea and various duties, fees, and taxes levied on domestic and foreign trade. During the Northern Sung, these commercial revenues rivaled the land tax; during the Southern Sung, they surpassed it. Confucian officials would continue to stress the primacy of land, but throughout late imperial China, commerce was a vital source of revenues.

A third change that strengthened emperors was the disappearance of the aristocracy. During the T'ang, the emperor had come from the same Sino-Turkic aristocracy of northwestern China as most of his principal ministers, and he was, essentially, the organ of a state that ruled on behalf of this aristocracy. Aristocrats monopolized

the high posts of government. They married among themselves and with the imperial family. They called the emperor the Son of Heaven, but they knew he was one of
them. During the Sung, in contrast, government officials were commoners, mostly products of the examination system. They were separated from the emperor by an enormous social gulf and saw him as a person apart. Able emperors took advantage of this.

The Sung examination system was larger than that of the T'ang, if smaller than
in later dynasties. Whereas only 10 percent of officials had been recruited by examination during the T'ang, the Sung figure rose to over 50 percent and included the most
important officials. The first examination was given at regional centers. The applicant took the examination in a walled cubicle under close supervision. To ensure impar-
tiality, his answers were recopied by clerks and his name was replaced by a number
before his examination was sent to the officials who would grade it. Of those who sat
for the examination, only a tiny percentage passed. The second hurdle was the metropolitan examination at the national capital, where the precautions were equally elaborate. Only one in five, or about two hundred a year, passed. The average successful
applicant was in his mid-thirties. The final hurdle was the palace examination, which
rejected a few and assigned a ranking to the others.

To pass the examinations, the candidate had to memorize the Confucian classics,
interpret selected passages, write in the literary style, compose poems on themes given
by the examiners, and propose solutions to contemporary problems in terms of Confucian philosophy. The quality of the officials produced by the Sung system was impressive. A parallel might be drawn with nineteenth-century Britain, where students in the
classics at Oxford and Cambridge went on to become generalist bureaucrats. The
Chinese examination system that flourished during the Sung continued, with some inter-
ruptions, into the twentieth century. The continuity of Chinese government during
this millennium rested on the examination elite, with its common culture and values.

The social base of this examination meritocracy was triangular, consisting of land,
education, and office. Landed wealth paid the costs of education. A poor peasant or
city dweller could not afford the years of study needed to pass the examinations. Without passing the examinations, official position was out of reach. And without office,
family wealth could not be preserved. The Chinese pattern of inheritance, as noted
earlier, led to the division of property at each change of generation. Some families
passed the examinations for several generations running. More often, the sons of well-
to-do officials did not study as hard as those with bare means. The adage "shirt sleeves
to shirt sleeves in three generations" is not inappropriate to the Sung and later dynasties. As China had an extended-family or clan system, a wealthy official often provided
education for the bright children of poor relations.

How the merchants related to this system is less clear. They had wealth but were
despised by scholar-officials as grubby profit seekers and were barred from taking the
examinations. Some merchants avoided the system altogether—a thorough education
in the Confucian classics did little to fit a merchant's son for a career in commerce. Others bought land for status and security, and their sons or grandsons became eligible to

take the exams. Similarly, a small peasant might build up his holdings, become a land-lord, and educate a son or grandson. The system was steeply hierarchical, but it was not closed nor did it produce a new, self-perpetuating elite.

## SUNG CULTURE

As society and government changed during the T'ang-Sung transition, so too did culture. Sung culture retained some of the energy of the T'ang while becoming more intensely and perhaps more narrowly Chinese. The preconditions for the rich Sung culture were a rising economy, an increase in the number of schools and higher literacy, and the spread of printing. Sung culture was less aristocratic, less cosmopolitan, and more closely associated with the officials and the scholar-gentry, who were both its practitioners and its patrons. It also was less Buddhist than the T'ang had been. Only the Zen (Ch'an) sect kept its vitality, and many Confucians were outspokenly anti-Buddhist and anti-Taoist. In sum, the secular culture of officials that had been a sidestream in the T'ang broadened and became the mainstream during the Sung.

Chinese consider the Sung dynasty as the peak of their traditional culture. It was, for example, China's greatest age of pottery and porcelains. High-firing techniques were developed, and kilns were established in every area. There was a rich variety of beautiful glazes. The shapes were restrained and harmonious. Sung pottery, like nothing produced in the world before it, made ceramics a major art form in East Asia. It was also an age of great historians. Ssu-ma Kuang (1019–1086) wrote *A Comprehensive Mirror for Aid in Government*, which treated not a single dynasty but all Chinese history. His work was more sophisticated than previous histories in that it included a discussion of documentary sources and an explanation of why he chose to rely on one source rather than another. The greatest achievements of the Sung, however, were in philosophy, poetry, and painting.

### Philosophy

The Sung was second only to the Chou as a creative age in philosophy. A series of original thinkers culminated in the towering figure of Chu Hsi (1130–1200). Chu Hsi studied Taoism and Buddhism in his youth, along with Confucianism. A brilliant student, he passed the metropolitan examination at the age of eighteen. During his thirties, he focused his attention on Confucianism, deepening and making more systematic its social and political ethics by joining to it certain Buddhist and native metaphysical elements. As a consequence, the new Confucianism became a viable alternative to Buddhism among Chinese intellectuals. Chu Hsi became famous as a teacher at the White Deer Grotto Academy, and his writings were widely distributed. Before the end of the Sung, his Confucianism had become the standard interpretation used in the civil service examinations, and it remained so until the twentieth century.

If we search for comparable figures in other traditions, we might pick Saint Thomas Aquinas (1224–1274) of medieval Europe or the Islamic theologian al-Ghazali (1058–1111), each of whom produced a new synthesis or worldview that lasted for centuries. Aquinas combined Aristotle and Latin theology just as Chu Hsi joined Confucian philosophy and metaphysical notions from other sources. Because Chu Hsi used terms such as the *great ultimate* and because he emphasized a Zen-like meditation called "quiet sitting," some contemporary critics said his Neo-Confucian philosophy was a Buddhist wolf in the clothing of a Confucian sheep. This was unfair. Whereas Aquinas would make philosophy serve religion, Chu Hsi made religion or metaphysics serve philosophy. In his hands, the great ultimate (identified with the *li* or principles that make things what they are) lost its otherworldly character and became a constituent of all things in the universe. Perhaps the Chu Hsi philosophy may be characterized as innerworldly.

Later critics often argued that Chu Hsi's teachings encouraged metaphysical speculation at the expense of practical ethics. Chu Hsi's loyal followers replied that, on the contrary, his teachings gave practical ethics a systematic underpinning and positively contributed to individual moral responsibility. What was discovered within by Neo-Confucian quiet sitting was just those positive ethical truths enunciated by Confucius over a thousand years earlier. The new metaphysics did not change the Confucian social philosophy.

Chu Hsi himself advocated the selection of scholar-officials through schools, rather than by examinations. It is ironic that his teachings became a new orthodoxy that was maintained by the channelizing effect of the civil service examinations. Historians argue, probably correctly, that Chu Hsi's teachings were one source of stability in late imperial China. Like the examination system, the imperial institution, the scholar-gentry class, and the land system, his interpretation of Confucianism contributed to continuity and impeded change. Some historians go further and say that the emergence of the Chu Hsi orthodoxy stifled intellectual creativity during later dynasties—which probably is a slight overstatement. There were always contending schools.

## Poetry

Sung poets were in awe of those of the T'ang, yet Sung poets were also among China's best. A Japanese scholar of Chinese literature wrote:

> T'ang poetry could be likened to wine, and Sung poetry to tea. Wine has great power to stimulate, but one cannot drink it constantly. Tea is less stimulating, bringing to the drinker a quieter pleasure, but one which can be enjoyed more continuously.[9]

[9]Kojiro Yoshikawa, *An Introduction to Sung Poetry*, trans. by Burton Watson (Cambridge, MA: Harvard University Press, Harvard-Yenching Institute Monograph Series, 1967), p. 37.

---

### Su Tung-p'o Imagined on a Wet Day, Wearing a Rain Hat and Clogs

After Su's death, a disciple wrote these lines:

---

*How does the sentiment in this poem relate to the Confucian humanism encountered in the document in Chapter 2?*

---

When with tall hat and firm baton he stood
    in council,
The crowds were awed at the dignity of the
    statesman in him.

But when in cloth cap he strolled with cane
    and sandals,
He greeted little children with gentle
    smiles.

Reprinted by permission of the publisher. From *An Introduction to Sung Poetry*, by Kojiro Yoshikawa, trans. by Burton Watson, Cambridge, MA: Harvard University Press, Copyright © 1967 by the Harvard-Yenching Institute Monograph Series, p. 122.

---

The most famous poet of the Northern Sung was Su Tung-p'o (1037–1101), a man who participated in the full range of the culture of his age: He was a painter and calligrapher, particularly knowledgeable about inks; he practiced Zen and wrote commentaries on the Confucian classics; he superintended engineering projects; and he was a connoisseur of cooking and wine. His life was shaped by politics. He was a conservative, believing in a limited role for government and social control through morality. (The other faction in the Sung bureaucracy was the reformers, who stressed law and institutions and a bigger role for government.)

Passing the metropolitan examination, Su rose through a succession of posts to become the governor of a province—a position of immense power. While considering death sentences, which could not be carried over into the new year, he wrote:

> New Year's Eve—you'd think I could go home early
> But official business keeps me.
> I hold the brush and face them with tears:
> Pitiful convicts in chains,
> Little men who tried to fill their bellies,
> Fell into the law's net, don't understand disgrace.
> And I? In love with a meager stipend
> I hold on to my job and miss the chance to retire.
> Do not ask who is foolish or wise;
> All of us alike scheme for a meal.
> The ancients would have freed them a while at New Year's—
> Would I dare do likewise? I am silent with shame.[10]

---

[10]Yoshikawa, p. 119.

Eight years later, when the reformers came to power, Su himself was arrested and spent one hundred days in prison, awaiting execution on a charge of slandering the emperor. Instead, he was released and exiled. He wrote, "Out the gate, I do a dance, wind blows in my face; our galloping horses race along as magpies cheer."[11] Arriving at his place of exile, he reflected:

Between heaven and earth I live,
One ant on a giant grindstone,
Trying in my petty way to walk to the right
While the turning of the mill wheel takes me endlessly left.
Though I go the way of benevolence and duty,
I can't escape from hunger and cold.[12]

But exile was soon turned to art. He farmed a plot of land at the "eastern slope," from which he took his literary name, Tung-p'o. Of his work there, he wrote:

A good farmer hates to wear out the land;
I'm lucky this plot was ten years fallow.
It's too soon to count on mulberries;
My best bet is a crop of wheat.
I planted seed and within the month
Dirt on the rows was showing green.
An old farmer warned me,
Don't let seedlings shoot up too fast!
If you want plenty of dumpling flour
Turn a cow or sheep in here to graze.
Good advice—I bowed my thanks;
I won't forget you when my belly's full.[13]

After 1086, the conservatives regained control of the government, and Su resumed his official career. In 1094, another shift occurred and Su was again sent into exile on the distant southern island of Hainan. After still another shift, Su was on his way back to the capital when he died in 1101.

## Painting

In the West, penmanship and painting are quite separate, one merely a skill and the other esteemed as an art. In China, calligraphy and painting were equally appre-

[11]Yoshikawa, p. 117.
[12]Yoshikawa, p. 105.
[13]Yoshikawa, pp. 119–120.

ciated and were seen as related. A scholar spent his life with brush in hand. The same qualities of line, balance, and strength needed for calligraphy carried over to painting. Chinese calligraphy is immensely pleasing even to the untutored Western eye, and it is not difficult to distinguish between the elegant strokes of Hui-neng, the last emperor of the Northern Sung, and the powerful brushwork of the Zen monk Chang Chi-chih.

Sung painting was varied—of birds or flowers; of fish or insects; of horses, monkeys, or water buffalo; of scholars, emperors, Buddhas, or Taoist immortals. But its crowning achievement was landscapes. Sung landscapes are quite different from those of the West. Each stroke of the brush on silk or paper was final. Mistakes could not be covered up. Each element of a painting was presented in its most pleasing aspect; the painting was not constrained by single-point perspective. Paintings had no single source of illumination with light and shadow but an overall diffusion of light. Space was an integral part of the painting. A typical painting might have craggy rocks or twisted pine trees in the foreground, then mist or clouds or rain to create distance, and in the background the outlines of mountains or cliffs fading into space. If the painting contained human figures at all, they were small in a natural universe that was very large. Chinese painting thus reflected the same worldview as Chinese philosophy or poetry. The goal of the painter was to grasp the inner reality of the scene and not to be bound up in surface details.

In paintings by monks or masters of the Zen school, the presentation of an intuitive vision of an inner reality became even more pronounced. Paintings of Bodhidharma, the legendary founder of the Zen sect, are often dominated by a single powerful downstroke of the brush, defining the edge of his robe. Paintings of patriarchs tearing up sutras or sweeping dust with a broom from the mirror of the mind are almost as calligraphic as paintings of bamboo. A Yuan dynasty painting in the style of Shih K'o shows the figure of a monk or sage who is dozing or meditating. A Zen "broken ink" landscape might contain rocks, water, mountains, and clouds, each represented by a few explosive strokes of the brush.

## CHINA IN THE MONGOL WORLD EMPIRE: THE YUAN DYNASTY (1279–1368)

The Mongols created the greatest empire in the history of the world. It extended from the Caspian Sea to the Pacific Ocean; from Russia, Siberia, and Korea in the north to Persia and Burma in the south. Invasion fleets were even sent to Java and Japan, although without success. Mongol rule in China is one chapter of this larger story.

## RISE OF THE MONGOL EMPIRE

A nomadic people, the Mongols lived to the north of China on grasslands where they raised horses and herded sheep. They lived in felt tents called yurts—they sometimes called themselves "the people of the felt tents." Women performed much of the work and were freer and more easygoing than women in China. Families belonged to clans, and related clans to tribes. Tribes would gather during the annual migration from the summer plains to winter pasturage. Chiefs were elected, most often from noble lineages, for their courage, military prowess, judgment, and leadership. Like Manchu or Turkic, the Mongol tongue was Altaic.

The Mongols believed in nature deities and in the sky god above all others. Sky blue was their sacred color. They communicated with their gods through religious specialists called *shamans*. Politically divided, they traded and warred among themselves and with settled peoples on the borders of their vast grassland domains.

The founder of the Mongol Empire, Temujin, was born in 1167, the son of a tribal chief. While Temujin was still a child, his father was poisoned. He fled and after wandering for some years, he returned to the tribe, avenged his father, and in time became chief himself. Through his shrewd policy of alliances and remarkable survival qualities, by the time he was forty he had united all Mongol tribes and had been elected

**Map 3–3   The Mongol Empire in the late thirteenth century.**   Note the four khanates: the Golden Horde in Russia, the Ilkhanate in Persia, Chagadai in Central Asia, and the Great Khanate extending from Mongolia to southern China.

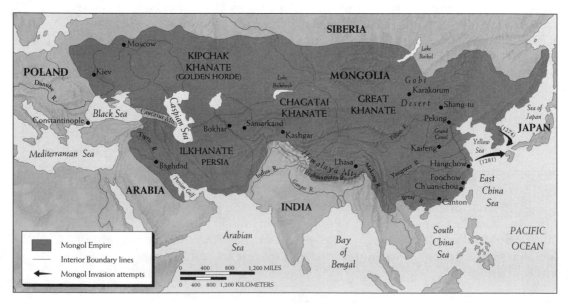

their great khan, or ruler. It is by the title *Genghis* (also spelled *Jenghiz* or *Chinggis*) *Khan* that he is known to history. Genghis possessed an extraordinary charisma, and his sons and grandsons also became wise and talented leaders. Why the Mongol tribes, almost untouched by the higher civilizations of the world, should have produced such leaders at this point in history is difficult to explain.

A second conundrum is how the Mongols, who numbered only about a million and a half, created the army that conquered vastly denser populations. Part of the answer is institutional. Genghis organized his armies into "myriads" of ten thousand troops, with decimal subdivisions of one thousand, one hundred, and ten. Elaborate signals were devised so that, in battle, even large units could be manipulated like the fingers of a hand. Mongol tactics were superb: Units would retreat, turn, flank, and destroy their enemies. The historical record makes amply clear that Genghis's nomadic cavalry had a paralytic effect on the peoples they encountered. Peerless horsemen, the Mongol's most dreaded weapon was the compound bow, short enough to be used from the saddle yet more powerful than the English longbow (a 150-pound pull versus a 100-pound pull).

They were astonishingly mobile. Each man carried his own supplies. Trailing remounts, they covered vast distances quickly. In 1241, for example, a Mongol army had reached Hungary, Poland, and the shore of the Adriatic and was poised for a further advance into Western Europe. But when word arrived of the death of the great khan, the army turned and galloped back to Mongolia to help choose his successor.

When this army encountered walled cities, it learned the use of siege weapons from the enemies it had conquered. Chinese engineers were used in campaigns in Persia. The Mongols also used terror as a weapon. Inhabitants of cities that refused to surrender in the Near East and China were put to the sword. Large areas in north China and Szechwan were devastated and depopulated in the process of conquest. Descriptions of the Mongols by those whom they conquered dwell on their physical toughness and pitiless cruelty.

But the Mongols had strengths that went beyond the strictly military. Genghis opened his armies to other nomadic peoples of the steppe. As long as they complied with the military discipline demanded of his forces, they could participate in his triumphs. In 1206, Genghis promulgated laws designed to prevent the normal wrangling and warring between tribes that would undermine his empire. Genghis also obtained thousands of pledges of personal loyalty from his followers, and he appointed these "vassals" to command his armies and staff his government. This policy gave to his forces an inner coherence that countered the divisive effect of tribal loyalties.

The Mongol conquests were all the more impressive in that, unlike the earlier Arab expansion, they lacked the unifying force of religious zeal. To be sure, at an assembly of chiefs in 1206, an influential shaman revealed that it was the sky god's will that Genghis conquer the world. Yet other unabashedly frank words attributed to Genghis may reveal a truer image of what lay behind the Mongol drive to conquest: "Man's highest joy is in victory: to conquer one's enemies, to pursue them, to deprive them of their possessions, to make their beloved weep, to ride on their horses, and to embrace their wives and daughters."[14]

Genghis divided his far-flung empire among his four sons, who, aided by their sons, completed the conquest. Trade and communications were maintained between the parts, but over several generations, each of the four khanates became independent. The khanate of Chagatai was in Central Asia and remained purely nomadic. A second khanate of the Golden Horde ruled Russia from the lower Volga. The third was in Persia. The fourth, led by those who succeeded Genghis as great khans, centered first on Mongolia and then China.

## MONGOL RULE IN CHINA

The standard theory used in explaining Chinese history is that of the dynastic cycle. A second theory explains the history in terms of the interaction between the settled people of China and nomads of the steppe. When strong states emerged in China, their wealth and population enabled them to expand militarily onto the steppe. But when China was weak, as was just as often the case, steppe peoples overran China. To review briefly:

1. During the Han dynasty (206 B.C.E.–220 C.E.), the most pressing problem in foreign relations was the Hsiung Nu empire to the north.
2. During the centuries that followed the Han, various nomadic peoples invaded and ruled northern China.
3. The energy and institutions of these Sino-Turkic rulers of the northern dynasties shaped China's reunification during the Sui (581–618) and T'ang (618–907) dynasties. The Uighur Turks also played an ongoing role in T'ang defense policy.
4. Northern border states became even more important during the Sung. The Northern Sung (960–1126) bought peace with payments of gold and silver to the Liao. The Southern Sung (1126–1279), for all of its cultural brilliance, was little more than a tributary state of the Chin, which had expanded into northern China.

From the very start of the Mongol pursuit of world hegemony, the riches of China were a target. But Genghis proceeded cautiously, determined to leave no enemy at his back. He first disposed of the Tibetan state to the northwest of China and then of the Manchu state of Ch'in that ruled north China. Mongol forces took Peking in 1227,

---

[14]J. K. Fairbank, E. O. Reischauer, and A. M. Craig, *East Asia, Tradition and Transformation* (Boston: Houghton Mifflin, 1989), p. 164.

the year Genghis died. They went on to take Loyang and the southern reaches of the Yellow River in 1234, and all of north China by 1241. During this time, the Mongols were interested mainly in loot. Only later did Chinese advisers persuade them that more wealth could be obtained by taxation.

Kublai, a grandson of Genghis, was chosen as the great khan in 1260. In 1264, he moved his capital from Karakorum in Mongolia to Peking. It was only in 1271 that he adopted a Chinese dynastic name, the Yuan, and the Chinese custom of hereditary succession. Then, as the ruler of a Chinese dynasty, he went to war with the Southern Sung. Once the decision was made, the Mongols swept across southern China. The last Sung stronghold fell in 1279.

Kublai Khan's rule in Peking reflected the mixture of cultural elements in Mongol China. From Peking, Kublai could rule as a Chinese emperor, which would not have been possible in Karakorum. He adopted the Chinese custom of hereditary succession. He rebuilt Peking as a walled city in the Chinese style. But Peking was far to the north of any previous Chinese capital, away from centers of wealth and population; to provision it, the Grand Canal had to be extended. From Peking, Kublai could look out onto Manchuria and Mongolia and maintain ties with the other khanates. The city proper was for the Mongols. It was known to the West as *Cambulac*, "the city (*baliq*) of the khan." Chinese were segregated in an adjoining walled city. The palace of the khan was designed by an Arab architect; its rooms were Central Asian in style. Kublai also maintained a summer palace at Shangtu (the "Xanadu" of Samuel Taylor Coleridge's poem) in Inner Mongolia, where he could hawk and ride and hunt in Mongol style.

Early Mongol rule in northern China was rapacious and exploitative, but it later shifted toward Chinese forms of government and taxation, especially in the south and at the local level. Because it was a foreign military occupation, civil administration was highly centralized. Under the emperor was a Central Secretariat, and beneath it were ten "Moving Secretariats," which became the provinces of later dynasties. These highly centralized institutions and the arbitrary style of Mongol decision making accelerated the trend toward absolutism that had started during the previous dynasty.

About four hundred thousand Mongols lived in China during the Yuan period. For such a tiny minority to control the Chinese majority, it had to stay separate. One measure was to make military service a monopoly of Mongols and their nomadic allies. Garrisons were established throughout China, with a strategic reserve on the steppe. Military officers were always regarded as more important than civil officials. A second measure was to use ethnic classifications in appointing civil officials. The highest category was the Mongols, who held the top civil and military posts. The second category included Persians, Turks, and other non-Chinese, who were given high civil posts. The third category was northern Chinese, including Manchus and other border peoples, and the fourth was southern Chinese. Even when the examination system was sporadically revived after 1315, the Mongols and their allies took an easier examination; their quota was as large as that for Chinese; and they were appointed to higher offices.

## Marco Polo Describes the City of Hangchow

Marco Polo was a Venetian. In 1300, Venice had a population of more than one hundred thousand and was one of the wealthiest Mediterranean city-states. But Polo was nonetheless unprepared for what he saw in China. Commenting on Hangchow, China's capital during the Southern Sung, he first noted its size (ten or twelve times larger than Venice), then its many canals and bridges, its streets "paved with stones and bricks," and its location between "a lake of fresh and very clear water" and "a river of great magnitude." He spoke of "the prodigious concourse of people" frequenting its ten great marketplaces and of its "capacious warehouses built of stone for the accommodation of merchants who arrive from India and other parts." He then described the life of its people.

---

*Europeans who read Marco Polo's account of China thought it was too good to be true. Would you agree?*

---

Each of the ten market-squares is surrounded with high dwelling-houses, in the lower part of which are shops, where every kind of manufacture is carried on, and every article of trade is sold; such, amongst others, as spices, drugs, trinkets, and pearls. In certain shops nothing is vended but the wine of the country, which they are continually brewing, and serve out fresh to their customers at a moderate price. The streets connected with the market-squares are numerous, and in some of them are many cold baths, attended by servants of both sexes, to perform the offices of ablution for the men and women who frequent them, and who from their childhood have been accustomed at all times to wash in cold water, which they reckon highly conducive to health. At these bathing places, however, they have apartments provided with warm water, for the use of strangers, who from not being habituated to it, cannot bear the shock of the cold. All are in the daily practice of washing their persons, and especially before their meals.

In other streets are the habitations of the courtesans, who are here in such numbers as I dare not venture to report; and not only near the squares, which is the situation usually appropriated for their residence, but in every part of the city they are to be found, adorned with much finery, highly perfumed, occupying well-furnished houses, and attended by many female domestics. These women are accomplished, and are perfect in the arts of blandishment and dalliance, which they accompany with expressions adapted to every description of person, inso-

---

The net result was an uneasy symbiosis. Chinese officials directly governed the Chinese populace, collecting taxes, settling disputes, and maintaining the local order. Only a small number of these officials ever learned to speak Mongolian, yet without their positive cooperation, Mongol rule in China would have been impossible. The Mongols, concentrated in Peking, large cities, and in garrisons, spoke Mongolian among

much that strangers who have once become so enchanted by their meretricious arts, that they can never divest themselves of the impression. Thus intoxicated with sensual pleasures, when they return to their homes they report that they have been in Kin-sai [Hangchow], or the celestial city, and pant for the time when they may be enabled to revisit paradise.

The inhabitants of the city are idolaters, and they use paper money as currency. The men as well as the women have fair complexions, and are handsome. The greater part of them are always clothed in silk, in consequence of the vast quantity of that material produced in the territory of Kin-sai, exclusively of what the merchants import from other provinces. Amongst the handicraft trades exercised in the place, there are twelve considered to be superior to the rest, as being more generally useful; for each of which there are a thousand workshops, and each shop furnishes employment for ten, fifteen, or twenty workmen, and in a few instances as many as forty, under their respective masters. The natural disposition of the native inhabitants of Kin-sai is pacific, and by the example of their former kings, who were themselves unwarlike, they have been accustomed to habits of tranquility. The

management of arms is unknown to them, nor do they keep any in their houses. Contentious broils are never heard among them. They conduct their mercantile and manufacturing concerns with perfect candour and probity. They are friendly towards each other, and persons who inhabit the same street, both men and women, from the mere circumstance of neighbourhood, appear like one family. In their domestic manners they are free from jealousy or suspicion of their wives, to whom great respect is shown, and any man would be accounted infamous who should presume to use indecent expressions to a married woman. To strangers also, who visit their city in the way of commerce, they give proofs of cordiality, inviting them freely to their houses, showing them hospitable attention, and furnishing them with the best advice and assistance in their mercantile transactions. On the other hand, they dislike the sight of soldiery, not excepting the guards of the grand khan, as they preserve the recollection that by them they were deprived of the government of their native kings and rulers.

Excerpt from *The Travels of Marco Polo*, 1908, from Everyman's Library. Reprinted by permission of David Campbell Publishers, London, pp. 290–301.

themselves and usually did not bother to learn Chinese. A few exceptions wrote poetry in Chinese and painted in the Chinese style. Communication was through interpreters. When a Chinese district magistrate sent a query to the court, the ruling was made in Mongolian. (The Mongols had borrowed the alphabet of the Uighurs to transcribe their tongue.) A word-for-word translation in Chinese was written below the Mongolian and passed back down to the magistrate. As the two languages are syntactically different, the resulting Chinese was grotesque.

## FOREIGN CONTACTS AND CHINESE CULTURE

Diplomacy and trade within the greater Mongol Empire brought China into contact with other higher civilizations for the first time since the T'ang period. Persia and the Arab world were especially important. Merchants, missionaries, and diplomats voyaged from the Persian Gulf and across the Indian Ocean to seaports in southeastern China. The Arab communities in Canton and other ports were larger than they had been during the Sung. Camel caravans carrying silks and ceramics left Peking to pass through the central Asian oases and on to Baghdad. Although the Mongols did not favor Chinese merchants and most trade was in other hands, Chinese trade also expanded. Chinese communities became established in Tabriz, the center of trading in western Asia, and in Moscow and Novgorod. It was during this period that knowledge of printing, gunpowder, and Chinese medicine spread to western Asia. Chinese ceramics influenced those of Persia as Chinese painting influenced Persian miniatures.

In Europe, knowledge of China was transmitted by the Venetian trader Marco Polo, who said he had served Kublai as an official between 1275 and 1292. His book, *A Description of the World*, was translated into most European languages. Many readers doubted that a land of such wealth and culture could exist so far from Europe, but the book excited an interest in geography. When Christopher Columbus set sail in 1492, his goal was to reach Polo's Zipangu (Japan).

Other cultural contacts were fostered by the Mongol toleration or encouragement of religion. Nestorian Christianity, spreading from Persia to Central Asia, reentered China during the Mongol era. The mother of Kublai Khan was a Christian of this sect. Churches were built in main cities; also, several papal missions were sent from Rome to the Mongol court. An archbishopric was established in Peking; a church was built, sermons were preached in Turkish or Mongolian, and choirboys sang hymns. Kublai sent Marco Polo's father and uncle with a letter to the pope asking for a hundred intelligent men acquainted with the seven arts.

Tibetan Buddhism with its magical doctrines and elaborate rites was the religion most favored by the Mongols. But Chinese Buddhism also flourished. Priests and monks of all religions were given tax exemptions. It is estimated that half a million Chinese became Buddhist monks during the Mongol century. The foreign religion that made the greatest gains was Islam, which became permanently established in Central Asia and western China. Mosques were built in the Islamic areas, in Peking, and in southeastern port cities. Even Confucianism was regarded as a religion by the Mongols, and its teachers were exempted from taxes. But as the scholar-gentry rarely obtained important offices, they saw the Mongol era as a time of hardship.

Despite these wide contacts with other peoples and religions, the high culture of China appears to have been influenced almost not at all—partly because China had little to learn from other areas, and partly because the centers of Chinese culture were in the south, the last area to be conquered and the area least affected by Mongol rule. Also, in reaction to the Mongol conquest, Chinese culture became conservative and turned in on itself. Scholars wrote poetry in the style of the Sung. New schools of painting developed, but the developments were from within the Chinese tradition, and the greatest Yuan paintings continued the style of the Sung. Yuan historians wrote the official history of the dynasty that preceded it. The head of the court bureau of historiography was a Mongol, but the histories produced by his Chinese staff were in the traditional mold. As the dynasty waned, unemployed scholars wrote essays expressing loyalty toward the Sung and satirizing the Mongols. Their writings were not censored: The Mongols either could not read them, did not read them, or did not care.

The major contribution to Chinese arts during the Yuan was by dramatists, who combined poetic arias with vaudeville theater to produce a new operatic drama. Performed by traveling troupes, the operas used few stage props. They relied for effect on makeup, costumes, pantomime, and stylized gestures. The women's roles were usually played by men. Except for the arias—the highlights of the performance—the dramas used vernacular Chinese, appealing to a popular audience. The unemployed scholars who wrote the scripts drew on the entire repertoire of the Sung storyteller. Among stock figures of the operas were a Robin Hood-like bandit; a famous detective-judge; the T'ang monk who traveled to India; warriors and statesmen of the Three Kingdoms; and romantic heroes, villains, and ghosts. Justice always triumphed, and the dramas usually ended happily. In several famous plays, the hero gets the girl, despite objections by her parents and seemingly insurmountable obstacles, by passing the civil service examinations in first place. As the examinations were not in effect during most of the Yuan, this resolution of the hero's predicament is one that looked back to the Sung pattern of government. Yuan drama continued almost unchanged in later dynasties, and during the nineteenth century, it merged with a form of southern Chinese theater to become today's Peking Opera.

## LAST YEARS OF THE YUAN

Despite the Mongol military domination of China and the highly centralized institutions of the Mongol court, the Yuan was the shortest of China's major dynasties. Little more than a century elapsed between Kublai's move to Peking in 1264 and the dynasty's collapse in 1368. The rule of Kublai and his successor had been effective, but thereafter a decline set in. By then, the Mongol Empire as a whole no longer lent strength to its parts. The khanates became separated by religion and culture as well as by distance. Even tribesmen in Mongolia rebelled now and then against the great khans in Peking, who, in their eyes, had become too Chinese. The court at Peking, too, had never really gained legitimacy. Some Chinese officials served it loyally to the end, but most Chinese saw the government as carpetbaggers and saw Mongol rule as a military occupation. When succession disputes, bureaucratic factionalism, and pitched battles between Mongol generals broke out, Chinese showed little inclination to rally in support of the dynasty.

Problems also arose in the countryside. Taxes were heavy and some local officials were corrupt. The government issued excessive paper money and then refused to accept it in payment for taxes. The Yellow River changed its course, flooding the canals that carried grain to the capital. At great cost and suffering, a labor force of 150,000 workers and 20,000 soldiers rerouted the river to the south of the Shantung peninsula. Further natural disasters during the 1350s led to popular uprisings. The White Lotus sect preached the coming of Maitreya. Regional military commanders, suppressing the rebellions, became independent of central control. Warlords arose. The warlord who ruled Szechwan was infamous for his cruelty. Important economic regions were devastated and in part depopulated by rebellions. At the end, a rebel army threatened Peking, and the last Mongol emperor and his court fled on horses to Shangtu. When that fell, they fled still deeper into the plains of Mongolia.

## IMPERIAL CHINA IN HISTORICAL PERSPECTIVE

Rough parallels between China and Europe persisted until the sixth century C.E. Both saw the rise and fall of great empires. At first glance, the three-and-one-half centuries that followed the Han dynasty appear remarkably similar to the comparable period after the collapse of the Roman Empire: Central authority broke down, private armies arose, and aristocratic estates were established. Barbarian tribes, once allied to the empires, invaded and pillaged large areas. Otherworldly religions entered to challenge earlier official worldviews. In China, Neo-Taoism and then Buddhism challenged Confucianism, just as Christianity challenged Roman conceptions of the sociopolitical order.

But from the late sixth century C.E., a fundamental divergence occurred. Europe tailed off into centuries of feudal disunity and backwardness. A ghost of empire lingered in the European memory. But the reality, even after centuries had passed, was that tiny areas like France (one-seventeenth the size of China), Italy (one-thirty-second), or Germany (one-twenty-seventh) found it difficult to establish an internal unity, much less recreate a pan-European or pan-Mediterranean empire. This pattern of separate little states has persisted in Europe until today. In contrast, China, which is about the size of Europe and geographically no more natural a political unit, put a unified empire back together again, attaining a new level of wealth, power, and culture, and unified rule has continued until the present. What is the explanation?

One reason the empire was reconstituted in China was that the victory of Buddhism in China was less complete than that of Christianity in Europe. Confucianism survived within the aristocratic families and at the courts of the Six Dynasties, and the idea of a united empire was integral to it. It is difficult even to think of Confucianism apart from the idea of a universal ruler, aided by men of virtue and ability, ruling "all under Heaven" according to Heaven's Mandate. In contrast, the Roman concept of political order was not maintained as an independent doctrine. Moreover, empire was not a vital element in Christian thought—except perhaps in Byzantium, where the empire lasted longer than it did in Western Europe. The notion of a "Christian king" did appear in the West, but basically, the kingdom sought by Jesus was not of this world.

A second consideration was China's greater cultural homogeneity. It had a common written language that was fairly close to all varieties of spoken Chinese. Minority peoples and even barbarian conquerors—apart from the Mongols—were rapidly Sinicized. In contrast, after Rome, the Mediterranean fell apart into its component cultures. Latin became the universal language of the Western church, but for most Christians it was a foreign language, a part of the mystery of the Mass, and even in Italy it became an artificial language, separate from the living tongue. European languages and cultures were divisive forces.

A third factor was the combination in the post-Han northern Chinese states of economic strength based on Chinese agriculture with the military striking force of a nomadic cavalry. There was nothing like it in Europe. Such a northern state reunified China in 589 C.E.

A fourth and perhaps critical factor was China's greater population density. The province (called a *circuit* at the time) of Hopei had a registered population of 10,559,728 during the eighth century C.E. Hopei was about one-third the size of France, which in the eleventh century had a population of about two million. That is to say, even comparing China with France three centuries later, China's population density was fifteen times greater. (This comparison, it should be noted, is with a nonrice-producing area of China. Rice paddy areas were even more densely populated.) Greater population density resulted in a different kind of history.

Population density helps explain why the Chinese could absorb barbarian conquerors so much more quickly than could Europe. More cultivators provided a larger agricultural surplus to the northern kingdoms than that enjoyed by comparable kingdoms in Europe. Greater numbers of people also meant better communications and a better base for commerce. To be sure, the centuries that followed the Han saw a decline in commerce and cities. In some areas, money went out of use to be replaced by barter or the use of silk as currency. But the economic level remained higher than in early medieval Europe.

Several of the factors that explain the Sui-T'ang regeneration of a unified empire apply equally well or better to the Sung and subsequent dynasties. As schools were established and literacy rose, Confucianism and the ideal of a unified China became more widely accepted. Chinese culture was more homogeneous and less open to outside influences in the tenth century than it had been four centuries earlier. The population had also grown, with the Yangtze basin emerging as a new center of gravity.

The cyclic regeneration of centralized bureaucratic government—even under outside conquerors—can also be analyzed in terms of the interests it served. For the military figure who established the dynasty, the bureaucratic state was a huge tax machine that supported his armies and bestowed on him revenues beyond the imaginings of contemporary European monarchs. Government by civilian officials also offered some promise for the security of his progeny by acting as a counterweight against army generals. For the scholar-gentry class, service to the state was the means to maintain family wealth, power, and status. Nothing mattered more. For merchants, a strong state was not an unmixed blessing: It might tax their profits or establish monopolies on the commodities they traded, but it also provided order and stability. More often than not, commerce expanded during such periods. For farmers, the picture was also unclear. Taxation was often exploitative, but orderly exploitation was usually preferable to rapacious warlords, bandits, or marauding armies.

Comparisons across continents are difficult, but it seems likely that T'ang and Sung China had longer stretches of good government than any other part of the contemporary world. Not until the nineteenth century would comparable bureaucracies of talent and virtue appear in the West.

## REVIEW QUESTIONS

1. Why could China recreate its empire—just 400 years after the fall of the Han—when Rome could not? Are there similarities between the Ch'in–Han transition and that of the Sui-T'ang? Between Han and T'ang expansion and contraction?

2. How did the Chinese economy change between the T'ang, the Northern Sung, and the Southern Sung? The polity? China's relationships to surrounding states?

3. What do Chinese poetry and art tell us about Chinese society? About women? About war?

4. What drove the Mongols to conquer most of the known world? How could their military accomplish the task? Once they had conquered China, how did they rule it? What was the Chinese response to Mongol rule?

## SUGGESTED READINGS

*General*

BOL, P. K. *The Culture of Ours* (1992). An intellectual history of the T'ang through the Sung dynasties.

CAHILL, J. *Chinese Painting* (1960). An excellent survey.

FAIRBANK, J. K. *China: A New History* (1992). The summation of a lifetime engagement with Chinese history.

KIERMAN, F. A. JR., AND FAIRBANK, J. K., EDS. *Chinese Ways in Warfare* (1974). Chapters by different authors on the Chinese military experience from the Chou to the Ming.

*Sui and T'ang*

EBREY, P. B. *The Aristocratic Families of Early Imperial China* (1978).

McMullen, D. *State and Scholars in Tang China* (1988).

Owen, S. *The Great Age of Chinese Poetry: The High T'ang* (1980).

Pulleyblank, E. G. *The Background of the Rebellion of An Lu-shan* (1955). A study of the 755 rebellion that weakened the central authority of the T'ang dynasty.

Reischauer, E. O. *Ennin's Travels in T'ang China* (1955). China as seen through the eyes of a ninth-century Japanese Marco Polo.

Schafer, E. H. *The Golden Peaches of Samarkand* (1963). A study of T'ang imagery.

Teiser, S. *The Ghost Festival in Medieval China* (1988). On T'ang popular religion.

Twitchett, D. ed. *Sui and T'ang China, 589–906*, Part 1 (1984). (Part 2, also in *The Cambridge History of China*, is forthcoming.)

Wang, G. W. *The Structure of Power in North China During the Five Dynasties* (1963). A study of the interim period between the T'ang and the Sung dynasties.

Wright, A. F. *The Sui Dynasty* (1978).

*Sung*

Chang, C. S. and Smythe, J. *South China in the Twelfth Century* (1981). China as seen through the eyes of a twelfth-century Chinese poet, historian, and statesman.

Gernet, J. *Daily Life in China on the Eve of the Mongol Invasion* (1962).

Haeger, J. W., ed. *Crisis and Prosperity in Sung China* (1975).

Hymes, R. *Statesmen and Gentlemen* (1987). On the transformation of officials into a local gentry elite during the twelfth and thirteenth centuries.

Liu, J. T. C. and Golas, P. J., eds., *Change in Sung China: Innovation or Renovation?* (1969).

Rossabi, M. *China Among Equals* (1983). A study of the Liao, Ch'in, and Sung empires and their relations.

Tu, W. M. *Confucian Thought, Selfhood as Creative Transformation* (1985).

Yoshikawa, K. *An Introduction to Sung Poetry*, trans. by B. Watson (1967).

*Yuan*

Allsen, T. T. *Mongol Imperialism* (1987).

Dardess, J. W. *Conquerors and Confucians: Aspects of Political Change in Late Yuan China* (1973).

Franke, H. and Twitchett, D., eds. *Alien Regimes and Border States, 710–1368* (to appear soon as Vol. 6 of *The Cambridge History of China*).

Langlois, J. D. *China Under Mongol Rule* (1981).

Latham, R. trans. *Travels of Marco Polo* (1958).

Martin, H. D. *The Rise of Chingis Khan and His Conquest of North China* (1981).

Morgan, D. *The Mongols* (1986).

The great Manchu emperor Ch'ien Lung (r. 1736–1795).

*chapter four*

# Late Imperial China: The Ming (1368–1644) and Ch'ing (1644–1912) Dynasties

## CHAPTER OUTLINE

The Ming and the Ch'ing were China's last dynasties. The first was Chinese, the second a dynasty of conquest in which the ruling house and an important segment of the military were foreign (Manchus). They were nevertheless remarkably similar in their institutions and pattern of rule, so much so that historians sometimes speak of "Ming–Ch'ing despotism" as if it were a single system. In one respect the Ming and Ch'ing were just the last in the long parade of the centralized bureaucratic regimes of imperial China. In the T'ang recreation of centralized empire, the Chinese had forged a form of government so efficient, and so closely geared to the deeper familial and educational constitution of the society, that, thereafter, they rebuilt such a government after each dynastic breakdown. This pattern clearly continued during the Ming and Ch'ing, giving these dynasties' histories a recognizable cyclical cast.

But noncyclical trends that cut across dynastic lines may have been more important. China's population, which had been stable within a narrow range for over a millennium from the Han to the Sung, experienced unprecedented growth during the Ming and Ch'ing. In this regard the Ming–Ch'ing set China on the path to becoming what it is today. Commerce and the institutions that served it reached higher levels than ever before. The eighteenth- and nineteenth-century diaspora of Chinese to Southeast Asia and farther, while beyond the scope of this volume, was a consequence of both population pressure and export institutions. Another change occurred in the balance of power between China and the steppe that had been a fundamental dimension of all Chinese history down to the nineteenth century. Simply put, firearms initially gave Europe little advantage in China but gave China a tremendous edge against steppe cavalry. The result was the Chinese subjugation of the non-Chinese populations of Tibet, Central Asia, and a part of Mongolia.

This chapter underlines the dynamism of China during these late centuries. If we refer to the Ming–Ch'ing as "late imperial China" or as a "late traditional society," it is to avoid labels such as "medieval" or "early modern," which suggest that China may be located somewhere along the continuum of European history. But "late imperial" and "late traditional" should not be read to mean "late static." For in China, the economy grew, the society became more integrated, and the apparatus of government became more sophisticated than ever before. These advances shaped the Chinese response to Europe during the nineteenth century. But we must also note that during these centuries, Europe underwent an even more sweeping transformation. In fact, Greece and Rome apart, most of what seems important in European history—the

Renaissance, the Reformation, the scientific revolution, the formation of nation-states, the industrial revolution, the Enlightenment, and the democratic revolution—happened during the Ming and the Ch'ing dynasties in China. As we view China from the perspective of Europe, it appears to have been caught in a tar pit of slow motion. But such was not the case; it was actually the West that had accelerated.

## LAND AND PEOPLE

China's population doubled during the Ming, from about 60 million in 1368 at the start of the dynasty to about 125 million in 1644 at its end. The population then tripled during the early and middle Ch'ing dynasty, reaching about 410 million several decades into the nineteenth century. The new density of population contributed to the growth of commerce and the new prominence of the scholar-gentry class.

Population growth was paralleled by an increase in food supply. During the Ming, the spread of Sung agricultural technology and new strains of rice accounted for 40 percent of the higher yields, and newly cultivated lands for the rest. During the Ch'ing, half the increased food supply was due to new lands and the other half to better seeds, fertilizers, and irrigation. New crops introduced from America during the late Ming, such as maize, sweet potatoes, and peanuts (which could be planted on dry sandy uplands and were not competitive with rice) also bolstered the food supply. By the nineteenth century, maize was grown in all parts of China.

In north China, the population had declined from 32 million to 11 million during the Mongol conquests. The Ming government repopulated its open lands, resettling villages, building water-control systems, and reopening the Grand Canal in 1415. The movement of people to the north continued until the nineteenth century. In the north, most farmers owned the land they worked and at times used hired labor. The land consisted mainly of irrigated dry fields, and the chief crops were millet, sorghum, and wheat.

South and southwest China also saw an influx of migrants from the densely populated lower Yangtze region, many settling in hilly or mountainous border areas that were agriculturally marginal. The White Lotus Rebellion of 1796–1804 occurred in such a recently settled area far from centers of governmental authority. The Miao Wars of the late eighteenth century also were precipitated by the movement of Chinese settlers into southwestern uplands previously left to the slash-and-burn agriculture of the Miao tribes. Other Chinese crossed over to the island of Taiwan or emigrated overseas. During the Ch'ing dynasty, large Chinese mercantile communities became established in Southeast Asia.

The Yangtze basin, meanwhile, became even more densely populated. The Lower Yangtze region and the delta, well supplied with waterways, had long been the rice basket of China, but from the late Ming, agricultural cash crops such as silk and cotton predominated. Cotton was so widely grown in the delta that food had to be brought in from other areas by the early nineteenth century. In the lower Yangtze, absentee landlords owned almost half of the land. A typical landlord's holdings were subdivided among tenants, who paid fixed rents in kind. South China also had extensive absentee landlords, but far more land was owned collectively by clans, which managed the land and distributed rents among their members.

There are many unanswered questions regarding the population growth during these six centuries. Was there a decline in the death rate and, if so, why? Or was it simply that new lands and technology raised the limit on the number of mouths that could be fed? Did the population oblige by promptly increasing? Certainly the Ming–Ch'ing era was the longest continuous period of good government in Chinese history. The good years of Ming rule were longer than such periods in earlier dynasties, and the transition to Ch'ing rule was quicker and less destructive. How much did these long periods contribute to population growth? Epidemic disease was not absent. In the great plagues from 1586 to 1589 and from 1639 to 1644, as many as 20 to 30 percent of the people died in the most populous regions of China, and in particular counties and villages the figure was higher. Another epidemic occurred in 1756 and a cholera epidemic from 1820 to 1822. The growth of China's population more than overcame such losses. Because of growth in agriculture and population, most accounts view the eighteenth century as the most prosperous in Chinese history. But by the early decades of the nineteenth century, Chinese living standards may have begun to decline. Ever-increasing numbers of people were no blessing.

## CHINA'S THIRD COMMERCIAL REVOLUTION

Commerce in China flourished between 300 B.C.E. and 220 C.E. (the late Chou through the Han dynasties), only to decline in the centuries of disunity that followed. In Chapter 2, we read Ssu-ma Ch'ien's description of wealthy Han merchants. Between 850 and 1250 (Late T'ang through Sung), commerce again surged, only to contract again during the Mongol conquest. At the end of the Mongol dynasty, warlords confiscated merchant wealth. Early Ming emperors, isolationist and agrarian in orientation, restricted the use of foreign goods, required licenses for junks, and attempted to encase foreign trade within the constraints of the tribute system. The early Ming also operated government monopolies, which stifled enterprise and depressed the southeastern coastal region by their restrictions on maritime trade and shipping. In the mid-sixteenth century, commerce started to grow again, buoyed up by the surge of population and agriculture and aided by a relaxation of government controls. If the growth during the Han and Sung dynasties may be called China's first and second commercial revolutions, respectively, then the expansion between 1500 and 1800 was the third. This revolution was partly the extension to other parts of China of changes begun earlier in the Yangtze area, but it had new features as well. By the early nineteenth century, China was the most highly commercialized nonindustrial society in the world.

One stimulus to commerce was imported silver, which played the role in the Ming–Ch'ing economy that copper cash had played during the Sung. The Chinese balance of international trade was favorable. Beginning in the mid-sixteenth century, silver from mines in western Japan entered China, and from the 1570s, Spanish galleons sailing from Acapulco to China via Manila brought in Mexican and Peruvian silver. In exchange, Chinese silks and porcelains were vended in the shops of Mexico City. The late Ming court opened silver mines in the southwestern provinces of Kweichow and Yunnan. In the eighteenth century copper mines were opened in south China. Also, private "Shensi banks" opened branches throughout China to facilitate the transfer of funds from one area to another and extend credit for trade. Eventually they opened offices in Singapore, Japan, and Russia as well.

As in Europe, so in China: the influx of silver and increased liquidity led to inflation and commercial growth. The price of land rose steadily. During the sixteenth century, the thirty or forty early Ming taxes on land that were payable in grain, labor service, and cash were consolidated into one tax payable in silver, the so-called Single Whip Reform. To obtain the silver, farmers sold their grain in the market, prompting some to switch from grain to cash crops. Moreover, by the early nineteenth century there were six times as many farm families as in the mid-fourteenth century.

Urban growth between 1500 and 1800, responding to flourishing local markets, was mainly at the level of intermediate market towns. These towns grew more rapidly than the population as a whole and provided the link between local markets and larger provincial capitals and cities such as Peking, Hangchow, and Canton. The commercial integration of local, intermediate, and large cities was not entirely new, having occurred during the Sung dynasty in the lower Yangtze region. But now it spread over all of China. Interregional trade also gained. Where Sung trade between regions was mainly in luxury goods such as silk, lacquerware, porcelains, medicines, and paintings, early Ch'ing traders also dealt in staples such as grain, timber, salt, iron, and cotton. Not that China developed a national economy. Seven or eight regional economies, each the size of a large European nation, were still the focus for most economic activity. But a new level of trade developed among them, especially where water transport made such trade economical. A final feature of eighteenth-century Chinese economic life was the so-called "putting out" system in textiles, under which merchant capitalists organized and financed each stage of production from fiber to dyed cloth.

## Women and the Commercial Revolution

The Confucian family ideal changed little during the Ming and Ch'ing dynasties. A woman was expected to obey first her parents, then her husband, and finally her son—when he became the new family head. Physically, women became more restricted. Footbinding, which had begun among the elite during the Sung dynasty, spread through the upper classes during the Ming and to some commoners during the mid-to-late Ch'ing. Most girls were subjected to this cruel and deformative procedure.

### The Thin Horse Market[1]

In China, ancestors without descendants to perform the rites ran the danger of becoming hungry ghosts or wandering spirits. Consequently, having a son who would continue the family line was an act of filial piety. If a wife failed to produce an heir, an official, merchant, or wealthy landowner might take a concubine and try again. Or he might do so simply because he was able to, because it gave him pleasure, and because it was socially acceptable. For a poor peasant household, after a bad harvest and faced with high taxes, the sale of a comely daughter often seemed preferable to the sale of ancestral land.

*Concubines usually had no choice in the matter. But neither did many brides in premodern China. Was a woman better off as the wife of a poor peasant, experiencing hardship, hunger, and want, or as the concubine in a wealthy household with servants, good food, and the likelihood that her children would receive an education? What does the following passage tell us about attitudes toward women in premodern China?*

Upwards of a hundred people in Yangzhou earn a living in the "thin horse" business. If someone shows an interest in taking a concubine, a team of a broker, a drudge, and a scout stick to him like flies. Early in the morning, the teams gather to wait outside the doors of potential customers, who usually give their business to the first team to arrive. Any teams coming late have to wait for the next opportunity. The winning team then leads their customer to the broker's house. The customer is then served tea and seated to wait for the women. The broker leads out each of them, who do what the matchmaker tells them to do. After each of her short commands, the woman bows to the customer, walks forward, turns toward the light so the customer can see her face clearly, draws back her sleeves to show him her hands, glances shyly at him to show her eyes, says her age so he can hear her voice, and finally lifts her skirt to reveal whether her feet are bound. An experienced customer could figure out the size of her feet by listening to the noise she made as she entered the room. If her skirt made noise when she walked in, she had to have a pair of big feet under her skirt. As one woman finishes, another comes out, each house hav-

Even in villages, women with big—that is to say, normal—feet were sometimes considered unmarriageable. An exception to the rule was the Hakka people of south China. Hakka women with unbound feet worked in the fields alongside their male kinsmen. Another exception was the Manchus. One Manchu (Ch'ing) emperor even issued an edict against footbinding, but it was ignored by the Chinese.

As population grew and the size of the average landholding shrank, growing numbers of women worked at home, spinning, weaving, and making other products for the burgeoning commercial markets. As the woman's contribution to the household income grew, her voice in household decisions often became larger than Confucian doctrines would suggest. But the same commercial revolution also increased the num-

ing at least five or six. If the customer finds a woman to his liking, he puts a gold hair-pin in her hair at the temple, a procedure called "inserting the ornament." If no one satisfies him, he gives a few hundred cash to the broker or the servants.

If the first broker gets tired, others will willingly take his place. Even if a customer has the stamina to keep looking for four or five days, he cannot finish visiting all the houses. Nevertheless, after seeing fifty to sixty white-faced, red-dressed women, they all begin to look alike and he cannot decide which are pretty or ugly. It is like the difficulty of recognizing a character after writing it hundreds or thousands of times. Therefore, the customer usually chooses someone once his mind and eyes can no longer discriminate. The owner of the woman brings out a piece of red paper on which are listed the "betrothal presents," including gold jewelry and cloth. Once he agrees to the deal, he is sent home. Before he even arrives back at his lodgings, a band and a load of food and wine are already waiting there. Before long, presents he was to send are prepared

and sent back with the band. Then a sedan chair and all the trimmings—colorful lanterns, happy candles, attendants, sacrificial foods—wait outside for the customer's arrangement. The cooks and the entertainer for the wedding celebration also arrive together with foods, wine, candy, tables, chairs, and tableware. Without the customer's order, the colorful sedan chair for the girl and the small sedan chair for her companion are dispatched to get the girl. The new concubine performs the bowing ceremony with music and singing and considerable clamor. The next morning before noon the laborers ask for rewards from the man, then leave to prepare another wedding for another customer in the same manner.

[1]A horse market is for the sale of horses. A "thin horse" market is the market for concubines. The name implies a measure of criticism.

Reprinted with the permission of The Free Press, a division of Simon & Schuster, Inc. from *Chinese Civilization: A Sourcebook* by Patricia Buckley Ebrey. Copyright © 1993 by Patricia Buckley Ebrey.

ber of rich townsmen who could afford concubines and patronize tea houses, restaurants, and brothels.

## POLITICAL SYSTEM

One might expect these massive demographic and economic changes to have produced, if not a bourgeois revolution, at least some profound change in the political superstructure of China. They did not. Government during the Ming and Ch'ing was much like that of the Sung or Yuan, only improved and made stronger. Historians sometimes describe it as the "perfected" late imperial system. This system, they argue, was able to contain and use the new economic energies that destroyed the weaker late-feudal polities of Europe. The sources of strength of the perfected Ming–Ch'ing system were the spread of education, the use of Confucianism as an ideology, a stronger emperor, better government finances, more competent officials, and a larger gentry class with an expanded role in local society.

## The Role of Confucianism

Confucian teachings were more widespread in late imperial China than ever before. There were more schools in villages and towns. Academies preparing candidates for the civil service examinations grew in number. Publishing flourished, bookstores abounded, and literacy increased faster than population. The Confucian view of society was patriarchal. The family, headed by the father, was the basic unit. The emperor, the Son of Heaven and the ruler-father of the empire, stood at its apex. In between were the district magistrates, the "father-mother officials." The idea of the state as the family writ large was not just a matter of metaphor but carried with it duties and obligations that were binding at every level.

The sociopolitical worldview of Confucianism was also buttressed by Neo-Confucian metaphysics, which gave a unitary character to Ming and Ch'ing culture. This is not, of course, to deny the existence of different schools of Confucian thought. The vitality of late Ming thinkers was especially notable. Still, in comparison to Europe, where religious philosophies were less involved with the state and where a revolution in science was reshaping both religious and political doctrines, the greater unity and integration of the Chinese worldview cannot be denied.

## The Role of the Emperor

In Ming–Ch'ing times, the emperor was stronger than ever. The Secretariat of high officials that had coordinated government affairs during the Sung and the Yuan was abolished by the first Ming emperor, who himself made all important and many unimportant decisions. His successors, often aided by Grand Secretaries, continued this pattern of direct, personal rule. During the late fourteenth and fifteenth centuries the emperor was "the bottleneck official," without whose active participation the business of government would bog down.

Then, during the sixteenth and early seventeenth centuries, a series of emperors appeared who were not interested in government. One spent his days on wine, women, and sports; another filled his hours with Taoist rites; and still another, who never learned to write, passed his days making furniture. During these centuries, the emperor's authority was exercised either by Grand Secretaries or by eunuchs. But then the Ch'ing reestablished the pattern of personal government by emperors.

Emperors wielded despotic powers at their courts. They had personal secret police and prisons where those who gave even minor offense might be cruelly tortured. Even high officials might suffer the humiliating, and sometimes fatal, punishment of having their bared buttocks beaten with bamboo rods at court—a practice inherited from the Mongols. The dedication and loyalty even of officials who were cruelly mistreated attest to the depth of their Confucian ethical formation. One censor who had served three emperors ran afoul of a powerful eunuch. The eunuch obtained an imperial order and had the official tortured to death in 1625. In his deathbed notes to his sons, the official blamed the villain for his agonies but wrote that he welcomed death because his body belonged to his "ruler-father." An earlier mid-sixteenth-century incident involved Hai Jui, the most famous censor of the Ming period:

> Hai presented himself at the palace gate to submit a memorial denouncing some of the emperor's notorious idiosyncrasies. The emperor flew into a rage and ordered that Hai not be permitted to escape. "Never fear, sire," the eunuch go-between told the emperor. "He has said goodbye to his family, has brought his coffin with him, and waits at the gate!" Shih-tsung [the emperor] was so taken aback by this news that he forgave Hai for his impertinence.[1]

During the Ch'ing, the life-and-death authority of emperors did not diminish, but officials were generally better treated. As foreign rulers, the Manchu emperors took care not to alienate Chinese officials.

The Forbidden Palace of the emperors in Peking, rebuilt when the third Ming emperor moved the capital from Nanking to Peking, was an icon of the emperor's majesty. Unlike the Kremlin, which consists of an assortment of buildings inside a wall, the entire palace complex in Peking focused on the single figure of the ruler. Designed geometrically, its massive outer and inner walls, vast courtyards, and halls progress level by level to the raised area of the audience hall. During the T'ang, emperors had sat together with their grand councillors while discussing matters of government. In the Sung, officials stood in his presence. By the Ming, the emperor sat on an elevated dais above the officials, who knelt before him. Behind the audience hall were the emperor's private chambers and his harem. In 1425, the palace had 6,300 cooks serving 10,000 persons daily. These numbers later increased. At the start of the seventeenth century, there were 9,000 palace ladies and perhaps 70,000 eunuchs. The glory of the emperor extended even to his family, whose members were awarded vast estates in north China.

---

[1]C. O. Hucker, *China's Imperial Past* (Stanford, CA: Stanford University Press, 1975), p. 206.

## The Seven Transformations of an Examination Candidate

The Chinese civil service examination was a grueling ordeal. Like a chess tournament, it required physical strength. Chinese critics said, "To pass the provincial examination a man needed the spiritual strength of a dragon-horse, the physique of a donkey, the insensitivity of a wood louse, and the endurance of a camel." The following selection is by a seventeenth-century writer who never succeeded in passing.

*Is the style of this passage overdone or effective? What is distinctively Chinese about it?*

When he first enters the examination compound and walks along, panting under his heavy load of luggage, he is just like a beggar. Next, while undergoing the personal body search and being scolded by the clerks and shouted at by the soldiers, he is just like a prisoner. When he finally enters his cell and, along with the other candidates, stretches his neck to peer out, he is just like the larva of a bee. When the examination is finished at last and he leaves, his mind in a haze and his legs tottering, he is just like a sick bird that has been released from a cage. While he is wondering when the results will be announced and waiting to learn whether he passed or failed, so nervous that he is startled even by the rustling of the trees and the grass and is unable to sit or stand still, his restlessness is like that of a monkey on a leash. When at last the results are announced and he has definitely failed, he loses his vitality like one dead, rolls over on his side, and lies there without moving, like a poisoned fly. Then, when he pulls himself together and stands up, he is provoked by every sight and sound, gradually flings away everything within his reach, and complains of the illiteracy of the examiners. When he calms down at last, he finds everything in the room broken. At this time he is like a pigeon smashing its own precious eggs. These are the seven transformations of a candidate.

From I. Miyazaki, *China's Examination Hell*, trans. by C. Schirokauer. Copyright © 1976 Weatherhill, pp. 57–58.

## The Role of Bureaucracy

A second component of the Ming–Ch'ing system was the government itself. The formal organization of offices was little different from that in the T'ang or the Sung. At the top were the military, the censorate, and the administrative branch, and beneath the administration were the six ministries and the web of provincial, prefectural, and district offices. If there was an important difference from earlier dynasties, it was that government was better financed. The productivity of China became steadily larger, whereas the apparatus of government grew only slowly. Government finances had ups and downs, but as late as the 1580s huge surpluses were still accumulated at both the central and the provincial levels. These surpluses probably braked the process of dynastic decline. Only during the last fifty years of the Ming did soaring military expenses bankrupt government finances.

Then, in the second half of the seventeenth century, the Manchus reestablished a strong central government and restored the flow of taxes to levels close to those of the Ming. In fact, revenues were so ample that early in the eighteenth century, the emperors were able to freeze taxes on agriculture at the 1711 level and fix quotas for each province. The freeze contributed to the general prosperity of the eighteenth century but led to problems during the nineteenth century. Because agricultural productivity continued to rise, even though local officials collected some of the surplus, fixed quotas meant a declining share of the product. Both cultivators and gentry probably benefited from the new wealth, with the latter obtaining the larger share.

If the Ming–Ch'ing system can be spoken of as perfected, the good government it brought to China was largely a product of the ethical commitment and exceptional ability of its officials. No officials in the world today approach in power or prestige those of the Ming and the Ch'ing. When the Portuguese arrived early in the sixteenth century, they called these officials "mandarins." (This term began as a Sanskrit word for "counselor" that became Hindi, entered Malay, and was then picked up by the Portuguese and adopted by other Europeans.) As in the Sung, the rewards of an official career were so great that the competition to enter it was intense. As population grew and schools increased, entrance became even more competitive.

After being screened at the district office, a candidate first took the county examination. If he passed, he became a member of the gentry. He gained the cap and sash of the scholar and exemption from state labor service. Even this examination required years of arduous study. About half a million passed each year. The second hurdle was the provincial examination held every third year. Only one in one hundred or more was successful. The final hurdle was the metropolitan examination, also held triennially. During the Ming, fewer than ninety passed each year. As in earlier dynasties, regional quotas were set to prevent the Yangtze region from dominating the officialdom.

## The Role of Gentry

A final component in the Ming–Ch'ing system—not new but vastly more important than in earlier dynasties—was the gentry class. It was an intermediate layer between the elite bureaucracy above and villages below. The lowest tier of bureaucratic government was the office of the district magistrate. Though the population increased sixfold during the Ming and the Ch'ing, the number of district magistrates increased only from 1,171 to 1,470. Thus the average district, which had had a population of 50,000 in the early Ming and 100,000 in the late Ming, had two or three times that number by the early nineteenth century. The district magistrate came to his district as an outsider. The "law of avoidance," designed to prevent conflicts of interest, prevented him from serving in his home province. His office compound had a large staff of secretaries, advisers, specialists, clerks, and runners; but even then, he could not govern such a large population directly. To govern effectively, the magistrate had to obtain the cooperation of the local literati or gentry.

By *gentry* we do not mean a rural elite, like English squires. The Chinese gentry was largely urban, living in market towns or district seats. Socially and educationally, its members were of the same class as magistrates—a world apart from the less educated clerks, runners, and village headmen. They usually owned land, which enabled them to avoid manual labor and to send their children to private academies. As absentee landlords, whose lands were worked by sharecroppers, they were often exploitative; rebels at the end of the Ming attacked landlords as they did government offices. But gentry were also local leaders. They represented community interests, which they interpreted conservatively, vis-à-vis the bureaucracy. They performed quasiofficial functions on behalf of their communities: maintaining schools and Confucian temples; repairing roads, bridges, canals, and dikes; and writing local histories.

The gentry class was the matrix from which officials arose; it was the local upholder of Confucian values. During the mid-nineteenth century, at a time of crisis, it would become the sustainer of the dynasty.

## The Pattern of Manchu Rule

The collapse of the Ming dynasty in 1644 and the establishment of Manchu rule was less of a break than might be imagined. First, the transition was short. Second, the Manchus, unlike the Mongols, were already partially Sinicized at the time of the conquest. They had been vassals of the Chinese state during the Ming, organized by tribal units into commanderies. Even before entering China, they had had the experience of ruling over the Chinese who had settled in Manchuria to the north of the Great Wall.

In the late sixteenth century, an extremely able leader, Nurhaci, unified the Manchurian tribes and proclaimed a new dynasty. While still based in Mukden, the dynasty established a Confucian type of government with six ministries, a censorate, and other Chinese institutions. When the Ming collapsed and rebel forces took over China, the Manchus presented themselves as the conservative upholders of the Confucian order. The Chinese gentry preferred the Manchus to Chinese rebel leaders, whom they saw as bandits. After the Manchu conquest, a few scholars and officials became famous as Ming loyalists. Most, however, shifted their loyalty and served the new dynasty. The Ch'ing as a Chinese dynasty dates from 1644, when the capital was moved from Mukden to Peking. All of South China was taken by 1659, with the aid of Ming generals who switched their allegiance to the new regime.

As a tiny fraction of the Chinese population, the Manchus adopted institutions to maintain themselves as an ethnically separate elite group. One was their military organization. The basic unit was the banner—the unit took the name of its flag. There were eight Manchu banners, eight Mongol, and eight Chinese. There were more companies (of three hundred men each) in the Manchu banners than in either of the other two; together with their steppe allies, the Mongols, the Manchus outnumbered the Chinese by more than two to one. Furthermore, the Chinese banners were mainly of

Manchurian Chinese, who had been a part of the regime from its inception. Manchu garrison forces were segregated and not under the jurisdiction of Chinese officials. They were given stipends and lands to cultivate. They were not permitted to marry Chinese, their children had to study Manchu, and they were not permitted to bind the feet of their daughters. In 1668, northern and central Manchuria were cordoned off by a willow palisade as a Manchu strategic tribal territory closed to Chinese immigrants.

In addition to the banners, there were also Chinese constabulary forces known as "armies of the green standard." At first, the distinction between the banners and the Chinese military was critical. Later, as the dynasty became Sinicized, the ethnic basis of its military strength became less important.

A second particular feature of Manchu government was what has been termed "dyarchy": the appointment of two persons, one Chinese and one Manchu, to each key post in the central government. Early in the dynasty, the Chinese appointments were often bannermen or bondservants who were personally loyal to the Manchus. At the provincial level, Chinese governors were overseen by Manchu governor-generals. Beneath the governors, most officials and virtually all district magistrates were Chinese.

Another strength of the Manchu dynasty was the long reigns of two extremely able emperors, K'ang Hsi (1661–1722) and Ch'ien Lung (1736–1795). K'ang Hsi was born in 1654, ten years after the start of the dynasty. He ascended the throne at the age of seven, began to rule at thirteen, and held sway until his death in 1722. He was a man of great vigor. He rose at dawn to read memorials (official documents) before beginning his daily routine of audiences with officials. He sired thirty-six sons and twenty daughters by thirty consorts. He presided over palace examinations. Well versed in the Confucian classics, he won the support of scholars by his patronage of the *Ming History*, a new dictionary, and a 5,000-volume encyclopedia.

K'ang Hsi also displayed an interest in European science, which he studied with Jesuit court astronomers whom the Ch'ing had inherited from the Ming. He opened four ports to foreign trade and carried out public works, improving the dikes on the Huai and Yellow rivers and dredging the Grand Canal. During his reign he made six tours of China's southern provinces. K'ang Hsi, in short, was a model emperor. But he was also responsible for the various policies that sought to preserve a separate Manchu identity. Like Kublai Khan before him, he built a summer palace on the plains of Manchuria, where he hunted, hawked, and rode horseback with the freedom of a steppe lord.

Ch'ien Lung began his reign in 1736, fourteen years after the death of his grandfather K'ang Hsi, and ruled until 1795. During his reign, the Ch'ing dynasty attained its highest level of prosperity and power. Like his grandfather K'ang Hsi, he was strong, wise, conscientious, careful, and hard working. He visited South China on inspection tours. He patronized scholars on a grand scale: His *Four Treasures* of the classics, works on history, letters, and philosophy, put 15,000 copyists to work for almost fifteen years. (But he also carried out a literary inquisition against works critical of Manchu rule.)

Only in his last years did Ch'ien Lung lose his grip and permit a court favorite to practice corruption on an almost unprecedented scale. In 1796, the White Lotus

Rebellion broke out. Ch'ien Lung's successor put down the rebellion and permitted the corrupt court favorite to take his own life. After this time, the ample financial reserves that had existed throughout the eighteenth century were never reestablished. China nevertheless entered the nineteenth century with its government intact and with a peaceful and stable society. There were few visible signs of what was soon to come.

## FOREIGN RELATIONS

### Ming

Some scholars have contended that post-Sung China was not an aggressive or imperialist state. They cite its inability to resist foreign conquest; the civility, self-restraint, and gentlemanliness of its officials; and the Sung adage that good men should not be used to make soldiers just as good iron is not used to make nails. The early Ming convincingly disproves this contention. The first Ming emperor (r. 1368–1398) oversaw the vigorous expansion of China's borders. At his death, China controlled the northern steppe from Hami at the gateway of Central Asia to the Sungari River in Manchuria and had regained control of the southern tier of Chinese provinces as well. China expelled the Mongols from Yunnan in 1382 (see Map 4–1).

During the reign of the third Ming emperor (1402–1424), China became even more aggressive. The emperor sent troops into northern Vietnam, which became a Chinese province for two decades until, eventually, guerrilla attacks forced the Chinese troops to withdraw. He also personally led five expeditions into the Gobi Desert in pursuit of Mongol troops.

Whenever possible, the third emperor and his successors managed China's frontiers with the tribute system. In this system, the ambassadors of vassal kings acted out their political subordination to the universal ruler of the celestial kingdom. An ambassador approached the emperor respectfully, performed the kowtow (kneeling three times and bowing his head to the floor nine times), and presented his gifts. In return, the vassal kings were sent seals confirming their status, given permission to use the Chinese calendar and year-period names, and appointed to the Ming nobility.

The system conferred notable benefits on those willing to participate. While in Peking, the ambassadors were housed and fed in a style appropriate to their status. The gifts they received were usually more valuable than those they gave. In addition, they were permitted to trade private goods in the markets of the city. So attractive were these perquisites that some Central Asian merchants invented imaginary kingdoms of which they appointed themselves the emissaries. Eventually, China had to set limits on the size, frequency, and cargos of these missions.

The most far-ranging ventures of the third Ming emperor were the maritime expeditions that sailed to Southeast Asia, India, the Arabian Gulf, and East Africa

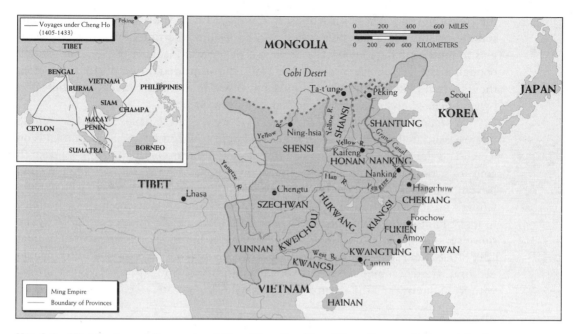

**Map 4-1   Ming Empire and the voyages of Cheng Ho.**   The ships of Cheng Ho, venturing beyond Southeast Asia and India, reached the coast of East Africa.

between 1405 and 1433. They were commanded by the eunuch Cheng Ho, a Muslim from Yunnan (see Map 4–1). The first of these armadas had sixty-two major ships and hundreds of smaller vessels and carried 28,000 sailors, soldiers, and merchants. Navigating by compass, the expeditions followed the sea routes of the Arab traders. Trade was not the primary purpose of the expeditions, although some eunuchs used the opportunity to make fortunes, and records show that giraffes, zebras, and other exotic items were presented at the Chinese court. The expeditions were likely intended to make China's glory known to distant kingdoms and to enroll them in the tribute system. Cheng Ho's soldiers installed a new king in Java. They captured and brought back to China hostile kings from Borneo and Ceylon, and they signed up nineteen other states as Chinese tributaries.

The expeditions ended as suddenly as they had begun. They were costly and offered little return at a time when the dynasty was fighting in Mongolia and building the new capital at Peking. What was remarkable about these expeditions was not that they came a half-century earlier than the Portuguese voyages of discovery, but that China had the necessary maritime technology and decided not to use it. China lacked the combination of restlessness, greed, faith, and curiosity that would motivate the Portuguese.

The chief threat to the Ming dynasty was the Mongols. In disarray after the collapse of their rule in China, the Mongols had broken into eastern, western, and southern tribes. The Chinese, "using the barbarian to control the barbarian," made allies of the southern tribes (those settled just north of the Great Wall) against the more fear-some grassland Mongols. This policy worked most of the time, but twice the Mongols formed confederations—pale imitations of the war machine of Genghis—strong enough to defeat Chinese armies. In the 1430s, they captured the emperor, and in 1550, they overran Peking. The Mongol forces involved in the latter attack were defeated by a Chinese army in the 1560s and signed a peace treaty in 1571.

A second foreign threat to the Ming dynasty was the Japanese and the Chinese pirates associated with them. Warrior-lords of decentralized Japan had begun raids on Korea and the northeastern Chinese coast during the thirteenth and early fourteenth centuries; they extended their activities down the coast to southeastern China and beyond during the fifteenth and sixteenth centuries. Hitherto, the sea coast had been China's most secure frontier. China built defenses and used a scorched-earth policy to make raiding less profitable, but mostly had to put up with the depredations. The most serious threat from Japan was Hideyoshi's invasions of Korea in 1592 and 1597–1598. Korea resisted with some initial success. China sent troops only after Japanese armies had occupied the entire Korean peninsula. Eventually, the Japanese armies withdrew, but by then the strain on Ming finances had severely weakened the dynasty.

## Ch'ing

The final foreign threat to the Ming was the Manchus—the mouse that swallowed the elephant. After coming to power in 1644, the Manchu court spent decades consolidating its rule within China. The last Ming prince was pursued into Burma and killed in 1662. But then the three Chinese generals who had helped the Manchus conquer the south revolted and were supported by a Sino-Japanese pirate state on Taiwan. Most Chinese troops in the Manchu armies remained loyal; the emperor K'ang Hsi was able to suppress the revolts by 1681. In 1683, he took Taiwan, which became a part of China for the first time (see Map 4–2).

As always, the principal foreign threats to China came from the north and northwest. Russia had begun expanding east across Siberia and south against the remnants of the Golden Horde during the reign of Ivan the Terrible (1533–1584). By the 1660s, Russian traders, trappers, and adventurers had reached the Amur River in northern Manchuria, where they built forts and traded with the eastern Mongols. One is reminded of the French penetration of Canada during the same decades. To prevent a rapprochement between the Russians and Mongols, K'ang Hsi set up military colonies in Manchuria during the 1680s and drove the Russians from the lower Amur. This victory during the early years of the reign of Peter the Great (1682–1725) led to the 1689 Treaty of Nerchinsk. Negotiated with the assistance of Jesuit translators, the treaty excluded Russia from northern Manchuria while permitting its caravans to visit Peking.

In the west the situation was more complex, with a three-corner relationship between Russia, the western Mongols, and Tibet. K'ang Hsi, and then Ch'ien Lung, campaigned against the Mongols, invaded Tibet, and in 1727 signed a new treaty

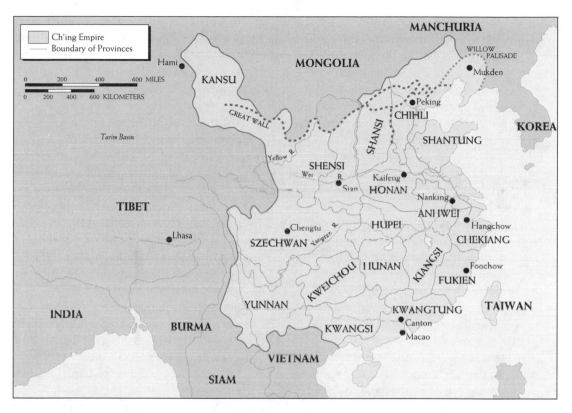

**Map 4–2  The Ch'ing Empire at its peak.**   The Willow Palisade was the line of demarcation between the Manchurian homeland of the Ch'ing rulers and China. Chinese were excluded from Manchuria.

with Russia. During the campaigns, the Chinese temporarily came to control millions of square miles of new territories. These areas became protectorates under a "barbarian management office," separate from the administration for China itself. It is a telling comment on the Chinese concept of empire that ever since that time, even after China's borders contracted during the nineteenth century, the Chinese have continued to insist that the Manchu conquests of non-Chinese peoples define their legitimate borders. The roots of the present-day contention over borders between China and the countries of the former Soviet Union go back to these events during the eighteenth century, as does the Chinese claim to Tibet.

## Contacts with the West

Europeans had made their way to China in the T'ang and the Yuan dynasties, but only with Europe's oceanic expansion during the sixteenth century did they arrive in large numbers. Some came as missionaries, of whom the most educated, calculating, disciplined, enterprising, and successful were the Jesuits. On first arriving in Ming China, they put on the robes of the Buddhist monk, but on learning something of the culture, they switched to the gowns of the Confucian scholar. They studied Chinese and the Confucian classics and engaged in conversation with scholars. They used their knowledge of astronomy, geography, engraving, and firearms to win entry to the court at Peking and appointments in the bureau of astronomy.

When the Manchus came to power in 1644, the Jesuits kept their position. They appealed to the curiosity of the court with instruments such as telescopes, clocks, and clavichords. They tried to propagate Christianity. They attacked Taoism and Buddhism as superstitions but argued that Confucianism as a rational philosophy complemented Christianity, just as Aristotle's teaching complemented Christian theology in Europe. They handled the problem of the Confucian rites of ancestor worship by interpreting them as secular and nonantagonistic to Christianity. A few high court officials were converted. K'ang Hsi was sympathetic to the scholarly personalities of the Jesuits and appreciated the cannon they cast but was unsympathetic to their religion: "I had asked [the Jesuit] Verbiest why God had not forgiven his son without making him die, but though he had tried to answer I had not understood him."[2]

Meanwhile, their Franciscan and Dominican rivals had reported to Rome that the Jesuits condoned the Confucian rites. The ensuing debate was long and complex, but in the end, papal bulls issued in 1715 and 1742 decided against the Jesuits and forbade Chinese Christians to participate in the family rites of ancestor worship. Thereupon the emperor banned Christianity in China, churches were seized, missionaries were forced to flee, and congregations declined.

Other Europeans came to China to trade. The Portuguese came first in the early sixteenth century but behaved badly and were expelled. They returned in mid-century and were permitted to trade only on a tiny peninsula at Macao that was walled off from China. They were followed by Dutch from the East Indies (Indonesia), by the British East India Company in 1699, and by Americans in 1784.

At first, the Westerners mingled with ships from Southeast Asia in a fairly open multiport pattern of trade. Then, during the early eighteenth century, the more restrictive "Canton system" evolved. Westerners could trade only at Canton. They were barred from entering the city proper but were assigned land outside its walls along the river. They could not bring their wives to China. They were subject to the harsh dispositions of Chinese law and were put under the control of official merchant guilds. Nevertheless, the trade was profitable to both sides.

The British East India Company developed a triangular commerce between China, India, and Britain that enabled the English to drink tea and wear silk. Private fortunes were built. For China, this trade produced an influx of specie, and the Chinese officials in charge grew immensely wealthy. Chafing under the various restric-

---

[2]J. D. Spence, *Emperor of China: A Self-Portrait of K'ang Hsi* (New York, Alfred A. Knopf, 1974), p. 84.

## Ch'ien Lung's Edict to King George III of England

The Chinese emperor rejected the requests of the 1793 Macartney mission for change in the restrictive Canton system. His edict reflects the Chinese sense of their superiority to other peoples and their belief that China was the "central kingdom" of the world.

*What philosophical principles underlie the emperor's sense of superiority?*

You, O King, are so inclined toward our civilization that you have sent a special envoy across the seas to bring to our Court your memorial of congratulations on the occasion of my birthday and to present your native products as an expression of your thoughtfulness. On perusing your memorial, so simply worded and sincerely conceived, I am impressed by your genuine respectfulness and friendliness and greatly pleased. . . .

The Celestial Court has pacified and possessed the territory within the four seas. Its sole aim is to do its utmost to achieve good government and to manage political affairs, attaching no value to strange jewels and precious objects. The various articles presented by you, O King, this time are accepted by my special order to the office in charge of such functions in consideration of the offerings having come from a long distance with sincere good wishes. As a matter of fact, the virtue and prestige of the Celestial Dynasty having spread far and wide, the kings of the myriad nations come by land and sea with all sorts of precious things. Consequently there is nothing we lack, as your principal envoy and others have themselves observed. We have never set much store on strange or ingenious objects, nor do we need any more of your country's manufactures. . . .

Reprinted with permission of the publisher from *China's Response to the West* by Ssu-yu Teng and John K. Fairbank, Cambridge, MA: Harvard University Press. Copyright © 1954, 1979 by the President and Fellows of Harvard College. Reprinted by permission of Harvard University Press.

tions, the British government in 1793 sent the Macartney mission to China to negotiate the opening of other ports, fixed tariffs, representation at Peking, and so on. The emperor Ch'ien Lung graciously permitted Macartney to present his gifts—which the Chinese described as tribute, even though Macartney refused to perform the kowtow—but he turned down Macartney's requests. Western trade remained encapsulated at Canton, distant from Peking and little noted elsewhere in China.

## CULTURE

One thing that can be said of Ming–Ch'ing culture, like population or agricultural crops, is that there was more of it. Whether considering gentry, scholar officials, or a professionalized class of literati, their numbers and works were far greater than in

**Late Imperial China**

**Ming Dynasty 1368–1644**

| | |
|---|---|
| 1368–1398 | Reign of first Ming emperor; Chinese armies invade Manchuria, Mongolia and eastern Central Asia |
| 1402–1424 | Reign of third Ming emperor; Chinese armies invade Vietnam and Mongolia |
| 1405–1433 | Voyage of Cheng Ho to India and Africa |
| 1415 | Grand Canal reopened |
| 1472–1529 | Wang Yang-ming, philosopher |
| 1592–1598 | Chinese army battles Japanese army in Korea |

**Ch'ing (Manchu) Dynasty 1644–1912**

| | |
|---|---|
| 1668 | Manchuria closed to Chinese immigrants (by Willow Palisade) |
| 1661–1722 | Reign of K'ang Hsi |
| 1681 | Suppression of revolts by Chinese generals |
| 1683 | Taiwan captured |
| 1689 | China and Russia sign Treaty of Nerchinsk |
| 1736–1795 | Reign of Ch'ien Lung |
| 1793 | Macartney mission |

previous dynasties. Even local literary figures and philosophers were likely to publish their collected works or have them published by admiring disciples. Bookstores came of age in the Ming: They sold the Confucian classics and commentaries on them; collections of T'ang and Sung poetry; as well as colored prints, novels, erotica, and collections of model answers for the civil service examinations.

Chinese culture had begun to turn inward during the Sung in reaction to Buddhism. This tendency was accelerated by the Chinese antipathy to Mongol rule and continued into the Ming and Ch'ing, when Chinese culture became virtually impervious to outside influences. Even works on mathematics and science translated into Chinese by the Jesuits left few traces in Chinese scholarship. Chinese cultural self-sufficiency, of course, reflected a tradition and a social order that had stood the test of time, but it also indicated a closed system of ideas with weaknesses that would become apparent in the nineteenth century. Orthodox thought during these five centuries was Chu Hsi Neo-Confucianism. From the mid- to the late Ming, some perturbations were caused by the Zen-like teachings of the philosopher Wang Yang-ming (1472–1529), whose activism caused him to be jailed, beaten, and at one point exiled in an otherwise illustrious official career.

Several other original thinkers' refusal to accept bureaucratic posts under the Ch'ing won them plaudits during the anti-Manchu nationalism of the early twentieth century, but they had only a limited influence on their own times. The most innovative was Ku Yen-wu, who wrote on both philology and statecraft. He used philology and historical phonetics to plumb the original meanings of the classics and contrasted their practical ethics with the "empty words" of Wang Yang-ming. Ku's successors extended his philological studies, developing empirical methods for textual studies, but lost sight of their implications for politics. The Manchus clamped down on unorthodox thought, and the seventeenth-century burst of creativity guttered out into a narrow, bookish, conservative scholasticism. Not until the end of the nineteenth century did thinkers draw from these studies the kind of radical inferences that philological studies of the Bible had produced in Europe.

Ming and Ch'ing Chinese esteemed most highly, and not without reason, the traditional categories of high culture: painting, calligraphy, poetry, and philosophy. Porcelains of great beauty were also produced. In the early Ming, the blue-on-white glazes predominated. During the later Ming and Ch'ing, more decorative wares with enamel painted over the glaze became widespread. The pottery industry of Europe was begun during the sixteenth century in an attempt to imitate these wares, and Chinese and Japanese influences have dominated Western ceramics down to the present. Chinese today, however, look back and see the novel as the characteristic cultural achievement of the Ming and Ch'ing.

The novel in China grew out of plot-books used by earlier storytellers. Like the stories, Chinese novels consisted of episodes strung together, and chapters in early novels often ended with an admonition to the reader not to miss the next exciting development. Ming and Ch'ing novels were usually written by scholars who had failed the examinations, a possible explanation for their caustic comments on officials. As most novels were written in colloquial Chinese, a medium not quite respectable in scholarly circles, their authors wrote under pseudonyms.

Two collections of lively short stories are available in English: *Stories from a Ming Collection* and *The Courtesan's Jewel Box*. Many stories (although not those in the two collections) were pornographic. In fact, the Ming may have invented the humorous pornographic novel. One example available in English is *The Carnal Prayer Mat*. This genre was suppressed in China during the Ch'ing and rediscovered in Japanese collections in the twentieth century.

Short descriptions of several major novels may convey something of their flavor:

1. *The Romance of the Three Kingdoms* was published in 1522. It tells of the political and military struggles in China in the aftermath of the Han dynasty. Like Shakespeare, the author, whose identity is uncertain, used a historical setting to create a dramatic world in which human character determines the outcome of events. More than twenty editions had appeared by the end of the Ming, and the novel was also extremely popular in Japan and Korea.

2. *All Men Are Brothers* (also translated as *The Water Margin*) tells of 108 bandit heroes who flee government repression during the late northern Sung, establish

## A Star in Heaven

Among the officials whose stories are told in *The Scholars* is Fan Chin, thin and sallow with a grizzled beard and threadbare linen gown, who finally passes the county examination at the age of fifty-four. On his return home, he is given a feast and advice by his domineering father-in-law, Butcher Hu. But when Fan Chin asks Hu for money to travel to the provincial examination, he gets the following reaction.

---

*Why did a satire such as* The Scholars *not undermine the premises on which Ch'ing society rested?*

---

Butcher Hu spat in his face and let loose a stream of abuse. "Don't forget who you are!" he bellowed. "Just passing one examination and you become like a toad thinking to dine on the flesh of a swan. I hear you passed the examination not because of your essay, but because the examiner took pity on your old age. Now, like a fool, you aspire to be an official. Don't you know that those who have passed the higher examination are all stars in heaven! Haven't you seen the Changs in the city? Those officials all have tons of money and generously proportioned faces and ears. Now look at you with your protruding mouth and monkey chin. Piss on the ground and take a good look at yourself in the puddle! A miserable creature like you can't even hope to swallow a swan's fart! Forget it!

[Fan Chin takes the examination anyway. When he returns home, he discovers that his family has been hungry for two days. Fan goes to the market to sell a chicken. In the meantime, heralds on horseback arrive to proclaim he has passed the provincial examination. Returning home, Fan sees the posted announcement and falls into a dead faint. When revived, he begins ranting incoherently. A herald suggests that Butcher Hu, whom Fan fears, bring him to his senses with a slap. Butcher Hu demurs.]

a hideout on a mountain amid marshes, and like Robin Hood avenge the wrongs perpetrated by corrupt officials. Separate episodes tell why each had to leave society and of their many daring and amusing adventures. Of all Chinese novels, this was the most popular. It was officially banned as subversive during the Ch'ing but was widely read nonetheless.

3. *The Golden Lotus* is a pornographic novel about the sexual adventures of an urban merchant. It gives vivid descriptions of individual women and satirical descriptions of venal officials and greedy monks. In the end, the hero dies of his excesses and his family—all six wives and their children—disintegrates. The early English translation of this novel had long passages in Latin to protect those

"He may be my son-in-law," he said, "but now he has become a member of the gentry, a star in heaven. How can I hit a star in heaven? I've heard from Buddhist priests that whoever strikes a star in heaven will be carried away by the King of Hell, struck one hundred times with an iron rod, consigned to the eighteenth hell, and never return to human form again. I wouldn't dare do it."

[Eventually Butcher Hu slaps him, and Fan recovers in time to receive a visit from a member of the local gentry, who is wearing "an official's gauze cap, sunflower-coloured gown, gilt belt and black shoes." "Sir," he says to Fan, "although we live in the same district, I regret that we have never become acquainted." After paying his respects, the visitor presents Fan with fifty taels of silver and a more appropriate house. Soon others give him land, goods, money, rice, and servants. The chapter ends with the maids cleaning up under the supervision of Fan Chin's wife after several days of feasting. Fan Chin's mother enters the courtyard.]

"You must be very careful," the old lady warned her daughter-in-law and the maids. "These things all belong to someone else, so don't break them."

The maids replied: "How can you say they belong to others, madam? They all belong to you."

"Oh no! How could our house have such things?" she said with a smile. "How can you talk of their belonging to others?" the maids replied in unison. "And not only these things, but all of us and the house, too, belong to you."

When the old lady heard this, she picked up the bowls and dishes of fine porcelain and the cups and chopsticks inlaid with silver and examined them one by one. She burbled: "These things are all mine." Laughing wildly, she fell over backward, choked on phlegm, and lost consciousness.

If you want to know what became of the old lady, please read the next chapter.

Translation by Shang Wei.

whose minds were not disciplined by the study of that language. Despite its literary merits, the book, like all of its genre, is proscribed in China today. Copies in universities are kept under lock and key.

4. *The Dream of the Red Chamber* (also translated as *The Story of the Stone*) is generally considered China's greatest novel. It tells the story of a youth growing up in a wealthy but declining family during the early Ch'ing. Critics praise its subtlety and psychological insight. Anthropologists mine the novel for information on the Chinese extended family and for its depiction of social relations. Like other Ming and Ch'ing novels, it was recognized as a respectable work of art only during the twentieth century, after Western novels entered China.

   **5.** *The Scholars* is a social satire of the early Ch'ing that pokes fun at scholars and
   officials.

## LATE IMPERIAL CHINA IN HISTORICAL PERSPECTIVE

   In the early Ming, China was "ahead" of Europe and the rest of the world by
most objective measures; by the late Ch'ing, it lagged "behind." What happened? In
most respects late imperial China had a "normal" history. It was Europe's breakthrough
to industrial production that was exceptional and needs explaining. Still, the arguments
and counterarguments as to why a comparable breakthrough did not occur in China
are illuminating.

   One often-cited argument is that China lacked the Protestant ethic that inspired
European capitalism. If by Protestant ethic we mean a strong family-centered ethic
with an emphasis on frugality, hard work, and saving, then China had one but nonetheless failed to industrialize. If we mean a Calvinist ethic that demands work as evidence
of salvation (or of the avoidance of damnation), then China did not have one. But if
industrialization requires such a deeply rooted religious ethic, why have Taiwan, Hong
Kong, Singapore, and then China itself been able to achieve explosive economic growth
during the past few decades?

   Another argument focuses on the absence of a scientific revolution in late imperial China. This was doubtless important. Was the lack of a Greek tradition of natural
philosophy and mathematics responsible? Or was it that China's best minds were occupied with mastering the Confucian classics, and not the natural world? The counter-
argument is that science made only a minimal contribution to England's early
industrialization: Not until the mid-nineteenth century was industry propelled by
science.

   Some scholars argue that in the early stage of an industrial revolution merchant
capital must be invested in industry, but that in late imperial China merchant capital
was more likely to be invested in land, which was honorable and secure from rapacious
officials. This argument has a measure of truth, but it applies to the Ming better than
to the Ch'ing.

   Still another argument stresses the importance of incentives and rewards. In England, the self-educated technicians who invented the water loom, steam engine, and
steam locomotive reaped enormous rewards and honors. In China, wealth and prestige were reserved for officials and gentry, who were political or literary in orientation
and despised those who worked with their hands. Nor were there patent laws for the
protection of inventors. But other scholars ask whether the Ming and Ch'ing were so
different from past dynasties when the Chinese had been brilliantly inventive. Whatever the explanation, all agree that substantial commercial growth during the Ming and
Ch'ing did not lead to an indigenous breakthrough to machine industry.

Another comparison concerns bureaucracy. Bureaucracy does for administration what the assembly line does for manufacturing: It breaks complex tasks into simple ones to achieve huge gains in efficiency. In the West, bureaucracies appeared only in recent centuries. They strengthened monarchies and then nation-states against landed aristocrats. They are viewed as a sign of modernity, the triumph of ability over hereditary privilege. In some respects, Chinese bureaucracy was similar: It was based on talent, it was reasonably efficient, and it strengthened the central state. Would-be officials in nineteenth-century Europe studied the Greek and Roman classics, whereas those of China studied the Confucian classics.

But in other regards, Western historians of Chinese bureaucracy feel as if they have passed through Alice's looking glass: What was recent in Europe had flourished for over a thousand years in China. Some say that China became "modern" a thousand years ago during the Sung, but they do not explain why officials became an obstacle to modernization during the nineteenth century. In Europe, kings used middle-class officials to advance their interests against those of hereditary landed aristocracies. But in China, the officials themselves were a segment of a landed gentry class in a society from which hereditary aristocracies had long since disappeared. Moreover, while Chinese merchants were clearly a middle class of sorts, they were not a bourgeoisie in that they displayed no political aspirations and had no parliament to represent their interests.

A final point that bears repetition was the Chinese disinterest in other civilizations and peoples, which they saw simply as barbarian. When the Jesuits tried to introduce science, the Chinese response was occasional curiosity and massive indifference. A few Jesuits were appointed as interpreters and court astronomers, or were used to cast cannon. This lack of interest in other civilizations may be explained by the coherence of its core institutions of government—the emperor, bureaucracy, the examination system, the gentry, and Confucian schools—that had been in place for centuries. Having proved their worth, they were so deeply rooted and internalized as to approximate a closed system.

## REVIEW QUESTIONS

1. Why did the economy grow in late traditional China?
2. How did the Ming and Ch'ing govern as well as they did for as long as they did?
3. How did Manchu rule resemble Mongol rule, and how did it differ? In what regards were K'ang Hsi and Ch'ien Lung indistinguishable from Chinese emperors?
4. Ming–Ch'ing foreign relations set the stage for China's nineteenth-century encounter with the West. How would you describe the setting?

## SUGGESTED READINGS

BODDE, D. AND MORRIS, C. *Law in Imperial China* (1967). Focuses on the Ch'ing dynasty (1644–1911).

CHANG, C. S. AND S. L. H. *Crisis and Transformation in Seventeenth Century China: Society, Culture, and Modernity* (1992).

CROSSLEY, P. *Translucent Mirror: History and Identity in Qing Imperial Ideology* (1999).

DE BARY, W. T. *Learning for One's Self: Essays on the Individual in Neo-Confucian Thought* (1991). A useful corrective to the view that Confucianism is simply a social ideology.

ELVIN, M. *The Pattern of the Chinese Past: A Social and Economic Interpretation* (1973). A controversial but stimulating interpretation of Chinese economic history in terms of technology. It brings in earlier periods as well as the Ming, Ch'ing, and modern China.

FAIRBANK, J. K., ED. *The Chinese World Order: Traditional China's Foreign Relations* (1968). An examination of the Chinese tribute system and its varying applications.

KAHN, H. L. *Monarchy in the Emperor's Eyes: Image and Reality in the Ch'ien-lung Reign* (1971). A study of the Chinese court during the mid-Ch'ing period.

LI YU, *The Carnal Prayer Mat*, trans. by P. Hanan (1990).

MOTE, F. AND TWITCHETT, D. EDS. *The Ming Dynasty 1368–1644*, Part 1 of *The Cambridge History of China*, Vols. 7 and 8 (1987).

NAQUIN, S. AND RAWSKI, E. S. *Chinese Society in the Eighteenth Century* (1987).

PARSONS, J. B. *The Peasant Rebellions of the Late Ming Dynasty* (1970).

PERDUE, P. C. *Exhausting the Earth, State and Peasant in Hunan, 1500–1850* (1987).

PERKINS, D. H. *Agricultural Development in China, 1368–1968* (1969).

RICCI, M. *China in the Sixteenth Century: The Journals of Matthew Ricci, 1583–1610* (1953).

ROWE, W. *Hankow* (1984). A study of a city in late imperial China.

SKINNER, G. W. *The City in Late Imperial China* (1977).

SPENCE, J. D. *Ts'ao Yin and the K'ang-hsi Emperor: Bondservant and Master* (1966). An excellent study of the early Ch'ing court.

SPENCE, J. D. *Emperor of China: A Self-Portrait of K'ang-hsi* (1974). The title of this very readable book does not adequately convey the extent of the author's contribution to the study of the early Ch'ing emperor.

STRUVE, L. A., TRANS. AND ED. *Voices from the Ming-Ch'ing Cataclysm* (1993). Readings from Chinese sources that describe the suffering and turmoil of a dynastic transition.

WAKEMAN, F. *The Great Enterprise* (1985). On the founding of the Manchu dynasty.

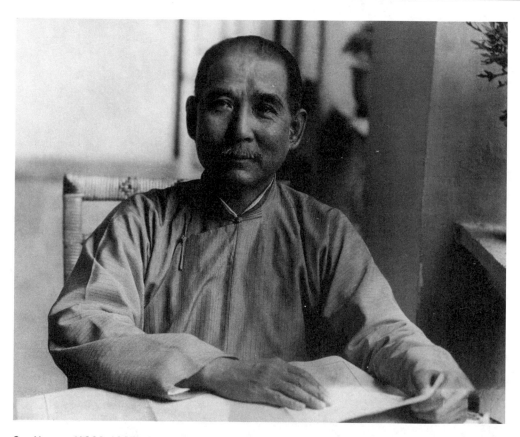

Sun Yat-sen (1866–1925), father of China's 1911 republican revolution. [Brown Brothers]

*chapter five*

# *Modern China (1839–1949)*

From the mid-nineteenth century, the West was the expanding, aggressive, imperialistic force in world history. Its industrial goods and gunboats reached every part of the globe. It believed in free trade and had the military might to impose it on others. It was the trigger for change throughout the world. But the response to the Western impact varied immensely according to the internal array of forces in each country. (Of course, it is well to remember that the "response to the West" was only one aspect of each country's history. In nineteenth-century China, hundreds of millions of people passed their entire lives without "responding" at all.)

Casting China's modern history in a positive light, we can say it was fairly successful in its response, for although it became subject to the so-called unequal treaties, it escaped the colonial fate of Asian countries such as India, Burma, Vietnam, Malaya, Indonesia, and Korea. Also, looking back from the perspective of the present, we note that Confucianism proved less of a barrier to science and modern ideas than did more otherworldly religions elsewhere. Unlike Islam, Hinduism, or Christianity, Confucianism was just secular enough to crumble in the face of the more powerful secularism of nineteenth-century science and its associated doctrines. Of course, many Confucian values, deeply embedded in the society, survived the philosophy of which they had once been a part. In fact, one of the "breakdown products" of the Confucian "political vocation" was a new and powerful nationalism.

But the picture of this century of Chinese history may also be colored in darker hues. We call it modern China, but it was not the century in which China became modern as much as the century in which it encountered the modern West. The first phase, from the Opium War (1839–1842) to the fall of the Ch'ing dynasty (1912), was, certain particulars apart, remarkably little affected by Western impact. Even after the Opium War, an event of much greater magnitude than Commodore Perry's visits to Japan in 1853 and 1854, it took seventy years for the dynasty to collapse. The ruling elite of Manchus and scholar-officials demonstrated a remarkable staying power. This was partly due to deeply internalized Confucian teachings, partly to a system of coherent institutions—central and local government offices, the examination system, schools, and family and clan organizations—and partly to a lack of viable alternatives. The dynastic system was also reinvigorated in the mid-nineteenth century by the effectiveness of local leaders in rebuilding after the devastation of the Taiping rebellions. Only in China's relations with the Western powers did traditional methods not work: Being confronted on its seaboard by nations more powerful than itself was a new experience for China. During the seventy years to 1912, the West grew stronger and China grew only more populous.

The second phase of China's modern history, from 1912 to the establishment of a Communist state in 1949, was an era of turmoil and suffering. The warlordism that broke out after the fall of the Ch'ing was a normal interdynastic phenomenon, and, other things being equal, might have led in time to a new dynasty. But other things were not. The radical critique of tradition by the May Fourth Movement spelled the end of the Confucian state. Warlordism was followed by a partial military unification and continual military campaigns, by war with Japan, and then, while most countries were returning to peace, by four bitter years of civil war. The darker view that China had in some sense "failed" during this modern century is not a Western view imposed on China; it is the view held by the Chinese themselves.

# THE CLOSE OF MANCHU RULE

## The Opium War and Its Aftermath

The eighteenth-century three-country trade—British goods to India, Indian cotton to China, and Chinese tea to Britain—was in China's favor. The silver flowing into China spurred the further monetization of Chinese markets. Then the British replaced cotton with Indian opium. By the 1820s, the balance of trade was reversed, and silver began to flow out of China.

A crisis arose in the 1830s when the British East India Company lost its monopoly on British trade with China. The opium trade became wide open. To check the evil of opium and the outflow of specie, the Chinese government in 1836 began to enforce an earlier ban on opium, closing the dens where it was smoked and executing Chinese dealers. In 1839, the government sent Imperial Commissioner Lin Tse-hsu to Canton to superintend the ban. He continued the crackdown on Chinese dealers and destroyed over 20,000 chests—a six-month supply—of opium belonging to foreign merchants. This action led to a confrontation between the Chinese and British.

War broke out in November 1839 when Chinese war junks clashed with a British merchantman. The following June, sixteen British warships arrived at Canton, and for the next two years, the British bombarded forts, fought battles, seized cities, and attempted negotiations. The Chinese troops, with their antiquated weapons and old-style cannon, were ineffective. The war was finally ended in August 1842 by the Treaty of Nanking, the first of the unequal treaties.

The treaty not only ended the tribute system, but also provided Britain with a superb deep-water port at Hong Kong, a huge indemnity, and the opening of five ports: Canton, Shanghai, Amoy, Ningpo, and Foochow. British merchants and their families were permitted to reside in the ports and to engage in trade; Britain could appoint a consul for each city; and British residents gained extraterritoriality, under

## Commissioner Lin Urges Morality on Queen Victoria

In 1839 the British in China argued for free trade and protection for the legal right of their citizens. The Chinese position was that behind such lofty arguments, the British were pushing opium.

*What does this document suggest about the Ch'ing dynasty's view of China's place in the world in 1839? Does it still view China as a universal empire?*

A communication: magnificently our great Emperor soothes and pacifies China and the foreign countries, regarding all with the same kindness. If there is profit, then he shares it with the peoples of the world; if there is harm, then he removes it on behalf of the world. This is because he takes the mind of heaven and earth as his mind.

The kings of your honorable country by a tradition handed down from generation to generation have always been noted for their politeness and submissiveness. We have read your successive tributary memorials saying, "In general our countrymen who go to trade in China have always received His Majesty the Emperor's gracious treatment and equal justice," and so on. Privately we are delighted with the way in which the honorable rulers of your country deeply understand the grand principles and are grateful for the Celestial grace. For this reason the Celestial Court in soothing those from afar has redoubled its polite and kind treatment. The profit from trade has been enjoyed by them continuously for two hundred years. This is the source from which your country has become known for its wealth. But after a long period of commercial intercourse, there appear among the crowd of barbarians both good persons and bad, unevenly. Consequently there are those who smuggle opium to seduce the Chinese people and so cause the spread of the poison to all provinces. Such persons who only care to profit themselves, and disregard their harm to others, are not tolerated by the laws of heaven and are unanimously hated by human beings. His Majesty the Emperor, upon hearing of this, is in a towering rage. . . .

We find that your country is sixty or seventy thousand *li* [three *li* make one mile, ordinarily] from China. Yet there are barbarian ships that strive to come here for trade for the purpose of making a great profit. The wealth of China is used to profit the barbarians. That is to say, the great

which they were subject to British and not Chinese law. The treaty also contained a "most-favored-nation" clause, a provision that any further rights gained by any other nation would automatically accrue to Britain as well. The treaty with Britain was followed in 1844 by similar treaties with the United States and France. The American treaty permitted churches in treaty ports, and the French treaty permitted the propagation of Catholicism.

After the signing of the treaties, Chinese imports of opium rose from 30,000 chests to a peak of 87,000 in 1879. Thereafter, imports declined to 50,000 chests in 1906,

profit made by barbarians is all taken from the rightful share of China. By what right do they then in return use the poisonous drug to injure the Chinese people? Even though the barbarians may not necessarily intend to do us harm, yet in coveting profit to an extreme, they have no regard for injuring others. Let us ask, where is your conscience? I have heard that the smoking of opium is very strictly forbidden by your country; that is because the harm caused by opium is clearly understood. Since it is not permitted to do harm to your own country, then even less should you let it be passed on to the harm of other countries—how much less to China!

Suppose there were people from another country who carried opium for sale to England and seduced your people into buying and smoking it; certainly your honorable ruler would deeply hate it and be bitterly aroused. We have heard heretofore that your honorable ruler is kind and benevolent. Naturally you would not wish to give unto others what you yourself do not want.

Now we have set up regulations governing the Chinese people. He who sells opium shall receive the death penalty and he who smokes it also the death penalty. Now consider this: if the barbarians do not bring opium, then how can the Chinese people resell it, and how can they smoke it? The fact is that the wicked barbarians beguile the Chinese people into a death trap. How then can we grant life only to those barbarians? He who takes the life of even one person still has to atone for it with his own life; yet is the harm done by opium limited to the taking of one life only? Therefore in the new regulations, in regard to those barbarians who bring opium to China, the penalty is fixed at decapitation or strangulation. This is what is called getting rid of a harmful thing on behalf of mankind.

[However] All those who within the period of the coming one year (from England) or six months (from India) bring opium to China by mistake, but who voluntarily confess and completely surrender their opium, shall be exempt from their punishment. This may be called the height of kindness and the perfection of justice.

and ended during World War I. But other kinds of trade did not grow as much as had been hoped, and Western merchants blamed the lack of growth on artificial restraints imposed by Chinese officials. They also complained that, despite the treaties, Canton remained closed to trade. The Chinese authorities, for their part, were incensed by the export of coolies to work under harsh conditions on plantations in Cuba and Peru. A second war broke out in 1856, which continued sporadically until Lord Elgin, the British commander, captured Peking in 1860. A new set of conventions and treaties provided for indemnities, the opening of eleven new ports, the stationing of foreign diplomats in Peking, the propagation of Christianity anywhere in China, and the legalization of the opium trade.

While the British fought China for trading rights, the Russians were encroaching on China's northern frontier. During the 1850s, Russia established settlements along the Amur River. In 1858, China signed a treaty ceding the north bank of the Amur to Russia, and in 1860, China signed another treaty giving Russia the Maritime Province between the Ussuri River and the Pacific. Some pockets of territory not covered by the treaty are still in dispute today.

## Rebellions Against the Manchus

Far more immediate a threat to Manchu rule than foreign gunboats and unequal treaties were the Taiping, Nien, and Muslim rebellions that convulsed China between 1850 and 1873 (see Map 5–1). The torment and suffering that they caused were unparalleled in world history. Estimates of those killed during the twenty years of the Taiping Rebellion range from twenty to thirty million. If one adds losses due to other rebellions, droughts, and floods, China's population dropped by sixty million and did not recover to prerebellion levels until the end of the dynasty in 1912.

The Taipings were begun by Hung Hsiu-ch'uan (1814–1864), a school teacher from a poor family in a minority Hakka group in the southern province of Kwangtung. Hung had four times failed to pass the civil service examinations. He became ill and saw visions. Influenced by Protestant tracts that he had picked up in Canton, Hung announced that he was the younger brother of Jesus and that God had told him to rid China of evil demons—including Manchus, Confucians, Taoists, and Buddhists. He formed an Association of God Worshipers. His followers cut off their queues as a sign of resistance to the Manchus, who called them "long-haired rebels." The Taipings began by attacking local Confucian temples, arousing the opposition of the gentry. The Taipings were soon joined by peasants, coal miners, charcoal workers, and unemployed transport workers. Hung proclaimed the Heavenly Kingdom of Great Peace in 1851 and two years later took Nanking and made it his capital. The fighting spread until the Taipings controlled most of the Yangtze basin; their expeditions eventually entered sixteen of the eighteen Chinese provinces. By that time, their army numbered almost a million.

The Taiping ideology joined Old Testament Christianity with an ancient text often used by reformers, the *Chou Rites*. The puritanical ethics of the Taipings came from the former, and the notion of sharing property equally came from the latter. The Taipings prohibited opium, tobacco, alcohol, gambling, adultery, prostitution, and footbinding. They upheld filial piety. They maintained that women were men's equals and appointed them to administrative and military posts. In short, like earlier rebels, the Taipings combined moral reform, religious fervor, and a vision of a transformed egalitarian society.

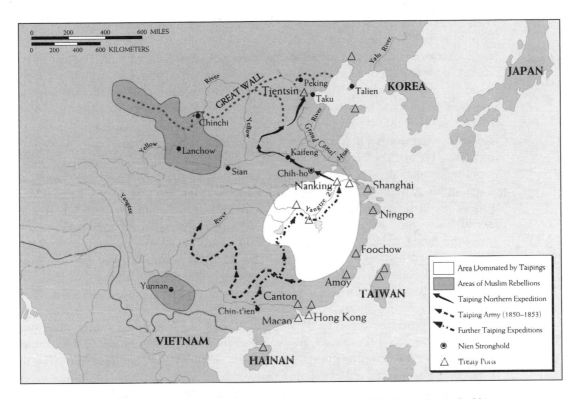

**Map 5–1  The Taiping, Nien, and Muslim rebellions.**   Between 1850 and 1873 China was wracked by rebellions that almost ended the Manchu dynasty. The dynasty was saved by Chinese "gentry armics."

The weaknesses of the movement were several. Most Taiping leaders were too poorly educated to govern effectively, and the Taipings could not draw on the gentry. When the Taiping area was divided into kingdoms, dissension broke out. The Taipings failed to cultivate the secret societies, which were also anti-Manchu. They also failed to cultivate Westerners, who had been neutral before the 1860 treaty settlements and aided the Manchus thereafter. In addition, many Taiping ideals remained unfulfilled; for example, land was not redistributed, and, although Taiping teachings emphasized frugality and the sanctity of monogamous marriage, Hung lived with many concubines in the midst of luxury.

The other rebellions were of lesser note but longer duration. The Nien were located to the north of the Taipings along the Huai River. They began as bandits who lived in walled villages, were organized in secret societies, and lived by raiding the surrounding countryside. Eventually they built an army, collected taxes, and ruled 100,000 square miles. The Ch'ing court feared that the Nien would join forces with the Taipings. The revolts of Muslims against Chinese in the southwest and the northwest lasted even longer. One rebel set up an Islamic kingdom with himself as sultan. Like the Taiping Rebellion, these several rebellions took advantage of the weakened state of the dynasty and occurred in areas that had few officials or Ch'ing military units.

Against these rebellions, the Manchu Banners and the Chinese Army of the Green Standard proved helpless: The one was useful only for defense, the other only against unarmed peasants. The first effective step was taken in 1852, when the court sent Tseng Kuo-fan (1811–1872) to Hunan Province in south-central China to organize a local army. Tseng was a product of the Confucian examination system and had served in Peking. He saw the Manchu government, of which he was an elite member, as the upholder of morality and the social order, and Chinese rebels as would-be destroyers of that order. Arriving in Hunan, he recruited members of the gentry as officers. They were of the class that, since the late Ming, had been growing in importance and performing many local government functions, in some cases organizing local militia. Not only were they Confucian, but as landlords they had the most to lose from rebel rule. They recruited soldiers from their local areas. At first Tseng's "Hunan Braves" held their ground; then they went on the offensive, stopping the Taipings' advance.

Until 1860, the Ch'ing court was dominated by Manchu conservatives who limited Tseng's role and dragged their feet in upholding the treaties. In 1860, the conservatives lost their footing when the British and the French occupied Peking. A reform government replaced the conservatives, began internal changes, adopted a policy of cooperation with the Western powers, and put Tseng in charge of suppressing the rebellions. Tseng appointed able officials to raise other regional armies. Li Hung-chang (1823–1901), with his Anhwei Army, was especially effective. Foreigners and Shanghai merchants gave their support; revenues from the customs service and foreign ships and weapons were essential to Tseng's armies. The Taipings collapsed when Nanking was captured in 1864 after protracted fighting. Tseng and Li suppressed the Nien by 1868, and the Muslim rebellions were put down five years later. Scholar-officials, relying on local gentry, had saved the dynasty.

## Self-Strengthening and Decline (1874–1895)

The two decades after the suppression of the mid-century rebellions illustrate the dictum that there is no single "correct" view of history. In comparison, for example, with the late Sung or the late Ming, the last decades of the nineteenth century look good. In view of the dynasty's advanced stage of administrative decentralization, the Chinese resiliency and capacity to rebuild after unprecedented destruction were impressive. Even on its borders, the Manchu state was able to maintain or regain some territories while losing others. But if we ask instead how effective China's response was to the West, or if we compare China's progress with that of Japan, then China during the same decades looks almost moribund. Historians often call these years the period of "self-strengthening" after a catchphrase in vogue at the time. This term is not inappropriate, as the list of new initiatives taken during the period is long. Yet, since the firepower of Western naval forces doubled each decade, the forces that China faced at the end of the century were vastly more formidable than those of the Opium War. Despite self-strengthening, China was relatively weaker at the end of the period than at the start.

In 1895, Li Hung-chang met with Itō Hirobumi of Japan to negotiate a peace treaty after China's defeat in the Sino-Japanese War. Itō asked with uncharacteristic bluntness: "Ten years ago when I was at Tientsin, I talked about reform with the Grand Secretary (Li). Why is it that up to now not a single thing has been changed or reformed?" Li replied: "Affairs in my country have been so confined by tradition that I could not accomplish what I desired. . . . Now in the twinkling of an eye ten years have gone by, and everything is still the same. I am even more regretful. I am ashamed of having excessive wishes and lacking the power to fulfill them. . ." Itō responded blandly: "The providence of heaven has no affection, except for the virtuous."[1] Considering that Li was the single most powerful figure in China during these decades, Ito's puzzlement was not surprising.

***The Court at Peking***   China's inability to act effectively is explained partly by the situation at the court. Prince Kung (1833–1898) and the empress dowager (1835–1908) were coregents for the young emperor. For a Manchu noble, Prince Kung was a man of ideas. After signing the treaties of 1860, he established in 1861 a new office directly under the Grand Council to handle the court's relations with foreign diplomats in Peking. The following year, he established a school to train Chinese in foreign languages. Over time, however, his position at the court grew weaker. Outmaneuvered by the empress dowager, he was ousted in 1884.

The empress dowager was the daughter of a Manchu official. She had become an imperial concubine and had produced the only male child of the former emperor. She was educated, clever, petty, strong-willed, and narrow-minded. She did not oppose change, except by circumstance, nor did she favor it. She had no conception of how to reform China. Her single goal was to gather political power into her own hands. She did this by forging a political machine of conservative bureaucrats, military commanders, and eunuchs, and by maintaining a balance between the court and the regional strength of the powerful governor-generals. The result was a court barely able to survive, too weak to govern effectively, and not inclined to do more than approve of initiatives taken at the provincial level.

***Regional Governments***   The most vital figures during these decades were a handful of governors-general whose names are legend: Tseng Kuo-fan, Li Hung-chang, Tso Tsung-t'ang, and Chang Chih-tung. Each had a staff of 200 or 300 and an army, and was in charge of two or three provinces. They were loyal to the dynasty that they

---

[1]S. Y. Teng and J. K. Fairbank, *China's Response to the West* (Cambridge, MA: Harvard University, Press, 1954), p. 126.

had restored in the face of almost certain collapse, and in return for their allegiance, they were allowed great autonomy.

Their first task was reconstruction. The rebellions in central China had destroyed the mulberry trees on which the silkworms fed, and those in the northwest, the irrigation systems. Millions were hungry or homeless. The leaders' response to these ills was massive and effective. Just as they had mobilized the gentry to suppress the rebellions, now they obtained their cooperation in rebuilding. They set up refugee centers and soup kitchens, reduced taxes in the devastated Yangtze valley, reclaimed lands gone to waste, began water-control projects, and built granaries. By the early 1890s, a considerable well-being had been restored to China's late dynastic society.

Their second task was self-strengthening—the adoption of Western arms and technology. The governors-general were keenly aware of China's weakness. To strengthen China, they built arsenals and shipyards during the 1860s and 1870s, and during the 1870s and 1880s, they began commercial ventures as well. The China Merchants Steam Navigation Company was established in 1872, the Kaiping Coal Mine in 1876, and then a telegraph company, short stretches of railways, and cotton mills. The formula applied in running these enterprises was "official supervision and merchant operation." The major decisions were made by scholar-officials like Tseng, but day-to-day operations were left to the merchants.

This division of labor led to contradictions. The Steam Navigation Company, for example, was funded partly by the government because private capital was inadequate. Li Hung-chang awarded the company a monopoly on shipments of the rice paid in taxes and official cargos to Tientsin and won tariff concessions for the company as well. For a time, these advantages enabled the company to compete successfully with foreign lines. But Li also used company ships to transport his troops; he took company funds to reward his political followers; and he interfered in the company by hiring and firing managers. Under these conditions, both investors and managers took their profits quickly and did not reinvest in the line. Soon British lines once again dominated shipping in China's domestic waters.

***Treaty Ports*** Conditions in the treaty ports, of which there were fourteen by the 1860s, were different from the rest of China. The ports were little islands of privilege where foreigners lived in mansions staffed with servants, raced horses at the track, participated in amateur theatricals, drank (in Shanghai, at the longest bar in the world), and went to church on Sunday. But the ports were also islands of security, under the rule of foreign consuls, where capital was safe from confiscation, trade was free, and "squeeze" (extortion by officials) was the exception and not the rule. Foreign companies quite naturally located in the ports. The Hong Kong and Shanghai Bank, for example, was funded in 1865 by British interests to finance international trade and to make loans to Chinese firms and banks. Chinese merchants were also attracted by these conditions and located their businesses on rented lands in the foreign concessions. Joint ventures, such as steamboats on the Yangtze, were begun by Chinese and foreign merchants. Well into the twentieth century, the foreign concessions (treaty port lands leased in perpetuity by foreigners) remained the vital sector of China's modern economy.

The effects of the treaty ports and of Western imperialism on China were largely negative. Under the low tariffs mandated by the treaties, Chinese industries had little protection from imports. Native cotton spinning was almost destroyed by imports of yarn—although the cloth woven from the yarn remained competitive with foreign cloth. Chinese tea lost ground to Indian tea and Chinese silk to Japanese silk, as these countries developed products of standard quality and China did not. China found few products to export: pig bristles, soybeans, and vegetable oils. The level of foreign trade stayed low, and China's interior markets were affected only slightly.

By the 1870s, the foreign powers had reached an accommodation with China. They counted on the court to uphold the treaties; in return, they became a prop for the dynasty during its final decades. By 1900, for example, the court's revenues from customs fees were larger than those from any other source, including the land tax. The fees were collected by the Maritime Customs Service, a notably efficient and honest treaty-port institution headed by an Irishman, Robert Hart, who saw himself as serving the Chinese government. In 1895 the Maritime Customs Service had 700 Western and 3,500 Chinese employees.

## The Borderlands

China's other foreign relations were with fringe lands inhabited by non-Chinese but which China claimed by right of past conquest or as tributaries. Often distant from the pressing concerns of Chinese government, the tributaries were nonetheless the mirrors in which China saw reflected its own self-image as a universal empire. During the late nineteenth century this image was strengthened in the northwest but dealt a fatal blow in Vietnam and Korea.

***The Northwest***   Along the sweep of its northern and western frontiers China confronted imperial Russia. Both countries had been expanding onto the steppe since the seventeenth century. Both had firearms. Caught in a pincers between them, the once proud, powerful, and independent nomadic tribes gradually were rendered impotent. Conservatives at the Manchu court ordered Tso Tsung-t'ang, who had suppressed Muslim rebels within China, to suppress a Muslim leader who had founded an independent state in Chinese Turkestan (the Tarim basin, the area of the old Silk Road). Tso led his army across 3,000 miles of deserts, and by 1878 he had reconquered the area, which was subsequently renamed Sinkiang, or the "New Territories." A treaty signed with Russia in 1881 also restored most of the Ili region in western Mongolia to Chinese control. These victories strengthened court conservatives who wished to take a stronger stance toward the West.

**Vietnam**   To the south was Vietnam, which had wrested its independence from China in 935 and periodically had repelled Chinese invasions thereafter. It saw itself as an independent and separate state, but it used the Chinese writing system, modeled its laws and government on those of China, and traded with China within the framework of the tribute system. China, more simply, saw Vietnam as a tributary that could be aided or punished as necessary.

During the 1840s, the second emperor of the Nguyen dynasty, which had begun in 1802, moved to reduce French influence and suppress Christianity. Thousands were killed, including French and Vietnamese priests. The French responded by seizing Saigon and the three provinces of Cochin China in 1859, establishing a protectorate over Cambodia in 1864, and taking three more provinces in 1867 and Hanoi in 1882. China, flush with confidence after its victories in Central Asia, in 1883 sent troops to aid its tributary. The result was a two-year war in which French warships ranged the coast of China, attacking shore batteries and sinking ships. In 1885, China was forced to sign a treaty abandoning its claims to Vietnam. By 1893 France had brought together Vietnam, Cambodia, and Laos to form the Federation of Indochina. Newly founded Cantonese newspapers contributed to a rising Chinese nationalism with inflammatory articles attacking French aggression. Indochina remained under French control until 1940.

**Korea**   A third area of contention was Korea, strategically located between Russia, China, and Japan. Korea was an ancient state, about the size of England, Scotland, and Wales combined. Like Vietnam, Korea was a proud nation with an independent identity. Even while drawing heavily on Chinese laws, philosophy, history, and institutions, it had developed a distinctive culture and way of life. Unlike Vietnam, Korea saw itself as a tributary of China. Even at his own court the Korean ruler styled himself as a king and not an emperor. It was the only rim area of China that accepted the tribute system on Chinese terms.

During the last decades of the long Choson dynasty, (1392–1910) the Korean state was weak. It hung on to power, in part, by enforcing a policy of seclusion almost as total as that of Tokugawa Japan, which won it the name of the *Hermit Kingdom*. Its only foreign ties were its tribute relations with China and its trade and occasional diplomatic missions to Japan. In 1876, Japan "opened" Korea to international relations, using much the same tactics that Perry had used twenty-two years earlier against Japan. Japan then contended with China for influence in Korea's internal politics. Conservatives and moderate reformers in Korea looked to China for support. Radical reformers, weaker and fewer in number, looked to Japan, arguing that only sweeping changes such as those that had occurred in Japan would enable Korea to survive. The radicals, however, were soon suppressed.

In 1893, a popular religious sect unleashed a rebellion against the weak and corrupt Seoul government. When the government requested Chinese help to suppress the rebellion, China sent troops, but Japan sent more, and in 1894, war broke out between China and Japan. China and the Western powers expected an easy Chinese victory, but they had not understood the changes occurring within Japan. Japan won handily. Neither the Chinese fleet nor the Chinese armies were a match for the discipline and the superior tactics of the Japanese. It was after this war that Taiwan became Japan's first colony. Japan's victory sent reverberations throughout China. For the first time many became convinced that basic changes were necessary.

## FROM DYNASTY TO WARLORDISM (1895–1926)

China was ruled by officials who had mastered the Confucian classics and the historical and literary tradition that had developed along with them. This intellectual formation was highly resistant to change. For most officials, living in China's interior, the foreign crises of the nineteenth century were "coastal phenomena" that, like bee stings, were painful for a time but then forgotten. Few officials realized the magnitude of the foreign threat.

China's defeat in 1895 by Japan, another Asian nation and one for which China had had little regard, came as a shock. The response within China was a new wave of reform proposals. The most influential thinker was K'ang Yu-wei (1858–1927), who described China as "enfeebled" and "soundly asleep atop a pile of kindling." For this state of affairs, K'ang blamed the "conservatives." They did not understand, he argued, that Confucius himself had been a reformer and not simply a transmitter of past wisdom. Confucius had invented the idea of a golden age in the past in order to persuade the rulers of his own age to adopt his ideas. All of history, K'ang continued, was evolutionary—a march forward from absolute monarchy to constitutional monarchy to democracy. Actually, K'ang was not well versed in Western ideas; he equated the somewhat mystical Confucian virtue of humanity (*jen*) with electricity and ether. Nonetheless, his reinterpretation of the essentials of Confucianism removed a major barrier to the entry of Western ideas into China.

In 1898, the emperor himself became sympathetic to K'ang's ideas and, on June 11, launched "one hundred days of reform." He took as his models not past Chinese monarchs but Peter the Great and the Japanese Meiji Emperor. Edicts were issued for sweeping reforms of China's schools, railroads, police, laws, military services, bureaucracy, post offices, and examination system. But the orders were implemented in only one province; conservative resistance was nationwide. Even at the court, after the one hundred days the empress dowager regained control and ended the reforms. K'ang and most of his associates fled to Japan. One reformer who remained behind was executed.

The response of the Western powers to China's 1895 defeat has been described as "carving up the melon." Each nation tried to define a sphere of interest, which usually consisted of a leasehold along with railway rights and special commercial privileges. Russia gained a leasehold at Port Arthur in the area that it had denied to Japan

### Liang Ch'i-ch'ao Urges the Chinese to Reform (1896)

Next to K'ang Yu-wei, Liang Ch'i-ch'ao (1873–1929) was the most influential thinker of late Ch'ing China.

*What kind of reform program do you imagine Liang advocated?*

On the *Harm of Not Reforming*. Now here is a big mansion which has lasted a thousand years. The tiles and bricks are decayed and the beams and rafters are broken. It is still a magnificent big thing, but when wind and rain suddenly come up, its fall is foredoomed. Yet the people in the house are still happily playing or soundly sleeping and as indifferent as if they have seen or heard nothing. Even some who have noted the danger know only how to weep bitterly, folding their arms and waiting for death without thinking of any remedy. Sometimes there are people a little better off who try to repair the cracks, seal up the leaks, and patch up the ant holes in order to be able to go on living there in peace, even temporarily, in the hope that something better may turn up. These three types of people use their minds differently, but when a hurricane comes they will die together. . . . A nation is also like this. . . .

India is one of the oldest countries on the great earth. She followed tradition without change; she has been rendered a colony of England. Turkey's territory occupied three continents and had an established state for a thousand years; yet, because of observing the old ways without change, she has been dominated by six large countries, which have divided her territory. . . . The Moslems in central Asia have usually been well known for their bravery and skill in warfare, and yet they observe the old ways without changing. The Russians are swallowing them like a whale and nibbling them as silkworms eat mulberry leaves, almost in their entirety.

The age of China as a country is equal to that of India and the fertility of her land is superior to that of Turkey, but her conformity to the defective ways which have accumulated and her incapacity to stand up and reform make her also like a brother of these two countries. . . . Whenever there is a flood or drought, communications are severed, there is no way to transport famine relief, the dead are abandoned to fill the ditches or are disregarded, and nine out of ten houses are emptied. . . . The members of secret societies are scattered over the whole country, waiting for the chance to move. Industry is not developed, commerce is not discussed, the native goods daily become less salable. . . . "Leakage" [i.e., squeeze] becomes more serious day by day and our financial sources are almost dried up. Schools are not well-run and students, apart from the "eight-legged" essays, do not know how to do a thing. The good ones are working on small researches, flowery writing, and miscellaneous trifles. Tell them about the vast oceans, they open their eyes wide and disbelieve it.

Reprinted by permission of the publisher from *China's Response to the West* by Ssu-Yu Teng and John K. Fairbank, Cambridge, MA: Harvard University Press. Copyright © 1954, 1979 by the President and Fellows of Harvard College.

An American view of the "Open Door." The combination of high self-esteem and anti-foreignism at the turn of the century was not a Chinese monopoly. [Bettmann Archive]

in 1895; Germany acquired one in Shantung; Britain got the New Territories adjoining Kowloon at Hong Kong. New ports and cities were opened to foreign trade. The United States, busy acquiring the Philippines and Guam, was in a weaker position in China. So it enunciated an "open-door" policy: equal commercial opportunities for all powers and the preservation of the territorial integrity of China.

There was in China at this time an antiforeign religious society known as the Boxers. The Chinese name translates more literally as the "Righteous and Harmonious Fists." The Boxers had rituals, spells, and amulets that they believed made them impervious to bullets. They rebelled first in Shantung in 1898, and, gaining court support, entered Peking in 1900. The court declared war on the treaty powers, and there followed a two-month siege of the foreign legation quarter. Support for the rebellion was fueled by pent-up resentments against decades of foreign encroachments. Eventually an international force captured Peking, won a huge indemnity, and obtained the right to maintain permanent military forces in the capital. In the aftermath of the Boxer Rebellion, the Russians occupied Manchuria.

The defeat of the Boxers convinced even conservative Chinese leaders of the futility of clinging to old ways. A more powerful reform movement began, with the empress dowager herself positioned in its vanguard. But as the movement gained momentum, the dynasty could not stay far enough in front and eventually was overrun.

Educational reforms began in 1901. Women, for the first time, were admitted along with men to the newly formed schools. In place of Confucianism, the instructors taught science, mathematics, geography, and an anti-imperialist version of Chinese history that fanned the flames of nationalism. Western doctrines such as classical economics, liberalism, socialism, anarchism, and social Darwinism were also introduced. Most entered via translations from Japanese, and in the process, the modern vocabulary coined by Japanese scholars was implanted in China. By 1906, there were 8,000 Chinese students in Japan, which had become a hotbed of Chinese reformist and revolutionary societies.

Military reforms were begun by Yuan Shih-k'ai (1859–1916), whose New Army drew on Japanese and Western models. Young men from gentry families, spurred by patriotism, broke with the traditional Chinese animus against military careers and joined the New Army as officers. They were loyal to their commanders and to their country, not to the Manchu dynasty.

Political reforms began with a modification of the examination system to accommodate the new learning. Then, in 1905 the examination system was abolished altogether. Henceforth, officials were to be recruited from the graduates of the new schools and those who had studied abroad. Provincial assemblies were formed in 1909, and a consultative assembly with some elected members was established in Peking in 1910. These representative bodies were intended to rally the new gentry nationalism in support of the dynasty, but they turned into forums for the expression of ideas and interests at odds with those of the dynasty.

In sum, during the first decade of the twentieth century, the three vital components of the imperial system—Confucian education, bureaucracy, and gentry—had been discarded or modified in ways that even a few decades earlier would have been unimaginable. These changes sparked the 1911–1912 revolution. It began with an uprising in Szechwan province against a government plan to nationalize the main railways. The players were:

1. Gentry who stood to lose their investments in the railways.

2. Ch'ing military commanders who broke with Peking, declaring their provinces independent.

3. Sun Yat-sen (1866–1925), a republican revolutionary. Born a peasant, he had learned English and become a Christian in Hawaii; he then studied medicine

in Canton and Hong Kong. He organized the Revolutionary Alliance in Tokyo in 1905, and was associated with the Nationalist Party (Kuomintang) formed in 1912.

4. Yuan Shih-k'ai, a general who was called on by the court to preserve the dynasty. Instead, he arranged for the last child emperor to abdicate in February 1912, for Sun to step aside, and for himself to become president of the new Republic of China.

An election was held in 1913, which the Nationalists won. Yuan thereupon had their leader assassinated, crushed the pro-Nationalist military-governors of the southern provinces who supported them, and forced Sun Yat-sen and other revolutionaries to flee again to Japan. Yuan emerged as the uncontested ruler of China. Mistaking the temper of the times, in December 1915 he proclaimed a new dynasty with himself as emperor. The idea of yet another dynasty met implacable opposition from all quarters, forcing Yuan to abandon the attempt. He died three months later. After Yuan, a national government continued to exist in Peking, but China fell into the hands of warlord armies. A few were concerned for local welfare but most were despots who cruelly exploited the populations they controlled. The years until the late twenties were a time of agony, frustration, and travail for the Chinese people, but they also were a time of intense intellectual ferment.

## CULTURAL AND IDEOLOGICAL FERMENT: THE MAY FOURTH MOVEMENT

In the century after the Opium War, China's leading thinkers responded to the challenge of the West in terms of four successive modes of thought:

1. During the 1840s and the 1850s, and into the 1860s, the key event in China was the Taiping Rebellion. The success of Confucian gentry in putting down the rebellion and in reestablishing the social order underlined for most Chinese the effectiveness, vitality, and validity of traditional doctrines.

2. From the 1860s to the 1890s, the dominant intellectual modality was "*ti-yung* reformism." The essence (*ti*) was to remain Chinese, but useful contrivances (*yung*) could be borrowed from the West. This formula enabled a restabilized China to borrow and reform in small ways like building arsenals and railroads, while remaining Chinese at the core. It was the ideology of the "self-strengthening" movement.

3. Then, during the decade after the turn of the century (the last decade of dynastic rule), the *ti-yung* distinction came to be seen as inadequate. The *ti* itself was reinterpreted. The dominant view was that of K'ang Yu-wei, who argued that

Confucius had been a reformer and that Confucianism, properly understood, was a philosophy of change. This kind of thought was behind the rash of reforms of 1900–1911.

4.  The fourth stage was a period of freedom and vigorous experimentation with new Western doctrines which began in 1914 and extended into the 1920s. It is called the *May Fourth Movement* after an incident in Peking in 1919 in which thousands of students protested the settlement at Versailles that awarded former German possessions in Shantung to Japan. The powerful nationalism that led the students to demonstrate in the streets changed the complexion of Chinese thought. Instead of appealing to tradition, leading thinkers began to judge ideas in terms of their value in solving China's problems. It was also not accidental that this era of intellectual ferment corresponded almost exactly with the period of warlord rule—which afforded a breathing space between the ideological constraints of the old dynasty and those of the nationalist and Communist eras that would follow.

Scholars who returned from abroad during the last years of Manchu rule often located in the safety of the treaty ports. During the May Fourth era, however, the center of advanced thought was Peking. Ts'ai Yuan-p'ei (1868–1940), who had been minister of education under the republic, became the chancellor of Peking University, and Ch'en Tu-hsiu (1879–1942) became his dean of letters. Both men had had a classical education and had passed the traditional examinations. Ts'ai joined the party of Sun Yat-sen and went to study in Germany, where he earned a Ph.D. After the fall of Yuan Shih-k'ai, he made Peking University into a haven for scholars who had returned from study in Japan or the West.

Ch'en Tu-hsiu, a francophile, had studied in Japan. In 1915, he launched *New Youth*, a magazine that played a role in the intellectual revolution of early twentieth-century China comparable to the *cahiers* in the French Revolution or the pamphlets of Thomas Paine in the American Revolution. In his magazine, Ch'en placed the blame for Chinese ills on the teachings of Confucius. He called for a generation of progressive, cosmopolitan, and scientific youth who would uphold the values of liberty, equality, and fraternity.

The greatest modern Chinese writer was Lu Hsun (1881–1936). Like most other leading intellectuals of the period, he had been born in a scholar-official family. He went to Japan for eight years to study medicine but switched in mid-course to literature. His first work, *A Madman's Diary*, appeared in *New Youth* in 1918. Its protagonist is a pathetic figure whose madness takes the form of a belief that people eat people. Lu Hsun's message was that only the vision of a madman could truly comprehend an abnormal and inhumane society.

As the May Fourth Movement developed, ideas propounded in Peking quickly spread to the rest of China, especially to its urban centers. Protest demonstrations against imperialist privilege broke out in Shanghai, Wuhan, and Canton, as they had in the capital. Nationalism and anti-imperialist sentiment were stronger than liberal-

## Ch'en Tu-hsiu's "Call to Youth" in 1915

Struggle, natural selection, and organic process are the images of Ch'en Tu-hsiu. How different from those of Confucianism!

*How does Ch'en's "Call to Youth" relate to the political conditions in China in 1915?*

The Chinese compliment others by saying, "He acts like an old man although still young." Englishmen and Americans encourage one another by saying, "Keep young while growing old." Such is one respect in which the different ways of thought of the East and West are manifested. Youth is like early spring, like the rising sun, like trees and grass in bud, like a newly sharpened blade. It is the most valuable period of life. The function of youth in society is the same as that of a fresh and vital cell in a human body. In the processes of metabolism, the old and the rotten are incessantly eliminated to be replaced by the fresh and living. . . . According to this standard, then, is the society of our nation flourishing, or is it about to perish? I cannot bear to answer. As for those old and rotten elements, I shall leave them to the process of natural selection. . . . I only, with tears, place my plea before the young and vital youth, in the hope that they will achieve self-awareness, and begin to struggle.

What is the struggle? It is to exert one's intellect, discard resolutely the old and the rotten, regard them as enemies and as the flood or savage beasts, keep away from their neighborhood and refuse to be contaminated by their poisonous germs. Alas! Do these words really fit the youth of our country? I have seen that, out of every ten youths who are young in age, five are old in physique; and out of every ten who are young in both age and physique, nine are old in mentality. Those with shining hair, smooth countenance, a straight back and a wide chest are indeed magnificent youths! Yet if you ask what thoughts and aims are entertained in their heads, then they all turn out to be the same as the old and rotten, like moles from the same hill. . . . It is the old and rotten air that fills society everywhere. One cannot even find a bit of fresh and vital air to comfort those of us who are suffocating in despair.

ism, although there were few thinkers who did not speak of democracy. Only members of an older generation of reformers, such as K'ang Yu-wei or Liang Ch'i-ch'ao, came full circle and, appalled by the slaughter of World War I and the evils of Western materialism, advocated a return to traditional Chinese philosophies.

At the onset of China's intellectual revolution, Marxism had small appeal. Marx's critique of capitalist society did not fit Chinese conditions. More popular was the anarchism of Peter Kropotkin, who taught that mutual aid was as much a part of evolution

## Lu Hsun

Like Ch'en Tu-hsui and other writers of the May Fourth Movement, Lu Hsun saw China's old society as rotten and corrupt. Only after a radical reform, he felt, would the Chinese be able to realize their human potential.

### Making An Argument

I dreamed I was in a primary school classroom preparing to write a composition, and I asked my teacher how to make an argument.

"That's hard." Looking at me sharply over the rim of his glasses, he said: "Let me give you an example."

"A son was born to a family and the entire household was overjoyed. When the boy was one month old, they brought him out and displayed him to guests—expecting, naturally, to hear predictions of good fortune.

One said, 'This child will become rich.' For his words he was thanked profusely.

One said, 'This child will become an official.' He received compliments in turn.

But another guest said, 'One day this child will die.' He was soundly beaten by the entire household.

That the child will die is inevitable, while to say he will become rich or attain high position is probably a lie. Those who lie are rewarded while those who speak the truth are beaten. You. . .

'But sir, I don't want to lie, and I don't want to be beaten, so how should I speak?'

In that case you can say: 'Aha! This child. Just look at him! Oh my. Hehe! He! Hehehehe!' "

### Observations

Downstairs a man is dying,
Next door the family is listening to a
    victrola,
Across the lane they are playing with
    children.
Upstairs two persons are laughing with
    abandon, and there is the clack of
    mahjong tiles.
In a boat on the river a woman is wailing
    for her dead mother.

Human grief and joy do not extend to
    others;
I feel only that they are noisy.

It is in woman's nature to be a mother and
    to be a daughter—but not to be a wife.
A wifely nature is something forced—a
    mixture of her motherly and daughterly
    natures.

On seeing short sleeves,
they immediately think of bare arms,
they immediately think of the naked body,
they immediately think of the sexual
    organs,
they immediately think of copulation,
they immediately think of promiscuity,
they immediately think of illegitimate
    children.
Only at this level is the imagination of the
    Chinese capable of advancing by leaps
    and bounds.

Translation by Albert Craig.

as the struggle for survival. But after the Russian Revolution of 1917, Marxism–Leninism entered China. The Leninist definition of imperialism as the last crisis stage of capitalism had an immediate appeal, for it put the blame for China's ills on the West and offered feudal China the possibility of leapfrogging over capitalism to socialism. As early as 1919, an entire issue of *New Youth* was devoted to Marxism. Marxist study groups formed in Peking and other cities. In 1919, a student from Hunan, Mao Tsetung, who had worked in the Peking University library, returned to Changsha to form a study group. Ch'en Tu-hsiu was converted to Marxism in 1920. Instructed in organizational techniques by a Comintern agent, Ch'en and others formed the Chinese Communist Party in Shanghai in 1921; Chou En-lai (1898–1976) formed a similar group in Paris during the same year. The numbers involved were small but grew steadily.

## NATIONALIST CHINA

### Kuomintang Unification of China and the Nanking Decade (1927–1937)

Sun Yat-sen had fled to Japan during the 1913–1916 rule by Yuan Shih-k'ai. He returned to Canton in 1916, but despite his immense personal attractiveness as a leader, he was a poor organizer, and his Kuomintang (KMT), or Nationalist Party, made little headway. For a time in 1922, he was driven out of Canton by a local warlord. From 1923 Sun began to receive Soviet advice and support. With the help of Comintern agents like Michael Borodin, he reorganized his party on the Leninist model, with an executive committee on top of a national party congress, and, below this, provincial and county organizations and local party cells.

Since 1905 Sun had enunciated his "three principles of the people": nationalism, people's livelihood, and people's rights. Sun's earlier nationalism had been directed against Manchu rule; it was now redirected against Western imperialism. The principle of people's livelihood was defined in terms of equalizing landholdings and nationalizing major industries. By "people's rights," Sun meant democracy, although he argued that full democracy must be preceded by a preparatory period of tutelage under a single party dictatorship. Sun sent his loyal lieutenant Chiang Kai-shek (1887–1975) to the Soviet Union for study. Chiang returned after four months with a cadre of Russian advisers and established a military academy at Whampoa to the south of Canton in 1924. The cadets of Whampoa were to form a "party army." Sun died in 1925. By 1926, the Whampoa Academy had graduated several thousand officers, and the KMT army numbered almost 100,000. The KMT had grown to become the major political force in China, with 200,000 members; its leadership was divided between a left and a right wing.

The growth of the party was spurred on by changes occurring within Chinese society. Industries arose in the cities. Labor unions were organized in tobacco and textile factories. New ventures were begun outside the treaty ports, and chambers of commerce were established even in medium-sized towns. Entrepreneurs, merchants, officials, journalists, and the employees of foreign firms formed a new and politically conscious middle class.

The quicksilver element in cities was the several million students at government, Catholic, and Protestant schools. In May 1925, students demonstrated against the treatment of workers in foreign-owned factories at Shanghai. Police in the international settlement fired on the demonstrators, killing thirteen and wounding fifty. The incident further inflamed national and anti-imperialist feelings, and strikes and boycotts of foreign goods were called throughout China. Those in Hong Kong lasted for fifteen months.

Under these conditions, the Chinese Communist Party (CCP) also grew, and in 1926, it had about 20,000 members. The party was influential in student organizations, labor unions, and even within the KMT. By an earlier agreement, Sun had permitted CCP members to join the KMT as individuals but had enjoined them from organizing CCP cells within the KMT. Moscow approved of this policy; it felt that the CCP was too small to accomplish anything on its own and that by working within the KMT, its members could join in the "bourgeois, national, democratic struggle" against "imperialism and feudal warlordism." Chou En-lai, for example, became deputy head of the Political Education Department of the Whampoa Academy.

By 1926, the KMT had established a base in the area around Canton, and Chiang Kai-shek felt ready to march north against the warlord domains. He worried about the growing Communist strength, however, and before setting off he ousted the Soviet advisers and CCP members from the KMT offices in Canton. The march north began in July. By the spring of 1927, Chiang's army had reached the Yangtze, defeating, and often absorbing, warlord armies as it advanced (see Map 5–2).

After entering Shanghai in April 1927, Chiang carried out a sweeping purge of the CCP—against its members in the KMT, against its party organization, and against the labor unions that it had come to dominate. Hundreds were killed. The CCP responded by trying to gain control of the KMT left wing, which had established a government at Wuhan, and by armed uprisings. Both attempts failed. The surviving CCP members fled to the mountainous border region of Hunan and Kiangsi to the southwest and established the "Kiangsi Soviet." The left wing of the KMT, disenchanted with the Communists, rejoined the right wing at Nanking, China's new capital. Chiang's army continued north, took Peking, and gained the nominal submission of most northern Chinese warlords in 1928. By this time, most foreign powers had recognized the Nanking regime as the government of China.

Chiang Kai-shek was the key figure in the Nanking government. By training and temperament he believed in military force. He was unimaginative, strict, feared more than loved, and, in the midst of considerable corruption, incorruptible. Chiang venerated Sun Yat-sen and his "three principles of the people." The grandeur of Sun's tomb in Nanking surpassed that of the Ming emperors. But where Sun, as a revolutionary, had looked back to the zeal of the Taiping rebels, Chiang, trying to consolidate his rule

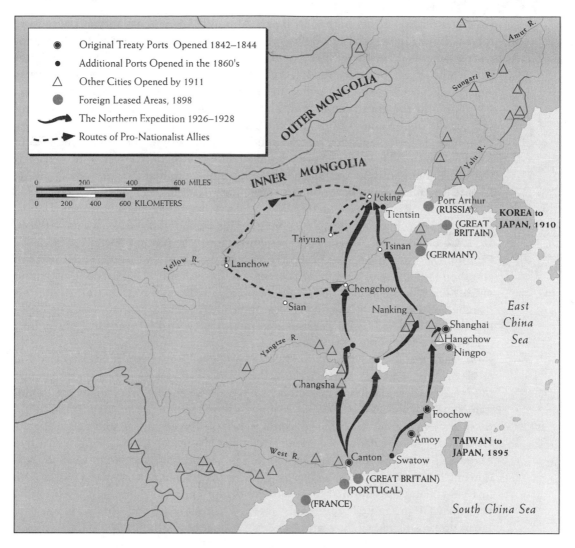

**Map 5-2   The Northern Expeditions of the Kuomintang.**   These expeditions, from 1926 to 1928, unified most of China under the Nationalist (Kuomintang) government of Chiang Kai-shek, inaugurating the Nanking decade. Warlord armies continued to hold power on the periphery.

over provincial warlords, looked back to Tseng Kuo-fan, who had put down the rebels and restabilized China. Like Tseng, Chiang was conservative and, though a Methodist, often appealed to Confucian values. The New Life Movement begun by Chiang in 1934 was an attempt to revitalize these values.

Chiang's power rested on the army, the party, and the government bureaucracy. The army was dominated by the Whampoa clique, which was personally loyal to

Chiang, and by officers trained in Japan. After 1927 Soviet military advisers were replaced by German advisers. They reorganized Chiang's army along German lines with a general staff system. The larger part of KMT revenues went to the military, which was expanded into a modernized force of 300,000. Whampoa graduates also controlled the secret military police and used it against Communists and any others who opposed the government. The KMT was a dictatorship under a central committee. Chiang became president of the party in 1938.

The densely populated central and lower Yangtze provinces were the area of KMT strength. The party, however, was unable to control outlying areas occupied by warlords, Communists, and Japanese. Some gains were made during the Nanking decade: Chiang's armies defeated the northern warlords in 1930, put down a rebellion in Fukien in 1934, and extended their control over southern and southwestern China two years later. But some areas remained under the sway of warlords until 1949. In 1931, Chiang launched a series of campaigns against the Kiangsi Soviet. In 1934, the Communists were forced to abandon their mountain base and flee to the southwest and then to Shensi province in northwestern China. Of the 90,000 troops that set out on this epic "Long March" of 6,000 miles, only 20,000 survived. It was during this march that Mao Tse-tung wrested control of the CCP from the Moscow-trained, urban-oriented leaders and established his unorthodox view that a revolutionary Leninist party could base itself on the peasantry.

The Japanese had held special rights in Manchuria since the Russo-Japanese War of 1905. When Chiang's march north and the rise of Chinese nationalism threatened the Japanese position, field-grade officers of Japan's Kwantung Army engineered a military coup in 1931 and, in 1932, proclaimed the independence of Manchukuo, their puppet state. In the years that followed, Japanese forces moved south as far as the Great Wall. Chinese nationalism demanded that Chiang resist, but Chiang, well aware of the disparity between his armies and those of Japan, said that the internal unification of China must take precedence over war against a foreign power. On a visit to Sian in 1936 Chiang was captured by a northern warlord and held until he agreed to join with the CCP in a united front against Japan. The following year, a full-scale war with Japan broke out, and China's situation again changed.

## War and Revolution (1937–1949)

In 1937, the KMT controlled the larger part of China and was recognized nationally and internationally as its government, whereas the CCP survivors of the Long March had just begun to rebuild their strength in arid Shensi, an area too remote for Chiang's army to penetrate. But by 1949, CCP forces had conquered China, including border areas never under KMT rule, and Chiang and the KMT were forced to flee to Taiwan. What had happened?

The war with Japan was the key event. It began in July 1937 as an unplanned clash at Peking and then spread. Battlefield victories soon convinced the Japanese

**MODERN CHINA**

**Close of Manchu Rule**

| | |
|---|---|
| 1839–1842 | Opium War |
| | Close of Manchu Rule |
| 1850–1873 | Taiping and other rebellions |
| 1870s–1880s | Self-strengthening movement |
| 1894–1895 | Sino-Japanese War |
| 1898 | One hundred days of reform |
| 1898–1900 | Boxer Rebellion |
| 1912–1912 | Republican revolution overthrows Ch'ing dynasty |

**Warlordism**

| | |
|---|---|
| 1912–1916 | Yuan Shih-k'ai president of Republic of China |
| 1916–1928 | Warlord era |
| 1919 | May Fourth Movement |

**Nationalist China**

| | |
|---|---|
| 1924 | Founding of Whampoa Military Academy |
| 1926–1928 | March north and Kuomintang reunification of China |
| 1928–1937 | Nanking decade |
| 1934–1935 | Chinese Communists' Long March to Yenan |
| 1937–1945 | War with Japan |
| 1945–1949 | Civil war and the establishment of the People's Republic of China |

military leaders to abandon negotiations in favor of a knockout blow. Peking and Tientsin fell within a month, Shanghai was attacked in August, and Nanking fell in December. During the following year, the Japanese took Canton and Wuhan and set up puppet regimes in Peking and Nanking. In 1940, frustrated by trying to work with Chiang, a rival party leader and many of his associates joined the Japanese puppet government. Japan proclaimed its "New Order in East Asia," which was to replace the system of unequal treaties. It expected that Chiang, as well, would recognize his situation as hopeless and submit. Instead, in 1938 he relocated his capital in Chungking, far to the west behind the gorges of the Yangtze. He was joined by thousands of Chinese, students and professors, factory managers and workers, who moved from occupied to free China.

Chiang's stubborn resistance to the Japanese won admiration from all sides. But the area occupied by the Japanese included just those eastern cities, railways, and densely populated Yangtze valley territories that had constituted the KMT base. The withdrawal to Chungking cut the KMT off from most of the Chinese population, programs for modernization ended, and the KMT's former tax revenues were lost.

Inflation increased geometrically, reducing the real income of officials, teachers, and soldiers alike. By the end of World War II and during the early postwar years, salaries were paid in large packages of almost worthless money, which was immediately spent for food or goods possessing real value. Inflation led to demoralization and exacerbated the already widespread corruption.

The United States sent advisers and military equipment to strengthen Chiang's forces after the start of the war in the Pacific. The advisers, however, were frustrated by Chiang, who wanted not to fight the Japanese but to husband his forces for the anticipated postwar confrontation with the Communists. Within his own army, a gap divided officers and men. Conditions in camps were primitive, food poor, and medical supplies inadequate. The young saw conscription almost as a sentence of death. Chiang's unwillingness to commit his troops against the Japanese also meant that the surge of anti-Japanese patriotism was not converted to popular support for the KMT.

For the Communists, the Japanese occupation was an opportunity. Headquartered at Yenan, they consolidated their base in Shensi province. They began campaigns to promote literacy and production drives to promote self-sufficiency. Soldiers farmed so as not to burden the peasants. The CCP abandoned its earlier policy of expropriating lands in favor of reductions in rents and interest. (This change led to the widespread American view that the CCP were not Communists but agrarian reformers, despite their protests to the contrary.) They took only those provincial and county offices needed to ensure their control and shared the rest with the KMT and other parties. They expanded village councils to include tenants and other previously excluded strata. But while compromising with other political and social groups, they strengthened their party internally.

Party membership expanded from 40,000 in 1937 to 1.2 million in 1945. Schools were established in Yenan to train party cadres. Even as the party expanded, orthodoxy was maintained by a rectification campaign begun in 1942. Those tainted by liberalism, individualism, or other impure tendencies were criticized and made to confess their failings and repent at public meetings. Mao's thought was supreme. To the Chinese at large, Mao represented himself as the successor to Sun Yat-sen, but within the Communist Party, he presented himself as a theoretician in the line of Marx (1818–1883), Engels (1820–1895), Lenin (1870–1924), and Stalin (1879–1953).

Whereas the KMT ruled through officials and often in cooperation with local landlords, the Communists learned to operate at the grass-roots level. They infiltrated Japanese-controlled areas and also penetrated some KMT organizations and military units. CCP armies were built up from 90,000 in 1937 to 900,000 in 1945. These armies were supplemented by a rural people's militia and by guerrilla forces in nineteen mountainous "base areas." By most accounts, the Yenan leadership and its party, army, and mass organizations possessed a cohesion, determination, and high morale that were conspicuously lacking in Chungking.

### Mao on the Peasant Movement in Hunan

The following excerpts are from Mao Tse-tung's 1927 "Report on an Investigation of the Peasant Movement in Hunan." While the more orthodox, Moscow-trained leaders of the Chinese Communist Party still put their trust in the urban proletariat, Mao emphasized the revolutionary potential of the peasantry.

*Does Mao's report seem overly optimistic or does it accurately foretell what would happen during the thirties and forties? What does it say of Mao's belief in the Marxist notion of class struggle?*

The present upsurge of the peasant movement is a colossal event. In a very short time, in China's central, southern and northern provinces, several hundred million peasants will rise like a mighty storm, like a hurricane, a force so swift and violent that no power, however great, will be able to hold it back. They will smash all the trammels that bind them and rush forward along the road to liberation. They will sweep all the imperialists, warlords, corrupt officials, local tyrants and evil gentry into their graves. Every revolutionary party and every revolutionary comrade will be put to the test, to be accepted or rejected as they decide. There are three alternatives. To march at their head and lead them? To trail behind them, gesticulating and criticizing? Or to stand in their way and oppose them? Every Chinese is free to choose, but events will force you to make the choice quickly. . . .

The peasants are clear-sighted. Who is bad and who is not, who is the worst and who is not quite so vicious, who deserves severe punishment and who deserves to be left off lightly—the peasants keep clear accounts, and very seldom has the punishment exceeded the crime. . . . A revolution is not a dinner party, or writing an essay, or painting a picture, or doing embroidery; it cannot be so refined, so leisurely and gentle, so temperate, kind, courteous, restrained and magnanimous. A revolution is an insurrection, an act of violence by which one class overthrows another. A rural revolution is a revolution by which the peasantry overthrows the power of the feudal landlord class. Without using the greatest force, the peasants cannot possibly overthrow the deep-rooted authority of the landlords which has lasted for thousands of years. The rural areas need a mighty revolutionary upsurge, for it alone can rouse the people in their millions to become a powerful force. . . .

*Selected Readings from the Works of Mao Tse-tung*, Peking: Foreign Languages Press, 1967, pp. 20–21, 25.

But the strength of the Chinese Communists as of 1945 should not be overstated. Most Chinese villagers were influenced by neither the CCP nor the KMT, and although intellectuals in free China had become disaffected with the KMT, most did not positively support the CCP. When the war in the Pacific ended in 1945, China's fate was unclear. The Soviet Union allowed CCP cadres to enter Manchuria, which it had seized during the last few days of the war, and blocked the entry of KMT troops until the following year. But even the Soviet Union recognized the KMT as the government of China and expected it to win the postwar struggle. The Allies directed Japanese armies to surrender to the KMT forces in 1945. The United States flew Chiang's troops from Chungking to key eastern cities. His armies were by then three times the size of the Communists' and far better equipped.

A civil war broke out early in 1946. Both sides knew that the earlier united front had been a sham. Efforts by U.S. General George Marshall (1880–1959) to mediate were futile. Until the summer of 1947, KMT armies were victorious—even capturing Yenan. But the tide turned in July as CCP armies went on the offensive in north China. They captured American military equipment left by the KMT forces, and by October 1948 the KMT forces had been driven from Manchuria. In January of 1949, Peking and Tientsin fell. By late spring, CCP armies had crossed the Yangtze, taking Nanking and Shanghai. A few months later, all of China was in Communist hands. Many Chinese fled with Chiang to Taiwan or escaped to Hong Kong; they included not only KMT officials and generals but entrepreneurs and academics as well. Not a few subsequently made their way to the United States.

In China, apprehension was mixed with anticipation. The disciplined, well-behaved soldiers of the "Peoples' Liberation Army" were certainly a contrast to those of the KMT. As villages were liberated, lands were taken from landlords and given to the landless. In the cities, crowds gave every indication of welcoming the CCP troops as liberators. The feeling was widespread that the future of China was once again in the hands of the Chinese.

## MODERN CHINA IN HISTORICAL PERSPECTIVE

From the late nineteenth century, most non-Western countries coveted the military power and the material well-being that science and industry had produced in the West. They did not, however, wish to become Western, for that would have negated their own cultural identity. Still, they found it difficult to adopt Western technology without also borrowing a broad range of Western values and ideas. Nor was it easy to distinguish between what was truly modern and what was merely recent-Western.

The process of modernization may be broken down into three stages: The first is the development of *preconditions*, of a base or platform within a country's late traditional culture from which it can reach out for the ideas and institutions of the West. The second is *Westernization*, the actual borrowing, and the third is *assimilation*, the fusion of what has been borrowed with indigenous values and institutions.

In terms of preconditions, China appears fairly advanced. In place was a high level of literacy, a stress on education as the means of getting ahead, an ethic emphasizing frugality and saving, a family system well adapted to small enterprises, a vigorous market economy, and many of the cultural ingredients for a modern nationalism. But China also had liabilities. Chinese merchants had no experience of political participation; they were not, in that sense, a bourgeoisie. Local Chinese society furnished no stable base for would be builders—as evidenced by rebellions during the nineteenth century and local disorders thereafter. The polity was run by an examination system elite who viewed foreigners as barbarians. The ingrained assumption of "middle kingdom" superiority is clearly reflected in Commissioner Lin's letter to Queen Victoria praising British kings for their "politeness and submissiveness." Consequently, when it came to borrowing from the West, government by Confucian literati, long China's outstanding asset, became its chief liability. Until the end of the dynasty, the most that intellectuals could devise was limited reformulations of Confucianism. Large-scale Westernization and assimilation had to wait seventy years after the Opium War for the dynasty to collapse.

Then, in the maelstrom of the May Fourth Movement, intellectual changes occurred at a furious pace in China's main cities. But in the political chaos following the demise of the dynasty, doctrines alone could not provide stability. Nationalism emerged as common denominator of most Chinese thought. Sun Yat-sen appealed to it. The Kuomintang drew on it at the Whampoa Academy, during the march north, and in founding the Nanking government. Other groups drew on it, too, and eventually the Chinese Communist Party (CCP) won out.

It is beguiling to view the CCP officials as a new class of literati operating the machinery of a monolithic, centralized state, with the teachings of Marx and Lenin replacing those of Confucius and local party cadres replacing the Confucian gentry. But this interpretation is too simple. Communism stressed science, class conflict, and the establishment of an ideal social order to be realized in the future. It broke with the Confucian emphasis on metaphysics, social harmony, and a golden age in the distant past.

Communism itself was also modified in China. Marx had predicted that socialist revolutions would break out in advanced economies where the contradictions of capitalism were sharpest. Lenin had shifted the emphasis from spontaneous revolutions by workers to the small but disciplined revolutionary party, the vanguard of the proletariat. He thereby changed Communism into what it has been ever since: a movement capable of seizing power only in backward nations. At the level of doctrine, Mao Tse-tung modified Lenin's ideas only slightly—by theorizing that "progressive" peasants were a part of the proletariat. But he went beyond this theory in practice, virtually ignoring city workers while relying on China's villages for recruits for his armies, who were then indoctrinated using Leninist techniques. Despite its low level of technology, the People's Liberation Army, the Communist equivalent of a "citizen's army," was formidable in the field. It was also modern in the sense that it did not loot and despoil the areas it occupied.

But the organizational techniques that were so effective in creating a party and army would prove less so for economic development. It soon became clear that mass mobilization was no substitute for individual incentives.

## REVIEW QUESTIONS

1. Which had the greater impact on China, the Opium War or the Taiping Rebellion?

2. How did the Ch'ing (or Manchu) dynasty recover from the Taiping Rebellion? In what ways was the recovery inadequate to prevent the overthrow of the dynasty in 1912?

3. Did the May Fourth Movement prepare the way for the Nationalist revolution? For the Communist revolution? Or was it incidental to both?

4. In thinking about the rise of the Nationalists to power, how much weight do you give to ideas and how much to political and military organization? Was the balance different in the Communist rise to power?

## SUGGESTED READINGS

COBLE, P. M. *The Shanghai Capitalists and the Nationalist Government, 1927–1937* (1980).

EASTMAN, L. E. *The Abortive Revolution: China Under Nationalist Rule, 1927–1937* (1974).

EASTMAN, L. E. *Seeds of Destruction: Nationalist China in War and Revolution, 1937–1949* (1984).

ELVIN, M. AND SKINNER, G. W. *The Chinese City Between Two Worlds* (1974). A study of the late Ch'ing and the Republican eras.

ESHERICK, J. W. *The Origins of the Boxer Rebellion* (1987).

FAIRBANK, J. K. *China, a New History* (1992). A survey of the entire sweep of Chinese history; especially strong on the modern period. (Fairbank, the doyen of Chinese history, completed reading the page proofs the day before he died.)

FAIRBANK, J. K. AND TWITCHETT, D. EDS. *The Cambridge History of China*. Like the premodern volumes in the same series, the volumes on modern China represent a survey of what is known. Vols. 10–15, which cover the history from the late Ch'ing to the People's Republic, have been published, and the others will be available soon. The series is substantial. Each volume contains a comprehensive bibliography.

HAO, C. *Chinese Intellectuals in Crisis: Search for Order and Meaning, 1890–1911* (1987).

KUHN, P. A. *Rebellion and Its Enemies in Late Imperial China; Militarization and Social Structure, 1796–1864* (1980). A study of how the Confucian gentry saved the Manchu dynasty after the Taiping Rebellion.

LEVENSON, J. *Liang Ch'i-ch'ao and the Mind of Modern China* (1953). A classic study of a major Chinese reformer and thinker.

LU HSUN, *Selected Works* (1960). Novels, stories, and other writings by modern China's greatest writer.

REISCHAUER, E. O., FAIRBANK, J. K., AND CRAIG, A. M. *East Asia: Tradition and Transformation* (1989). The most widely read text on East Asian history. Contains ample chapters on Japan and shorter chapters on Korea and Vietnam, as well as coverage of China.

SCHIFFRIN, H. Z. *Sun Yat-sen, Reluctant Revolutionary* (1980). A biography.

SCHWARTZ, B. I. *Chinese Communism and the Rise of Mao* (1951). A classic study of Mao, his thought, and the Chinese Communist Party before 1949.

SCHWARTZ, B. I. *In Search of Wealth and Power: Yen Fu and the West* (1964). Study of a late-nineteenth-century thinker who introduced Western ideas into China.

SPENCE, J. D. *The Gate of Heavenly Peace: The Chinese and Their Revolution, 1895–1980* (1981). Historical reflections on twentieth century China.

SPENCE, J. D. *The Search for Modern China* (1990). A thick text that reads remarkably well.

TENG, S. Y. AND FAIRBANK, J. K. *China's Response to the West* (1954). Translations from Chinese thinkers and political figures, with commentaries.

WHITE, T. H. AND JACOBY, A. *Thunder Out of China* (1946). A view of China during World War II by two who were there.

The Chinese Cultural Revolution of the 1960's. Marchers hold a banner of Mao Tse-tung.
[Archive Photos]

## chapter six

# China, the Last Half Century

China's history since the rise to power of the Communist state in 1949 divides neatly into two periods: the China of Mao and China after Mao. During the first, which lasted until 1976, China was wracked by successive political convulsions. Mao Tse-tung (Mao Zedong) wanted "revolution" to continue, even under his own government. Millions died as a result. Moreover, in spite of gaining undisputed political authority over an area comparable to that of the Ch'ing Empire—an area that included the non-Chinese peoples of Tibet, Central Asia, Inner Mongolia, and Manchuria—the government was unable to tap effectively the energies and talents of its people. To be sure, the problems faced by the government were immense and there were accomplishments. Still, the contrast between the low productivity of the Chinese in China and the remarkable productivity of the same people in Hong Kong and Taiwan was startling.

A marked reversal of earlier "socialist" policies occurred after Mao's death in 1976. This era might be called the China of Teng Hsiao-p'ing (Deng Xiaoping). Teng and his associates maintained the dictatorship of the Communist Party, but also introduced many features of a market economy. The result was explosive growth and an export boom, first in southeastern coastal areas, where long-suppressed entrepreneurial abilities surfaced, and then throughout the country. Standards of living rose and the society became freer—though criticism of the government was not permitted and political dissidents were jailed. Though it was still a dictatorship, the China of Teng was no longer totalitarian.

## MAO'S CHINA

### Consolidation

Victory over the forces of Chiang Kai-shek (Jiang Jieshi) had come suddenly. The People's Republic of China was proclaimed in October 1949. Even after that, Chinese armies continued to push outward, conquering vast areas with non-Chinese populations. Tibet, for example, was seized in 1950. Once subdued, the areas inhabited by Tibetans, Uighur Turks, Mongols, and other minorities were designated "autonomous regions." Their governments were staffed mainly by members of the

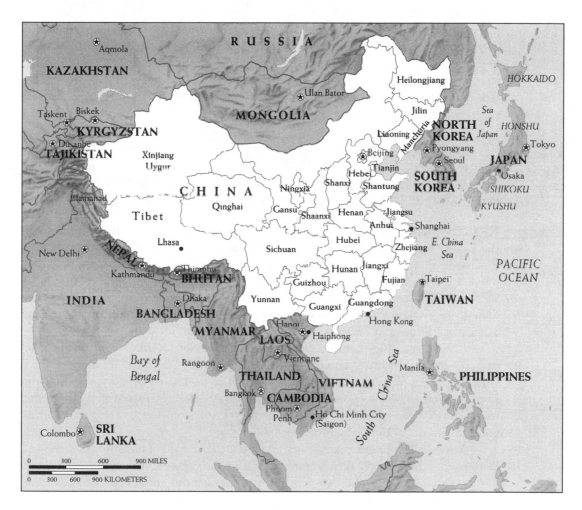

**Map 6–1    China in Contemporary Asia**

indigenous population but were tightly controlled by the Chinese. Their lands were occupied by Chinese army units and over time were settled by a sufficient number of Chinese immigrants to change their ethnic complexion. Also in 1950, Chinese troops entered the Korean War to preserve North Korea as a buffer state, and fought South Korean, American, and other UN troops to a standstill in mid-peninsula.

The Communists, who had gained power by war, found themselves the rulers of a country devastated and poor. The people were apprehensive. The Communist Party was small, with fewer than three million members in 1949. (By 1961 the figure would rise to seventeen million.) The new government proceeded cautiously. In central and south China officials appointed by the Nationalist government were left in place for a time. The Communist Party had its hand on all levers of power, but other parties were permitted to coexist. Liberals and other non-Marxist scholars continued to teach in universities. Two-thirds of the large industries were already owned by the state, but for a time the remaining third and small businesses were left in private hands. Under these moderate policies the economy began to recover. These early years were sometimes called the era of "New Democracy."

## The Soviet Model

In 1950, the Sino-Soviet Alliance was formed. Thereafter, in a piecemeal fashion, the Soviet model was adopted for the government, the army, the economy, and education. Mao was chairman of the Chinese Communist Party and the head of state. He ruled through the Standing Committee of the Political Bureau (the Politburo) of the party's Central Committee. Below the Politburo were regional, provincial, and district committees with party cells in every village, factory, school, and government office. Party members were called on to energize and enforce the local enactment of party policies. The party also tightly controlled the military and public security forces. The driving force behind this reorganization was the Leninism-Stalinism of Mao and other party leaders.

China's first five-year plan began in 1953. The Soviet Union sent financial aid as well as engineers and planners. Industries in Manchuria and the former treaty ports were integrated with those in the rest of China. Huge numbers of workers were mobilized to build new bridges, dams, roads, and railways. Better transport linked up what had formerly been isolated regional economies. Private businesses were nationalized and brought under bureaucratic control.

Rural society underwent two fundamental changes: land redistribution and collectivization. In the early fifties, teams of party cadres visited villages and held meetings at which landlords and rich peasants were denounced and made to confess their crimes. Some were rehabilitated, others were sent to labor camps, and hundreds of thousands—some scholars estimate several million—were executed. Their holdings were redistributed to the landless. Local responsibilities once borne by landlord gentry were shifted to peasant associations dominated by former tenant farmers, the most able of whom became local party cadres. Then two years later, in 1955 and 1956, before the new landowners had time to put down roots and entrench themselves, all lands were collectivized. The timing was important. In the Soviet Union collectivization had come six years after redistribution and was resisted by the *kulaks*, who had by then fully established their ownership of the land.

## The Great Leap Forward

During the first wave of "socialism," intellectuals and the universities became a target for thought reform. The Chinese slang term was *brainwashing*. This involved study

## Mao's View of China on the Eve of the Great Leap Forward

The following passage is from "Introducing a Cooperative," which Mao wrote in 1958. It was written just as he broke with the Soviet model of five-year plans in favor of a "mass mobilization" of the energies of the Chinese people.

*What was the basis of the optimism reflected in this passage? Why did the Great Leap Forward fail? Was Mao's view of the Chinese people as "blank" at fault? How could the masses be both "inspired" and "blank"?*

The political consciousness of the broad masses is rising rapidly. . . .

Judging from this, it will probably take less time than previously estimated for our industry and agriculture to catch up with that of the capitalist powers. In addition to the leadership of the Party, a decisive factor is our population of 600 million. More people mean a greater ferment of ideas, more enthusiasm and more energy. Never before have the masses of the people been so inspired, so militant and so daring as at present. . . .

Apart from their other characteristics, the outstanding thing about China's 600 million people is that they are "poor and blank". This may seem a bad thing, but in reality it is a good thing. Poverty gives rise to the desire for change, the desire for action and the desire for revolution. On a blank sheet of paper free from any mark, the freshest and most beautiful characters can be written, the freshest and most beautiful pictures can be painted. . . .

*Selected Readings from the Works of Mao Tse-tung,* Peking: Foreign Languages Press, 1967, p. 403.

and indoctrination in Marxism and group pressure to produce an atmosphere of insecurity and fear, followed by confession, repentance, and reacceptance by society. The indoctrination was intended to strengthen party control. But beyond this was the optimistic belief that the inculcation of correct moral doctrines could mobilize human energies on behalf of the state—perhaps a belief with distant Confucian roots. By 1956 Mao felt that intellectuals had been adequately indoctrinated and, concerned lest creativity be stifled, he said in a speech, "Let the hundred flowers bloom"—a reference to the lively discourse among the many schools of philosophy in ancient Chou China. To his surprise, intellectuals responded with a torrent of criticism that did not spare the Communist Party. Mao thereupon reversed his position, mounting an antirightist campaign and sending almost half a million writers and intellectuals to labor camps.

By the late fifties Mao was disappointed with the results of collectivization and the first five year-plan. In 1958 he abandoned a second plan (and the Soviet model) in favor of a mass mobilization to unleash the productive energies of the people. He called it the Great Leap Forward. One slogan was: "Hard work for a few years and happiness for a thousand." Campaigns were organized to accomplish vast projects, iron smelters were built in "backyards," and new instant industries were the order of the day. In the countryside, village-based collectives gave way to communes of 30,000 persons or more. The results were disastrous. Home-made iron was unusable, instant industries failed, and agricultural production plummeted. Scholars estimate that between 1958 and 1962 as many as twenty or thirty million Chinese may have starved to death. To control the damage, communes were broken into production brigades in 1959, and two years later these were further broken into production teams of forty households. Even these compromises could not overcome the ills of low incentives and collective responsibility; through most of the seventies agricultural production barely matched population growth.

During the late fifties, Sino-Soviet relations deteriorated. Disputes arose over borders. Chinese leaders were dissatisfied with the level of Soviet aid. They were embarrassed by the Soviet debunking of Stalin's cult of personality, since in China, Mao was still venerated as the "great helmsman." They felt Soviet revisionism had betrayed the principles of Marx, Lenin, and Stalin. For its part, the Soviet Union condemned China's Great Leap Forward as "leftist fanaticism" and resented Mao's view of himself, after Stalin's death, as the foremost theoretician and exponent of world Communism. In 1960, the Soviet Union halted its economic aid and withdrew its engineers from China, and by 1963 the split was visible to the outside world. Each country deployed about a million troops along their mutual border. Had relations between the two Communist countries been amicable, these troops, deployed elsewhere, might have changed the history of Southeast Asia and Eastern Europe. The Sino-Soviet split was arguably the single most important development in postwar international politics.

The years between 1960 and 1965 saw conflicting trends. The utter failure of the Great Leap Forward led some Chinese leaders to turn away from Mao's reckless radicalism toward more moderate policies. Mao kept his position as the head of the party but was forced to give up his post as head of state to another veteran Communist official. Yet even as the government moved toward more realistic goals and stable bureaucratic management, General Lin Piao (Lin Biao, 1908–1971) reestablished within the army the party committees and procedures for ideological indoctrination that had lapsed since the failure of the Great Leap Forward. A new mass movement was also begun to transform education.

## The Great Proletarian Cultural Revolution (1965–1976)

In 1965, Mao once again emerged to dominate Chinese politics. Mao the revolutionary, Mao the proponent of class struggle, had never been able to make the transition to Mao the ruler of an established state. When he looked at the Chinese Communist Party and the government bureaucracy, he saw a new privileged elite; when he looked at younger Chinese, he saw a generation with no experience of revolution. Mao feared that the Chinese revolution—his revolution—would end as a Soviet-style bureaucratic Communism run for the benefit of officials and not the people. The beginnings of such a system had already appeared. So he called for a new revolution to create a truly egalitarian culture.

Obtaining the backing of the army, Mao urged students and teen-aged youth to form bands of Red Guards. In the early feverish phase of the Cultural Revolution, the guards invoked the little red book containing Mao's sayings almost as holy scripture. Mass rallies were held. One rally in Peking (Beijing) was attended by millions of youths, who then made "long marches" back to their home provinces to carry out Mao's program. Universities were shut down as student factions fought. Teachers were beaten, imprisoned, and subjected to such extremes of humiliation that many committed suicide. An attack was launched on the "four olds," that is to say on China's traditional culture, in which books were burned and art destroyed. Stone Buddhist sculptures that had endured since the Sung dynasty were smashed or defaced. Things foreign also came under attack. Homes were ransacked for foreign books and Chinese who had studied abroad were persecuted. Even the borrowing of foreign technology was denigrated as "sniffing after foreigners' farts and calling them sweet." Red Guards attacked local party headquarters and government offices, and beat to death persons viewed as reactionaries, including some party cadres. High party officials were purged. The crippled apparatus of party and government was replaced by revolutionary committees. Chinese sometimes recall these events as a species of mass hysteria that even today they find difficult to comprehend.

Eventually Mao tired of the violence and near anarchy. In 1968 and 1969, he called in the army to take over the revolutionary committees. In 1969, a new Central Committee, composed largely of military men, was established, and General Lin Piao was named as Mao's successor. Violence came to an end as millions of students and intellectuals were sent to the countryside to work on farms. In 1970 and 1971, the revolutionary committees were reconstituted as party committees. Worsening relations with the Soviet Union also made China's leaders desire greater stability at home. In 1969 a pitched battle had broken out between Chinese and Russian troops over an island in the Ussuri River. After this encounter, the Chinese built bomb shelters in their main cities. It was just at this time that President Nixon began to withdraw U.S. troops from Vietnam. When he proposed a renewal of ties, China responded quickly. Nixon visited Peking in 1972, opening a new era of diplomatic relations.

The second phase of the Cultural Revolution, during the years between 1969 and 1976 ,was moderate only in comparison with what had gone before. On farms and in factories, ideology was still seen as an adequate substitute for economic incentives. Universities reopened, but students were admitted by class background, not by examination. In 1971, Lin Piao, Mao's heir, was purged. According to the official account, Lin tried to kill Mao and seize the government, but when his coup failed, he died in a plane crash as he tried to flee to the Soviet Union. Lin's place was taken by the so-called Gang of Four, which included Mao's wife and was abetted by the aging Mao. Class struggle was revived, and an official campaign was launched attacking the rightist "political swindlers" Lin Piao and Confucius.

## CHINA AFTER MAO

### Political Developments

Mao's death in 1976 brought immediate changes. Within four weeks, the Gang of Four and their radical supporters had been arrested. In this action, the role of the army was crucial. By the close of 1978 Teng Hsiao-p'ing (Deng Xiaoping, 1904–1997) had emerged as the dominant figure in Chinese politics. As a young man, Teng had spent eight years in France, and he was a veteran of the Long March. During the Cultural Revolution, he had twice been arrested; on one occasion he was paraded around Peking wearing a dunce cap. He was determined that such things would not happen again. He ousted his enemies, rehabilitated those purged during the Cultural Revolution, and put his supporters into office. Portraits of Mao were removed from most public places in August 1980. After the lunacy of the Cultural Revolution, the establishment of a "normal" Communist Party dictatorship came as a welcome relief. The people could now enjoy a measure of security and the prospect of material improvement in their lives.

There continued, however, a tension between the determination of the ruling party to maintain its grip on power and its desire to obtain the benefits of some liberalization. The tension was most visible in China's intellectual life. The government's repudiation of the Cultural Revolution led to an outpouring of stories, plays, and reports. In *Nightmare*, by Hsu Hui (Xu Hui), a mother whose son was killed during the Cultural Revolution asks, "Why? Why? Can anyone tell me why?" Liu Pin-yen (Liu Binyan) wrote of a corrupt officialdom that had "degenerated into parasitical insects that fed off the people's productivity and the socialist system." But the new leeway for criticism did not extend to the period of Teng's rule. Writers were regularly enjoined to be "led by the Communist Party and guided by Marx-Leninism." When a writer in 1983 overstepped the invisible line separating what was permissible from what was not, a short campaign was launched against "spiritual pollution." It was followed in 1985 and 1987 by other campaigns against "capitalist thinking" and "bourgeois democracy."

Universities returned to normal in 1977. Entrance examinations were reinstituted, purged teachers returned to their classrooms, and scientists and scholars were sent to study in Japan and the West. During the late seventies and early eighties students spent one afternoon a week studying party directives or the *Selected Works of Deng Xiaoping*. But far more influential was the new openness within China and the growing contacts with the wider world, as scholars returned from the West. Students also became aware of the prosperity achieved by Japan, Taiwan, and Hong Kong. They began to demand still greater freedoms with the hope that these would lead to political democracy. During the late 1980s, the ferment that marked Eastern Europe and the Soviet Union under Gorbachev also appeared in China: It was as if a new virus had entered the Communist world.

## Teng on the Cultural Revolution

Teng Hsiao-p'ing recognized Mao's "immortal service" to the people of China; he wrote that Mao's "contributions are primary and his mistakes secondary." But he also wrote that "we cannot discuss the defects in our system of Party and state leadership without touching upon Comrade Mao Zedong's mistakes in his later years." Teng's approach was more practical than ideological; he once said that if a cat catches mice, what difference does it make whether they are black or white. His criticisms of the Cultural Revolution in "On the Reform of the System of Party and State Leadership (1980)" provided a basis for extensive changes in many spheres of life in China.

---

*Do the problems of "bureaucracy" in China sound familiar? Or, in a highly centralized Communist state, were these problems magnified in a way that we find difficult to comprehend? How do these passages relate to policy changes in China during the Teng era?*

---

Bureaucracy remains a major and widespread problem in the political life of our Party and state. Its harmful manifestations include the following: standing high above the masses; abusing power; divorcing oneself from reality and the masses; spending a lot of time and effort to put up an impressive front; indulging in empty talk; sticking to a rigid way of thinking; being hidebound by convention; overstaffing administrative organs; being dilatory, inefficient and irresponsible; failing to keep one's word; circulating documents endlessly without solving problems; shifting responsibility to others; and even assuming the airs of a mandarin, reprimanding other people at every turn, vindictively attacking others, suppressing democracy, deceiving superiors and subordinates, being arbitrary and despotic, practising favouritism, offering bribes, participating in corrupt practices in violation of the law, and so on. Such things have reached intolerable dimensions both in our domestic affairs and in our contacts with other countries.

During the "Cultural Revolution," when someone got to the top, even his dogs and chickens got there too; likewise, when someone got into trouble, even his distant relatives were dragged down with him. This situation became very serious. Even now, the abominable practice of appointing people through favouritism and factionalism continues unchecked in some regions, departments and units. There are quite a few instances where cadres abuse their power so as to enable their friends and relations to move to the cities or to obtain jobs or promotions. It is thus clear that the residual influences of clannishness must not be underestimated.

*Selected Works of Deng Xiaoping,* Beijing: Foreign Languages Press, 1984, pp. 317, 318.

The new spirit came to a head in April and May of 1989, when hundreds of thousands of students, workers, and people from all walks of life demonstrated for democracy in Tienanmen Square in Peking and in dozens of other cities. Hunger strikes were held. Students published prodemocracy newspapers. Banners proclaimed slogans, among them "Give us freedom or give us death." A twenty-seven-foot, polystyrene and plaster Goddess of Democracy and Freedom was erected in the Square. At first government leaders disagreed on how to respond, but the hardline faction led by Teng won out and, in early June, sent in tanks and troops. Hundreds of students were killed, and leaders who did not escape abroad were jailed. The event defined the political climate in China for the decade that followed: considerable freedom was allowed in most areas of life, even intellectual life, but no challenge to the Communist Party was tolerated.

## Economic Growth

Developments in the economy were more promising. After taking power Teng said in a speech that "to be rich is glorious." His greatest achievement in the years after 1978 was to demonstrate in China the superiority of market incentives to central planning.

In China's villages, as the farm family became the basic unit of production, grain production rose from 305 million tons in 1978 to about 550 million in 1997, an increase of 80 percent. A local leader commented, "When people work for themselves, they work better." A similarly realistic view, that China "had wasted twenty years" on "radical leftist nonsense," was expressed in 1985 by General Secretary Hu Yao-pang (Hu Yaobang), who was later demoted. But even during the nineties agriculture had problems. Because the government bought up 30 percent of farmers' grain output at an artificially low price, farmers living near cities found it profitable to abandon grain production in favor of specialty crops such as fruit or the feedgrain required by China's rising consumption of meat. China already imported some of its food and there were gloomy estimates of future shortages.

State-operated enterprises—the surviving portion of the old centrally planned, command economy—were another sector of the economy. As late as 1982, their output constituted 74 percent of industrial production. But they employed twice the labor needed to run them efficiently, and because half of the enterprises ran at a loss, they were the chief source of problem loans at China's state-owned banks. They were, in effect, welfare establishments in which workers were paid little and had little incentive to work hard since they enjoyed the security of the so-called "iron rice bowl." As the free market sector grew faster, the state enterprise share of industrial production declined to 40 percent in 1997. Finally, the government announced that 10,000 of the 13,000 state enterprises would be sold by the year 2000. The "state ownership" required by the constitution would give way to "public ownership." That is to say, they would be privatized. The costs of such privatization would be high: defaulted loans, bankruptcies, unemployed workers, and a sudden rise in pensioners, but the drain on the state budget would end.

The main driver of the new economy was a variety of entrepreneurial ventures apart from those operated by the central government. These are often referred to collectively as the free market sector, but they included businesses run by villages, munic-

## The Chinese Economy in Transition

In this document, Executive Vice-Premier for the Economy Chu Jung-chi (Zhu Rongji) discusses key issues facing the Chinese economy at the end of 1995.

*What does Mr. Chu mean by "a socialist market economy"?*

### Pace of Reform

"At the 14th national congress of the Chinese communist party [October 1992], we decided to establish a socialist market economy. The pace of progress has generally been the same as we envisaged. Originally, we had anticipated more risk—but, as it turned out, we have seen less risk and more success."

### State Enterprise Reform

"In 1994 we carried out extensive reform measures in accordance with the market economic principles. So far, all these are concentrated in macro economic areas, meaning reforms in fiscal, banking, taxation, foreign trade, foreign exchange and investment sectors. We have not had time to focus on the micro aspects of the economy, and one of the key issues of the micro reforms is the state enterprises. Next year, we will spend more time and energy on the reform of the state enterprises."

### Regional Disparities

"The regional economic gap has always been a matter of concern to us, but this problem is caused by history. I am afraid in the short term the gap will not be narrowed—on the contrary, the gap might widen. At present, the focus in our work is to bring about rapid development in China's mid-west. However, we should not seek this objective at the expense of growth in the coastal areas."

### Tariff Reduction

"The current tariff level of China is very high . . . The average tariff level for developing countries is about 15 per cent, but now for China the level is 35 per cent . . . To be consistent with international practice, we will have to reduce tariffs to at least the average level of developing countries, 15 per cent, that is a must."

Reprinted by permission from the *Financial Times' Survey of China*, 20th November 1995. The Financial Times Ltd., London.

ipalities, and other public bodies, as well as those begun as private enterprises. There were also joint ventures with foreign firms. All were run for profit and were attuned to market forces. Employees in this sector doubled between 1984 and 1995. Chinese exports rose from $7 billion in 1975 to $183 billion in 1997. Between 1980 and 1994, the Chinese economy as a whole grew at double-digit rates, and though it slowed after 1995, it still grew faster than any other Asian economy.

The surge of such new enterprises began in special economic zones established along the border with Hong Kong, and quickly spread along the coast. Shanghai, with a population of fourteen million, became a city of skyscrapers and industrialists, and the site of China's first stock exchange. Shantung Province in the northeast attracted huge investments from Japan, South Korea, and the United States, and also achieved stunning growth, as did Manchuria, another industrial heartland. As entrepreneurs, cities, and local governments joined in, the tide of enterprise swept inland. Wuhan, a major communications hub and automobile manufacturer in central China, averaged growth of 16 or 17 percent during the early nineties. But in the hinterlands large areas remained undeveloped and mired in poverty; they clamored in vain for government assistance. To achieve growth, the government was willing to tolerate personal and regional inequities.

The factors that fueled this growth were clear: the entrepreneurial abilities of the Chinese; a huge surplus of fairly good-quality, cheap labor; a savings rate of 35–40 percent; a level of protectionism more than double that of other Asian nations; large investments from abroad; and open world markets. China, in effect, successfully used tariffs to shield its markets, while making use of cheap labor to flood foreign markets with goods and build up its currency reserves.

## Social Change

During the Mao years, farmers had been tied to their collective or village. Cities were closed to those without residence permits. City dwellers, whether they worked in factories, hospitals, schools, newspapers, or government offices, were members of "units." Like company towns, units provided their members with jobs, housing, food, child care, medical services, and pensions. Party cadres exercised near-total control over the unit's members. Block organizations exercised surveillance over the inhabitants and reported any infractions of "socialist morality" to the authorities.

Under Teng, controls were loosened. The police became less active—except against political dissidents—censorship was reduced, and ties with the outside world were allowed to develop. The "unit" also diminished in importance as food became more widely available in free markets and apartments were sold to their inhabitants on easy terms. Private housing brought with it the freedom to change jobs. As workers with higher salaries began to provide for their own needs, especially in the burgeoning private sector, life became freer and more enjoyable. The market economy fostered a greater reliance on individual decisions and initiatives.

The new prosperity and changing mores became increasingly evident. The blue Mao uniforms of the sixties were followed by suits, however ill-fitting, and later, for the young, by blue jeans, sneakers, colorful jackets, and designer sunglasses. By the nineties, innovative Chinese designers were holding fashion shows in Shanghai and Peking. Young people associated more freely, and in urban areas the earlier taboo against public displays of affection slowly relaxed. The "household treasures" of the sixties, radios and bicycles, gave way to stoves and refrigerators in the seventies, and, in the next decade, to washing machines and color televisions. Crowds gathered around displays of motorbikes in department stores. By the early nineties, motorbikes and pri-

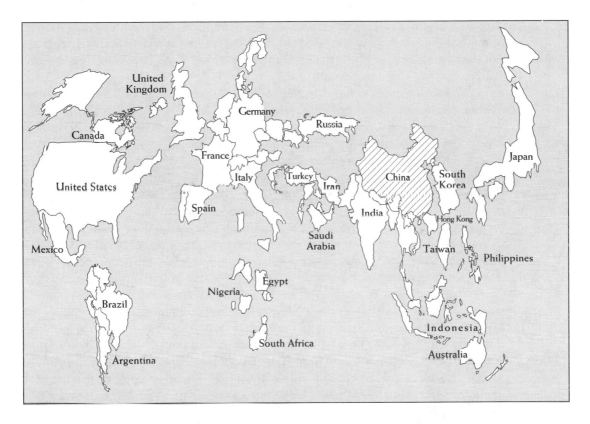

**Map 6–2   "How big is China's economy?"**   Economists give two quite different answers. Some ask how much it would cost in dollars to produce the goods and services consumed by the Chinese people. Their answer calculates the Chinese GDP (gross domestic product) as the second largest in the world, and the per capita GDP at about $3200. The above map showing the economic size of the countries of the world reflects such a calculation. Other economists take the actual cost of the same goods and services as measured in Chinese currency, and convert the figure to dollars at the current rate of exchange. By such a calculation, the Chinese GDP is only one quarter as large and the per capita figure is less than $1000.

vately owned cars competed in crowded streets with the flow of bicycles. Private restaurants opened and travel for pleasure became commonplace. In 1988, most passengers on airline flights within China were foreign; ten years later, most were Chinese.

The new wealth was unevenly distributed. The more successful entrepreneurs bought houses, cars, microwaves, computers, and cell phones. They traveled abroad and sent their children to private schools. As their lifestyle became more Western, they were sometimes called China's "new middle class," but in fact they constituted an upper class. Other city dwellers also participated in the new prosperity, but many just scraped by and unemployment remained high. Among the rural 70 percent of the population, the pace of change was slower. In prosperous belts near cities, the number of large brick houses and tractors impressed foreign visitors. But the lifestyle of those in remote regions continued almost unchanged, except for the most enterprising. In the West envy is green. In China the envy and resentment of the have-nots for the newly affluent is called "the red-eye disease."

Population remained a critical dimension of Chinese society. The story of population during the years after 1949 involved the four Ma's: Malthus, Marx, Ma Yin-ch'u (Ma Yinchu), and Mao Tse-tung (Mao Zedong). Malthus had claimed that population would expand geometrically whereas food would increase only arithmetically. Marx rejected the Malthusian hypothesis, along with classical economics, as myths of the capitalist stage of history. Professor Ma Yin-ch'u (1882–1982), the chancellor of Peking University, published in 1957 *New Principles on Chinese Population*, in which he argued that unchecked population growth would impede capital accumulation and depress living standards. Mao Tse-tung, faithfully following the teachings of Marx, purged Professor Ma and closed down population institutes at Chinese universities. What followed was a population increase from 550 million in 1949 to nearly a billion by 1981. Real growth occurred in the economy during the sixties and seventies, but the gains were eaten up by the extra mouths. In the face of this crisis, in 1981 the government adopted a national policy of one child per family. It recognized that the policy ran contrary to the deep-rooted Chinese sense of family, but argued that without it China's future would be bleak. Thereafter the increase slowed but by the year 2000 another quarter billion had been added to the population. Demographers predict the population will peak in 2030 at about a billion and a half. In recent decades parents have tended to spoil their single child; Chinese sociologists speak of a new generation of "little emperors."

## China's Relations with the World

From the fifties to the seventies, China isolated itself from the rest of the world. The Sino-Soviet split defined its relations to the north, the Cold War defined its relations with Japan, South Korea, Taiwan, and the United States. China gave aid to North Vietnam during the Vietnam War but then turned around and invaded Vietnam in 1979. In some measure China's relations with its neighbors reflected its internal political turmoil. As the turmoil ended during the eighties, changes set in. Economic growth gave China some leeway, and trade ties with the non-Communist world led China to look outward and adopt more moderate policies.

In the nineties, foreign relations seemed to improve across the board. Relations with Russia became amicable. China welcomed increased trade and investment from Taiwan and South Korea, despite its fear of Taiwan's growing independence and its continuing reluctant support for North Korea. China also worked to improve its relations with Southeast Asia. As the decade drew to an end, China emerged as the military and political heavyweight of East Asia, though Japan remained, even in recession, the predominant economic power. (See Map 6–2 on page 167).

## U.S. Foreign Policy: A Chinese Dissident's View

Wei Jingsheng, a Chinese advocate of democratic rights, was deported to the United States late in 1997. A year later, in a *New York Times* editorial, he criticized U.S. policy as pandering to Chinese tyranny.

*Should U.S. foreign policy be used to promote human rights even in poor countries with cultural traditions different from the West? Or should the United States avoid interference in the domestic politics of other nations and aim primarily at furthering American economic and security goals? What is foreign policy capable of achieving? Where should the balance be struck?*

### China's Diversionary Tactics

One year ago, after 18 years in a Chinese prison, I was "released" and sent here. A Chinese official said that if I ever set foot in China again, I would immediately be returned to prison. . . .

The State Department, in a report last January, used my forced exile as evidence that China was taking "positive steps in human rights" and that "Chinese society continued to become more open." These "positive steps" led the United States and its allies to oppose condemnation of China at a meeting of the United Nations Commission on Human Rights in April. In the months that followed, President Clinton and other Western leaders traveled to China, trumpeting increased economic ties and muting criticism on human rights.

Thus, without fear of sanction, the Chinese Government intensified its repression in 1998. Once the leaders achieved their diplomatic victories, they turned to their main objective: the preservation of tyrannical power. This year, about 70 people are known to have been arrested. . . .

Li Peng, the speaker of the National People's Party Congress, declared recently, "If an organization's purpose is to promote a multiparty system in China and to negate the leadership prerogatives to the Chinese Communist Party, then it will not be permitted to exist."

This statement clearly shows that the Communist Party's primary objective is to sustain its tyranny, and to do so it must deny the people basic rights and freedoms. We must measure the leaders' progress on human rights not by the "release" of individuals but by the people's ability to speak, worship and assemble without official interference and persecution.

China's relations with the United States were difficult. Both during the Cold War and afterwards, U.S. military alliances with Japan and South Korea, and its ties to Taiwan and the non-Communist nations of Southeast Asia, were the main countervailing force to Chinese hegemony in the region. China resented the U.S. presence as an intrusion in what it considered its own proper sphere of influence. The first step toward a new relationship was President Nixon's visit to China in 1972. The United States extended diplomatic recognition to China in 1979. From the eighties exports to the United States were vital to China's economic growth, and they became more so during the mid-nineties as the rest of East Asia slipped into recession. In 1996 the United States bought $54 billion of goods from China but sold China only $12 billion of its own products. Thereafter, the U.S. trade deficit with China continued to grow. The United States was unhappy with this imbalance; it protested Chinese piracy of hundreds of millions of dollars worth of U.S. movies, computer software, and CDs each year. The United States was also critical of Chinese human rights abuses, nuclear testing, and arms sales to Iran and Pakistan. Despite these areas of contention, the United States worked to better relations, hoping that a deeper Chinese engagement with the U.S. and the rest of the world would lead to a freer Chinese society. With Premier Chiang Tse-min's (Jiang Zemin) visit to the United States in 1997 and President Clinton's visit to China in 1998, U.S.–Chinese political ties continued to improve. In the year 2000 the U.S. House of Representatives voted to give China a permanent most-favored-nation status. This opens the way for the admission of China to the World Trade Organization, a further step toward a more open participation in the world economy.

## TAIWAN

Taiwan is a mountainous island less than a hundred miles off the coast of central China. A little larger than Belgium or Massachusetts, it has a population of twenty-three million. Originally, it was a remote and backward part of the Ch'ing empire; it became a Japanese colony in 1895 as a spoil of the Sino-Japanese War. The Japanese found it easy to rule since the Taiwanese lacked a strong sense of national identity and were accustomed to rule by officials from across the sea who spoke a language they could not understand. (Standard Chinese and the Fukien dialect spoken on Taiwan are mutually unintelligible.) The Japanese colonial government suppressed opium and bandits and eradicated epidemic diseases. It built roads and railroads, reformed the land system, and introduced improvements in agriculture. Before 1895 education had been the privilege of a tiny elite; the Japanese established "common schools," which, by the end of World War II, were attended by 71 percent of school age children. (In the Dutch East Indies and French Indochina the figure was about 10 or 15 percent.) Light industries were introduced and, during the thirties, textiles, chemicals, ceramics, and machine tools. Though these were mostly owned by Japanese and run in their interests, more benefits seem to have accrued to the local population than was the case in Korea, another Japanese colony.

Anticolonial feelings rose slowly. During the twenties Taiwanese petitioned for political reform and greater personal freedom. The Japanese made a few concessions, but after war with China began in 1937 they intensified their strict controls and assimilationist policies. At the end of the war the Taiwanese were happy to see the Japanese leave and welcomed mainland Kuomintang (Guomindang) officials as liberators. The new officials, however, saw the Taiwanese as Japanese collaborators; they looted the economy and ruled harshly. When Taiwanese protested in February 1947, the Kuomintang put down the demonstrators and over several months killed between eight to ten thousand Taiwanese, many of them community leaders. By the time Chiang Kai-shek and two million more military and civilian mainlanders fled to the island in 1949, its economy and society were in disarray. Mainlanders looked down on the Taiwanese, who, in turn, hated their new rulers and in private often compared them unfavorably to the Japanese.

In the mid-fifties, order was restored, and rapid economic growth followed. Heavy industries were put under state control; other Japanese-owned industries were sold to private parties. With the outbreak of the Korean War in 1950, U.S. aid became substantial. Foreign investment was welcomed. Light industries were followed by consumer electronics, steel and petrochemicals, and then by computers and semiconductors. From the late eighties trade and investments in China began. By the late nineties, Taiwan was the world's largest producer of monitors, keyboards, motherboards, and computer mice; the second in notebook PCs; and the fourth in integrated circuits. Taiwan traded with China and by the year 2000 had invested $40 billion in factories on the mainland to take advantage of China's cheap labor. In 1996, Taiwan's estimated per capita product was more than $13,000, half that of France but fifteen times that of mainland China. Though small, Taiwan had the healthiest economy in recession-ridden Asia.

Even with economic progress, government in Taiwan was authoritarian; until 1987 martial law was in effect and opposition parties were banned. The KMT (Kuomintang) maintained that its government, which it called the Republic of China, was the legitimate government of all of China. Posters on Taipei billboards proclaimed the official policy of eventually reconquering the mainland. As the self-proclaimed government of all of China, a minority of mainlanders were able to dominate the Taiwanese population.

Social changes began during the sixties. Education advanced, with rising numbers entering universities. Taiwanese and mainleaders began to intermarry. A new middle class emerged, and Taiwanese began to enter the KMT and attain minor political offices. Chiang Kai-shek died in 1976, the same year as Mao. Under his son, Chiang Ching-kuo, who was president from 1976 to 1988, Taiwan inched toward representative government. In 1987 martial law ended and opposition parties were permitted.

After Chiang Ching-kuo's death, Lee Teng-hui became president. A native Taiwanese, Lee was a graduate of a Taiwanese high school, Kyoto Imperial University, and Cornell. In March 1996, Lee was elected president in what he described as "the first free election in 5,000 years of Chinese history." During the election China tried to intimidate the voters by firing missiles into the waters off Taiwan, but the voters responded to this heavy-handedness by giving Lee a substantial majority of their votes. After the election, Lee spoke of Taiwan as a separate "state," a concept anathema to the government in Peking. He also reiterated the recent KMT line that Taiwan would consider reunification if China became free and democratic, but opined that this would not happen soon.

Another presidential election was held in March 2000 in which Ch'en Shui-pien, the candidate of the Democratic-Progressive Party, was elected. A Taiwanese, Ch'en was born in poverty, rose to become a corporate attorney and, in 1994, mayor of Taipei. His election victory, which ended fifty years of KMT rule, was hailed by one scholar as "the first peaceful transition of power from one political party to another in Taiwanese history and probably in all Chinese history." Though the central issue in the election was KMT corruption, a second issue was the Democratic-Progressive party's earlier espousal of Taiwan's independence. Ch'en's vice-president is Annette Lu, a feminist, Harvard Law School graduate, and outspoken advocate of Taiwan's independence. In the early eighties, such views had led the Kuomintang to imprison her for more than five years.

The Communist government in Peking, since 1949, had claimed that Taiwan was a province of China unlawfully controlled by a "bandit" government. It maintained that its relation with the island was a matter of internal Chinese politics, and refused diplomatic ties with any nation maintaining such ties with Taiwan. For almost thirty years, from the outbreak of the Korean War until 1979, Taiwan was a protégé of the United States, which ignored the mainland and supported Taiwan's claim to be the legitimate government of all China. In 1979, however, the United States changed its policy: it broke off formal diplomatic relations with Taipei and recognized Peking as the legitimate government of a China that included Taiwan. The United States, nonetheless, continued informal relations with Taiwan, and continued to trade with Taiwan and to sell it arms. Curiously, it was during the years of diplomatic limbo after the break in 1979 that Taiwan's economy grew and its society became more democratic.

As the new millennium began, both China and the United States were apprehensive about Taiwan. China worried that a freely elected democratic government would give Taiwan's government legitimacy in the eyes of the world. It denounced Vice-President Lu as a "scum" bent on promoting Taiwan's independence. (She replied that the Kuomintang had jailed her on the same charge.) China also worried that Taiwan's prosperity would make its people less willing to rejoin the mainland—a view lent credence by public opinion polls in Taiwan. It also spoke of using military force to retake the island. The United States, on its part, feared that within a decade or two China would have the military power to do just that. It cautioned President Ch'en not to speak of independence. (He replied that a declaration of independence was not necessary since Taiwan already functioned as an independent state.) Many in the U.S. Congress felt that the United States could not stand by and see this prosperous and democratic state it had helped to create be forcibly taken over by China. Taiwan remains the principal obstacle to smooth relations between the United States and China.

## CHINA, THE OUTLOOK

What China does affects other nations. When we think, for example, of population, our usual models are Western Europe and Japan, where population quadrupled in the process of industrialization and then began, almost as a natural process, to level off. But China already had a huge population to begin with, and could not afford a further quadrupling. Consequently, late in the day, it adopted extremely tough policies to limit births. At present, China imports grain. Whether it will be self-sufficient in foodstuffs in the future is a question. Many other nations, overpopulated and poor, are like China. They lack the leeway of Europe or Japan. As they experience the baleful consequences of soaring populations, they may look to the Chinese example for tough and effective policies.

China will also exert a growing influence on patterns of world trade. Japan's postwar leap to high technology, followed by the rapid advance of Taiwan, South Korea, Hong Kong, and Singapore, upset the prewar pattern in which advanced Western nations sold their manufactures to the rest of the world in exchange for raw materials and labor-intensive products. The East Asian combination of cheap labor and efficient manufacturing put great pressure on the United States and Europe, causing trade deficits, corporate restructuring, the relocation of jobs abroad, and a downward pressure on wages. But the pressure lessened as wages rose in the rim nations of East Asia. Then, in the mid-eighties, China, with its enormous population and extraordinarily cheap labor, emerged as an efficient producer. Even in the nineties, most of its exports were labor-intensive products, such as toys and bicycles, but it began to move toward value-added manufacturing. Four out of five mice for Apple computers are made by a Taiwan subsidiary in Suzhou, China by women paid $75 a month. If free trade remains the rule, the future impact of Chinese production on wages in the West and Japan will be enormous. But if the advanced nations act to protect their labor and markets, the effect on Chinese growth and on the world economy will also be immense. China's size and poverty pose a trade challenge of a different magnitude from that posed two decades earlier by the East Asian rim nations.

Rapid Chinese development—in combination with ongoing developments in India, South America, and elsewhere—will affect the supply of natural resources. In the early seventies a crisis occurred when the demand for oil outran the supply. There were shortages at the pumps, the price of oil soared, and wealth was transferred from industrial to oil-rich nations. Experts pointed out that the world's reserves of oil were dwindling. But then, new supplies came on line, OPEC. The cartel of producers, weakened, and the transfer of wealth slowed. But as China and other parts of the world industrialize, the demand for oil and other resources will rise steadily. At some point demand will again outstrip supply. How will this be handled? Of course, it is the developed nations, and not China, which are the major consumers of the world's resources. But China and other late developers will add to demand at the margin. China has huge reserves of soft coal and fair reserves of waxy oil. But already its large cities are more polluted than Bangkok, Mexico City, or cities in Eastern Europe. Will it be able to afford better grades of oil? What will be the consequences if it cannot? It is not difficult to imagine a world in which the exchange of natural resources and foodstuffs is managed far more than is the case today.

Another issue is the political consequences of economic growth. As its standard of living gradually rises, will China evolve toward some form of political democracy? At present China embodies a massive incongruity. The government is moving to abolish the socialist pattern of state-run industries and establish a market economy—complete with entrepreneurs and stock market; this destroys the rationale for Communist rule. Yet Party officials are determined to hang onto power and to do so are quite willing to jail their critics. Since there is no organized opposition and since the military is both well treated and tightly controlled, the situation is unlikely to change suddenly. But what of the longer term? Many in China desire more freedom. U.S. policy with its emphasis on human rights assumes that such a development is possible. Certainly, East Asian culture, if it can be spoken of in the singular, is no bar to representative government. Japan, and then South Korea and Taiwan, have followed checkered paths toward greater democracy. Their progress rested on rising standards of living, sizeable and highly educated middle classes, hybrid forms of Western and traditional ideas, and considerable U.S. influence. Are similar conditions appearing in China today? The answer is only very slowly. In comparison to Taiwan or South Korea, the Chinese standard of living is still low, despite having doubled during the past fifteen years. The percentage of the population with a higher education is also much lower. The influence of the United States is small. And, though China since Mao is again open to new Western ideas, and ready to reconsider its own cultural tradition in a piecemeal fashion, the climate of ideas in China is still not supportive of representative government. Even optimistic appraisals see democracy as several decades away.

## SUGGESTED READINGS

CHAN, A., MADSEN, R., AND UNGER, J. *Chen Village: A Recent History of a Peasant Community in Mao's China* (1984). The postwar history of a Chinese village.

CHANG, J. *Wild Swans: Three Daughters of China* (1992). A superbly readable novel of three female generations of a Chinese family.

CHENG, J.Y. S. *China in the Post-Deng Era* (1998). A multiple author view of the immediate future based on study of the recent past.

FAIRBANK, J. K. AND GOLDMAN, M. *China, a New History* (1998). An excellent updating of a splendid book.

FROLIC, B. M. Mao's People: Sixteen Portraits of Life in Revolutionary China (1987).

GOLD, T. State and Society in the Taiwan Miracle (1986). The story of economic growth in postwar Taiwan.

GOLDMAN, M. AND MACFARQUHAR, R., EDS. *The Paradox of China's Post-Mao Reforms* (1999).

GOLDMAN, M. *Sowing the Seeds of Democracy in China* (1994).

LIEBERTHAL, K. *Governing China, from Revolution through Reform* (1995).

LU HSUN, *Diary of a Madman and Other Stories* (1990).

MACFARQUHAR, R. AND FAIRBANK, J. K., EDS. *The Cambridge History of China: The People's Republic Part II*, Vol. 15 (1987).

MACFARQUHAR, R. *Politics of China, the Eras of Mao and Deng* (1997). A summary of some of the best research.

LIANG, H. Son of the Revolution (1983). An autobiographical account of a young man growing up in Mao's China.

LIU, B. People or Monsters? and Other Stories and Reportage from China After Mao (1983). Literary reflections on China.

MOTE, F. W. AND TWITCHETT, D., EDS. *The Cambridge History of China: The People's Republic Part I*, Vol. 14 (1987) A summary of some of the best research.

WHITE, G., ED. *In Search of Civil Society: Market Reform and Social Change in Contemporary China* (1996). An insightful look at the society.

WOLF, M. *Revolution Postponed: Women in Contemporary China* (1985).

ZHANG, X. AND SANG Y. *Chinese Lives: An Oral History of Contemporary China* (1987).

# Index